The Ride

The Improbable Life of Cowboy Freckles Brown,
an Unbeaten Bull Named Tornado,
and the Most Historic Eight Seconds in Rodeo History

By Ron J. Jackson, Jr.

Wild Horse Press
An Imprint of Wild Horse Media Group

Copyright © 2025
By Ron J. Jackson Jr.
Published By Wild Horse Press
An Imprint of Wild Horse Media Group
P.O. Box 331779
Fort Worth, Texas 76163
1-817-344-7036
www.WildHorseMedia.com
ALL RIGHTS RESERVED
Paperback 978-1-68179-385-6
Hardback 978-1-68179-386-3
ebook 978-1-68179-387-0

ALL RIGHTS RESERVED. No part of this book may be reproduced in any form without written permission from the publisher, except for brief passages included in a review appearing in a newspaper or magazine.

For my children and grandchildren …
Joseph (1991-2017)
Ashley
Tristan
Missouri
Emma
Shelby
Sage

"Dare to dream. Dare to live."

Contents

Introduction	vii
1. December 1, 1967	1
2. London Flats	9
3. "Freckles"	21
4. Sunlight Ranch	46
5. Legendary Journey	66
6. Love and War	84
7. Living the Dream	105
8. Black Smoke	125
9. A Phoenix Rising	134
10. Tornado	152
11. The Draw	163
12. The Ride	169
13. Living Legend	179
14. End of Days	199
Acknowledgments	223
Author Bio	229
Notes	230
Bibliography	256
Index	268

'The next best thing to a lie,' Joe Palmer wrote, *'is a true story nobody will believe'* and anybody who would believe the story of Freckles Brown ought to report himself.
— **Red Smith, sportswriter**

Introduction

Curiosity might be my greatest gift as a storyteller.

Ever since I was a child, curiosity has led me to explore for a deeper, fuller understanding of a subject or person who piqued my interest. Curiosity has served me well as a writer. Sometimes, that curiosity raged like a fire from within and my exploration only intensified with time. The more I learned, the more I journeyed in a relentless quest for knowledge and understanding.

The Ride is the result of one such journey.

I first heard the name Freckles Brown seventeen years ago as a staff writer for *The Oklahoman* newspaper in Oklahoma City. As I recall, my colleagues and I were discussing ideas for what would become an ongoing, award-winning series titled, "Stories of the Ages" — a collection of meaty articles that delved into Oklahoma's most iconic historical figures and episodes. The series explored everything from the collective psychological impact of John Steinbeck's *Grapes of Wrath* on Oklahomans to the state's largely hidden Black history.

"Ever heard the story of Freckles Brown?" asked Bryan Painter, a talented colleague who covered rodeo for years for our newspaper.

"No," I replied. "Who was he?"

Painter smiled and joyfully launched into an unvarnished version of a story about a beloved, over-the-hill bull rider who once faced the most feared bull in the sport of rodeo at the National Finals Rodeo in December of 1967 in Oklahoma City. The bull — a 1,725-pound Hereford-Brahman crossbreed named *Tornado* — had never been ridden in seven years.

Few, if any, gave the aged, diminutive bull rider a chance. Some even feared he might be killed.

The story needed no varnish. Such is the moment that Freckles Brown first entered my life. And I was hooked.

Instantly, I needed to know more. About Freckles. About *Tornado*. About that iconic moment. My curiosity led me to the Dickinson Research Center at the National Cowboy and Western Heritage Museum in Oklahoma City. Here, I read the archival files of Freckles, *Tornado*, and the bull's legendary owner, Jim Shoulders — "the Babe Ruth of Rodeo."

My research first produced a feature article for *The Oklahoman*'s Stories of the Ages series, titled, "The Ride." The 2011 article won a couple of first-place awards from the Associated Press, but more importantly, continued to feed that internal flame of curiosity. By then, I already knew Freckles Brown's showdown with *Tornado* would be the centerpiece for one of my upcoming books. I resumed my research into the life of Warren Granger "Freckles" Brown and *Tornado*, even as I published three other books: *Joe, the Slave Who Became an Alamo Legend* (2015); *Fight to the Finish: "Gentleman" Jim Corbett, Joe Choynski, and the Fight that Launched Boxing's Modern Era* (2019); and *Bebes and the Bear: Gene Stallings, Coach Bryant, and Their 1968 Cotton Bowl Showdown* (2019).

Through it all, Freckles never left my side. My journey to discover the man behind the legend led me down numerous trails in the American West. I traveled to the banks of the

North Platte River in eastern Wyoming where he grew up as the son of a farmer to the plush, rolling pastures of his own Kelly Bend Ranch in Soper, Oklahoma, where his descendants still reside and thrive. In Soper, the family graciously gave me full access to his private papers and photographs, including a collection of World War II-era letters he wrote to his beloved wife, Edith, while serving in the United States Army. I also journeyed to Willcox, Arizona, where he rode his first bull at age sixteen in 1937 and stared at the vast stretches of rangeland and mountains that still frame the remote township. And I walked in his footsteps in Wyoming's majestic Sunlight Basin where, as a starving teenager of the Depression, he found work on a dude ranch as a bronc buster.

Each stop gave me a piece of Freckles Brown.

Interviews with contemporaries such as Ferrell Butler, Myrtis Dightman, Ronnie Bowman, Bobby Berger, Bill Kornell, and Marvin Paul Shoulders added further texture to the man I sought to discover and the lively times in which he lived. Wiley Harrison, his son-in-law, escorted me into his inner circle of family — a privileged place away from the glaring spotlight of the rodeo arena. There, I methodically examined the flesh-and-blood man — a beautiful human worthy of remembrance. For what is life if left unexamined?

The Ride is the culmination of all that I learned about the improbable life of Freckles Brown, a bull named *Tornado*, and the most historic eight seconds in rodeo. May you enjoy the journey and ultimately the ride. Hold on tightly, though. It's gonna be wild.

Chapter One
December 1, 1967
"The tension could be felt like a heavy fog."
— Pete Logan, rodeo announcer

Fear spread swiftly throughout the State Fair Arena crowd that December night, just as the frigid norther swept over the Oklahoma City metro. Beyond the arena walls, sleet pelted the ground and ice blanketed roads, laying siege to the city with hazardous conditions. The dangerous weather struck an ominous chord in the arena, in ways seen and perhaps even unseen.[1]

Officially, the 8,000-seat arena was a sellout for the first night of the 1967 National Finals Rodeo. Oklahomans were driven by a sense of duty to support the national event. They hoped to cast a positive light on their state — one often associated with John Steinbeck's bestselling novel *The Grapes of Wrath*, which many felt depicted an unflattering image of "Okies" during the Great Depression. In fact, many of the state's public libraries still banned Steinbeck's book. So, Oklahomans purchased tickets for the Finals until there were none left to purchase. Yet only "some 4,112 spectators" were in attendance on this night, meaning nearly half of the ticket holders were either unable or unwilling to brave the ice storm.[2]

State pride obviously had its limits. Fear, in contrast, can often be a runaway train. A chatter of consternation and anticipation first gained steam in the arena when Pete Logan — the voice of rodeo — announced the bull riding matchups for the first round. Logan informed the crowd that Freckles Brown — rodeo's beloved, ageless wonder at forty-six — had drawn *Tornado*, arguably the rankest bull to ever burst from a bucking chute. The 1,725-pound bull hailed from the herd of one of the most decorated cowboys in rodeo history, Jim Shoulders, and like its owner, was already a *bona fide* legend.[3]

No cowboy had ever made a qualified ride on *Tornado*. The bull's unbeaten streak included those who tried in the previous six National Finals dating back to 1961. Cowboys voted *Tornado* the "Finals Bull of the Year" from 1962 to 1965. By December 1967, *Tornado's* exact number of conquests were already cloaked by mystique. Fertile ground for exaggeration. Numerous reporters claimed *Tornado* had bucked off 220 cowboys entering the 1967 Finals. Other claims ranged from 185 to "nearly 250." The truth is no one knew for certain how many cowboys *Tornado* flung skyward, not even Shoulders. Nor did the exact number really matter. All anyone needed to know about *Tornado* was that the bull was undefeated in six years, and that its feared reputation was well-earned.[4]

Some cowboys who drew *Tornado* were even known to "turn him out," rather than climb aboard and possibly face the bull's wrath in the arena. Shoulders witnessed this scenario occur on numerous occasions.[5]

Fear simply shadowed *Tornado*.

"*Tornado* was one the greatest barrel bulls of all-time," recalled Ferrell Butler, a legendary rodeo photographer who stood in the arena that night armed with his trusty German-made Rolleiflex T 75 mm camera. "I mean he'd throw a cowboy and then go to blasting away at the barrel, busting it all the way across the arena.

"Everybody was scared for Freckles that night. What would happen once he hit the ground? Freckles wasn't young anymore, and he wasn't as quick as he used to be. The question was whether he'd be able to get away in time once he landed on the seat of his pants."[6]

C.R. Boucher, a hardened, old-school cowboy from Montana, even expressed concerns privately about Freckles' safety. Officials selected the former world champion steer wrestler to serve at the Finals as a pickup man — a mounted rider whose job routinely kept cowboys safe by roping any runaway roughstock animals. "I remember ol' Boucher was ready to move in," Butler said. "He was gonna ride in and rope *Tornado* by the horns if he had to . . . yeah, the fear was real."[7]

So was Freckles.

At first glance Freckles didn't evoke images of the stereotypical, heroic cowboy. He cast a diminutive silhouette at 5-foot-7, 150 pounds, and always spoke in a soft, child-like voice. The great sportswriter Red Smith once described him as a "smiling little chipmunk of a man," and Red wasn't wrong.[8] Freckles had an oval face with a long, straight nose, flanked by puffy-round cheekbones. And when he smiled, which was often, his cheeks rose and pooched ever slightly like a chipmunk with a mouth full of pine nuts.

Kindness might have been his greatest gift. He sprinkled goodwill wherever he journeyed and was never known to express anger or utter a harsh word. "Everybody loved

Freckles," remembered Ronnie Bowman, one of the world's best bull riders in 1967 and a travel companion of Freckles for years. "He was just the most humble and nicest man you'd ever want to meet."⁹

Freckles oozed humility, and possessed a gentleness toward others that belied his physical and mental strength. Strangers were often shocked at how such a small man — and a gentle one, at that — could make a living riding 1,700-pound, raging bulls. They failed to read the signs. Although small, Freckles' physique was all skin, bones, and muscles. He ran everywhere, whether in a rodeo arena or on his ranch in southeastern Oklahoma. He would drop at random times and do pushups. Or stop at an overhead beam and do pullups. He also avoided fried foods, long before it entered the nation's collective health conscience. And for those who looked closely, his hands were another dead giveaway. They were rugged hands with bulging knuckles, molded by a lifetime of arduous work and three decades of bull riding. He rode his first bull in a rodeo at age sixteen in Willcox, Arizona, in 1937 — the same year Walt Disney's ground-breaking animation *Snow White and the Seven Dwarfs* premiered in

Freckles flashes his famous smile in this iconic photograph taken by DeVere Helfrich in 1957. (*DeVere Helfrich Rodeo Photographs, Dickinson Research Center, National Cowboy & Western Heritage Museum. 81.023.12514*)

theaters worldwide.[10]

Three decades later Freckles was still doing the one thing he loved most — rodeo. Throughout those years, his focus evolved. He rode bareback broncs, bulldogged, and even competed in team roping events before he finally concentrated on bull riding — a profession not known for longevity. Over the years he collected more than his share of shiny belt buckles, trophies, and championships. He also paid for his passion with his body.

And he never complained. Not once.

Doctors both marveled at his resilience and shook their heads at his stubbornness. Freckles broke his right leg four times, his left leg twice, his right ankle twice, and left ankle once. He also had his left foot smashed a couple times. In one thirteen-month period, he broke his leg three times. He broke his neck twice, and in one surgery, doctors used a piece of his hip bone to plug into his neck. In another operation, surgeons cut a piece of tendon from his upper left leg and tied it to a tendon in his left ankle. He additionally had a severed tendon in his right arm retied. He suffered two broken collar bones and countless broken ribs, as well as a number of shoulder and knee injuries. There were ruptured blood vessels in his groin, a ruptured blood vessel in his right thigh, and countless pulled muscles. Freckles also noted that he had suffered three concussions — a dubiously low count given his line of work and the era in which he rodeoed. Then there were two shoulder surgeries, one of which left a metal pin in one shoulder. Another operation required a metal screw in one ankle.

Naturally, given his humility, Freckles shrugged off the

long list of medical setbacks. He even dismissed the near-death encounters he had with a few of the meanest bulls on the Professional Rodeo Cowboys Association (PRCA)* circuit. One bull hooked him in the mouth, leaving a scar on the right side of his upper lip. He was lucky to escape with only a scar. Yet Freckles would merely smile at all he had endured in the arena, and quip that he was "a walking hardware store."[11] In truth, he was much more. He was nothing short of extraordinary. No one rides bulls for three decades.

No one, but Freckles. He miraculously remained one of the world's top fifteen best bull riders in 1967, and as he strode into the arena on that frigid night, he was just forty-five days shy of his forty-seventh birthday. He entered the Finals as the seventh highest money-earner in a field where the average age of his competitors was twenty-six.[12]

Still, Freckles remained a bit of an enigma. Beloved by all but understood by few. One could argue that only a handful of people truly understood the key to his success and longevity. That's because beyond a man's physical attributes are sometimes those sources of inspiration buried deep within the soul. There, where painful memories linger, a fire of determination can rage. This is the fire no one sees, perhaps not even by those closest to the heart.

Not everyone can tap into that fire to find resolve. Freckles clearly did. He knew hardships intimately as a child of the Great Depression. He left his family home as a teenager to find work, often laboring all day for no more than room and

---

*Note: Organized in 1936, the association was named the Cowboys' Turtle Association and, in 1945, was changed to the Rodeo Cowboys Association. In 1975, the name was changed to the Professional Rodeo Cowboys Association.

board. He knew the discipline and loneliness of living in a distant, cowboy line camp in the Arizona mountains, as well as the dangers of riding the rails from state to state in search of work. He felt the humiliation of begging for work in exchange for a meal, and the sting of another closed door. He also endured the pain of being rocked to sleep by hunger in an unfamiliar town park with a newspaper for a blanket.[13]

Life dealt Freckles several blows during his formative years, some he never saw being thrown. The Great Depression hit with such ghostly speed and power. Few emerged unscathed. At least a bull presented him with a fair fight — an opponent he could see.

Tornado — the "unrideable" bull — presented something far more for Freckles. Drawing *Tornado* meant the opportunity to ride the most ferocious bull in rodeo history on the sport's biggest stage. If successful, Freckles would be forever remembered as the first cowboy to tame the legendary bull.[14]

A buzz filtered through the crowd that night as Freckles strode toward the chutes. His black chaps flapped in rhythm with his quick steps, and a white Stetson sat firmly atop his head of neatly cropped brown hair. Freckles climbed to the top of chute number two, where he stared down at the awaiting *Tornado*. The behemoth, Hereford-Brahman crossbreed featured a massive body covered by red hair with a distinctive white face. Gouge marks peppered the bull's horns from six years of combat in the arena.

Dean Krakel, then the executive director of the National Cowboy Hall of Fame and Western Heritage Center in Oklahoma City, would later write, "You could see *Tornado's* sides heaving and hear his hooves striking against the heavy steel gate."[15]

Spectators were already standing.

"Ladies and gentlemen — Freckles Brown will come out of chute number two . . ." Logan announced as the crowd fell silent. The twenty-one-year veteran rodeo announcer then uncharacteristically choked-up and paused. He composed himself and began again: "Ladies and gentlemen, Freckles Brown will come out of chute number two — on a bull that has never been ridden — Jim Shoulders' great bull, *Tornado!*"[16]

Lives are often reduced to defining moments, and Freckles recognized this as his greatest defining moment. He now stood on a precipice. His destiny teetered on the outcome. Finally, the ageless wonder climbed into the chute and lowered onto *Tornado's* massive back.

Logan would later recall how the tension in the arena "could be felt like a heavy fog." Logan let the moment breath before leaning into the microphone.[17]

"If you believe he can do it," Logan whispered, "he will."[18]

Suddenly, Freckles nodded, and the chute's heavy gate burst open . . .

Chapter Two
London Flats

"My only desire since I was a little boy was to be a cowboy. I used to dream of working on a ranch and breaking horses and just being a good cowboy. I never even thought of being good enough to rodeo."

— **Warren Granger "Freckles" Brown**

The signs were everywhere in a place appropriately branded by history.

Warren Granger Brown showed all the traits during his childhood in Wyoming. The daredevil. The showman. The tough man. The thinker. The worker. The survivor. In sum — and given the staging ground from which he spent his adolescent years — it's no wonder he eventually became a famous rodeo cowboy. Even if Brown himself never envisioned such a life. Maybe rodeo stardom was his destiny, although a destiny is hard to recognize in a land where animals and people are often casualties.

Brown's earliest years were spent in Goshen County, a rugged, arid country in southeast Wyoming where tender hearts and minds could be swallowed whole. The lifeblood of the region proved to be the North Platte River, delivering hope to settlers, as well as explorers and immigrants lured by the next horizon. The river is a tributary of the Platte River and flows some 716 miles like a thick snake through Colorado, Wyoming, and Nebraska — part of the thoroughfare for westward expansion. The trail followed the Missouri River,

Platte River, and North Platte River west.

Explorer and agent Wilson Price Hunt of the Astor Expedition first wrote about the trail along the North Platte River in 1811. Mountain men like Jim Bridger and Jedediah Smith of the Rocky Mountain Fur Company rediscovered the trail in 1823, and the route soon became a major path for fur trappers headed to the Rocky Mountain Rendezvous each summer.

John C. Fremont also followed the route on the first of his five westward expeditions in 1842. He noted on July 14, of that year how his party camped at "Goshen Hole" on the North Platte River.[1] A short distance away Fremont first entered Fort Laramie, which was then in its infancy and would increasingly become a haven for travelers who sought refuge from the wilderness. Eventually, immigrants followed the north and south banks of the river on the Oregon (1843-1869), California (1843-1869), Mormon (1847-1869) and Bozeman (1863-1868) trails. In addition, between April 1860 and November 1861, the short-lived Pony Express carried mail along the same route from Missouri to California.[2]

Goshen County's long, rich history essentially featured countless folks who passed through on their way to somewhere else. Ironically, Brown's journey eventually carried him away, as well. Although not before he tasted enough of life's joys and hardships on a far-flung, Wyoming prairie to forge the foundation of the man he would become.

Brown's origins were indeed humble. Richard and Lucretia Brown celebrated the birth of their tenth and final child, Warren Granger, January 18, 1921, in Wheatland, Wyoming — forty-nine miles from their homestead near the

Goshen County town of Lingle. Snow thawed in Wheatland the day he was born, perhaps an omen of the joyful spirit about to embrace the world. The first known public mention of Warren's birth appeared in the *Guernsey Gazette* seventeen days later: "Mr. Richard Brown, wife and baby of Lingle passed through Guernsey Sunday night (January 30) en route to home from the Wheatland hospital, where Mrs. Brown has been a patient."[3]

Richard Granger Brown married Lucretia Wilson in 1901 on Christmas Day in Pettis County, Missouri. Richard was twenty-seven years old, and Lucretia six years his junior. Both were natives of Green Ridge, Missouri, but later homesteaded in the neighboring town of Windsor. A suggestion, or perhaps simple wanderlust, would forever change the course of their family history. Two of Richard's sisters taught school in Wyoming and sold the couple on prospective opportunities for homesteaders in their state. Then, in 1905, Richard and Lucretia loaded their belongings and ventured into Wyoming. They never looked back. Lucretia continued to travel to Washington, where her family lived in Ephrata — a town known more for its abundance of wild horses than its prospects for settlement.[4]

Richard, meanwhile, remained in Wyoming to build a temporary home for his young family near what was then the town of Wyncote in Goshen County. Wyncote essentially sprang up in 1900 as a section house for the Burlington Railroad line, located three miles southeast of Fort Laramie. Richard's 160-acre homestead sat two miles north of the North Platte River on the old Oregon Trail where wagons ruts were still visible. Settlers called the place London Flats.

An early-day photograph of Lucretia Wilson Brown and Richard Granger Brown, Freckles Brown's parents. *(Courtesy of the Harrison-Brown Family)*

The scarcity of wood forced him to build a crude, log home from toppled cottonwood trees, likely gathering timber along a nearby creek.[5]

Two major developments in the region preceded the family's move to Wyoming. The first occurred when the Burlington Railroad expanded westward from Northport, Nebraska, in 1900, stretching from the unincorporated Wyoming town of Torrington in what was then Laramie County through Fort Laramie and then to Guernsey in Platte County. Homesteaders increasingly rode the new line to farmland along the North Platte River, as well as the rich iron mines at Hartville and Sunrise north of Guernsey.[6]

Another major milestone transpired with the passage of the *Reclamation Act of 1902*. The act pumped money into irrigation projects for arid lands in twenty western states, including Wyoming. Revenue from the sales of semi-arid public lands were then used for construction and maintenance of irrigation projects. Revolving funds from the sale of newly irrigated lands were also used to support additional projects.[7]

As usual, the North Platte River gave life to these projects and to the future of folks like Richard and Lucretia Brown. Upon completion of their log home, Lucretia reunited with her husband and returned with their first daughter who had been born in Washington.[8]

Wyncote, consequently, vanished as quickly as it appeared. The railroad's failure to obtain enough land for a townsite sealed its fate. Soon, other sites to the east were being considered by railroad brass. Hiram D. Lingle, a capitalist from Indiana, moved quickly. He had built an irrigation canal from the North Platte River to feed his plush, 1,800-acre valley to the north. Later, the federal government decided to build an irrigation canal on the north side of the river. Authorities concluded the only feasible route was the one used by Lingle, and purchased the right-of-way from the entrepreneurial, Hoosier transplant.[9]

So, when Lingle learned of the railroad's desire to find another townsite for a depot, he shrewdly offered to donate land. The new town — unsurprisingly named Lingle — thus popped up overnight. A few buildings were moved from Wyncote. Others followed. One man moved his store to the new town — the Lingle Supply Company. Another man built a hotel, which later housed the U.S. post office and the *Lingle Review* newspaper. By the time Warren was born, Lingle boasted the largest population in Goshen County with 2,739 souls.[10]

In those early days, the streets of Lingle were often rutted and muddy. Cowboys routinely gathered at the railroad station to greet the train — a sight alone that signaled hope for a prosperous future. But the real hope rested in the minds, hands, and backs of the homesteaders. Richard embraced irrigation farming, even despite hostile resistance from ranchers who resented his use of prime grazing land for his crops. Brown stood his ground. In doing so, he provided a strong voice for the region's irrigation farmers — an act of courage Warren either learned about during his childhood or perhaps even witnessed firsthand.[11]

By the time Warren took his first steps, his father had already established a sustainable farm. The elder Brown irrigated his crops during the summer, growing potatoes, corn, beans, alfalfa, sugar beets, and hay.[12] "We always had plenty to eat," Warren later recalled, "but otherwise we were poor."[13]

The family's "temporary" log home would remain for the first nine years of Warren's life. The elder Brown eventually added a tar paper shack thirty yards from the main house, and this is where Warren slept during his earliest years with his elder brothers Parson and Bryson. A coal oil lantern served as their lone source of light, and on frigid days and nights, the three brothers huddled around the shack's pot-bellied stove. Still, Wyoming's winters could be merciless. Temperatures dipped sometimes to thirty-degrees below, and on those occasions, there was no way to escape the bitter cold that bit at their bones.[14]

Nor did Warren ever forgot the pain of those bites.

In 1930, the fifty-five-year-old Richard built a new house with two bedrooms in the basement where Warren slept with Bryson. Parson had moved by then, leaving six children still in the home — Lillian, twenty; Ella, nineteen; Bryson, seventeen; Orpha, fifteen; Mildred, eleven; and Warren, nine.[15] For the first time, they all lived under the same roof. The house also featured an indoor bathroom, and a windmill that provided running water in the house on a windy day. On calm days, Warren mused somebody had to go outside and manually pump the water.[16]

Neighbors called the Brown's new house the "most beautifully landscaped home in Goshen County."[17] The Browns proudly shouldered a lead role in their community during this period. They helped establish a church in Lingle and actively worked to create area schools. Those years were likely the best of times for Richard and Lucretia, who had certainly experienced the worst of times with the death of their first two sons.[18]

One son — Richard Brown, Jr. — died at age nineteen in August 1922 while Warren was still a toddler. He was taking business courses at Scottsbluff Community College in Nebraska when he passed, supposedly from "infantile paralysis." The second son appeared to have died at birth.[19]

Life, of course, did not stop for the grieving. Especially on a farm. Richard rotated crops — irrigating in the summer — raised cattle, and broke horses. Warren increasingly worked alongside his father as he grew older. He realized then as a child he did not want to be a farmer. Instead, on the rich soil fed by the North Platte River, Warren dreamed of being a cowboy.[20]

"Since I was a little ol' kid all I dreamed about was being a cowboy," Warren said decades later. "My whole life, all I thought about was being a cowboy . . . I thought if I could just be good enough to hold down a job on a ranch, I'd be tickled to death and ride a horse that didn't have any collar marks on it."[21]

Richard Brown planted the seeds for his youngest son's dreams, whether knowingly or unknowingly. He charged Warren with herding cattle during the summer. The solitude of those days offered Warren a chance to engage in something else he loved to do — read. In fact, he read everything he could get his hands on. He even consumed books while he herded cattle along sunny trails. Warren especially loved to read books by Will James. The popular Canadian-born writer and artist first captured the romance and authenticity of cowboy life with his 1922 award-winning publication of *Smoky the Cowhorse*. For the next twenty years James produced books related to the western cowboy, including his fictionalized autobiography *Lone Cowboy: My Life Story* in 1930. James essentially lionized the cowboy and his way of life with his books during Warren's formative years. In time, the heroic characters created by James began to foster Warren's dreams of a cowboy life.[22]

Yet as much as Warren loved to read, he loved to ride horses even more. In addition to farming, his father regularly broke horses for ranchers, likely even for some who opposed him in the early days. Richard taught his son how to break horses, and afterward Warren would take them out for long rides in the North Platte River countryside where they lived.[23]

The sense of freedom from those rides undoubtedly stirred Warren's imaginations.

Warren also exhibited a propensity for taking risks. Ross E.

Baker, Warren's childhood friend, witnessed Warren's daring on more than one occasion back then. Baker remembered Warren as "a showman" who always flashed "a pleased look" at his wild deeds, even when the two boys were caught in a neighbor's watermelon patch and staring down the barrel of a twelve-gauge shotgun.[24]

Baker recalled the first time Warren climbed on the back of a steer — a horned, Guernsey-Holstein cross yearling. The steer bolted across the corral and suddenly stopped, hurling young Warren into the air. Warren landed on his back, knocking the wind from his lungs but not the spirit from his soul. On another occasion Baker remembered a time when the two boys were swimming naked in the North Platte River. They corralled a neighbor's cattle along a fence, climbed aboard, and rode them unabashedly through the river. Warren kicked the cattle in the shoulders with his bare heels and waved wildly.[25]

"What a sight!" Baker marveled decades later. "That neighbor would have killed us at an early age if he had caught us."[26]

Danger sometimes courted Warren. Even then, he never seemed to lack determination or courage. He and Baker once participated in a Pony Express rerun for the Boy Scouts of America from Sacramento, California, to St. Joseph, Missouri. The event was probably part of the Diamond Jubilee of the Pony Express, sponsored by the Oregon Trail Memorial Association in 1935. The highlight of the Jubilee was the rerun. More than 300 Boy Scouts participated, carrying letters addressed to President Franklin D. Roosevelt from governors and other officials along the route from August 8 to August

23. Organizers assigned Warren to carry the mail from the old Fort Laramie Bridge to a point just east of Fort Laramie, where he would then hand his bag to Baker.[27]

Warren rode his old, tall horse *Slim* at a breakneck speed, but suddenly found himself jerking back the reins as he approached a train crossing. Warren spotted an oncoming train. At that critical moment his bit broke, prompting him to ride down the middle of the highway with little control. The fourteen-year-old Warren never panicked. He gripped tightly with his legs, likely grabbing his horse's mane, and survived the wild escapade. He also dutifully finished the job — a trait he exhibited time and again as he grew into manhood.[28]

Oddly, the diminutive Warren never seemed to be aware of his own physical limitations. Warren may have displayed this mindset best on Lingle's crude football field, where he loved to run with the ball on offense and then blast classmates in the open field for a tackle on defense. Warren would later say matter-of-factly, "I thought I was as big as anybody."[29]

He wasn't.

Warren's greatest power might have been his mind. He grew to embrace whatever challenges enticed him most, and to always live large. Ironically, Warren's love of football changed the course of his life in another profound way in 1935. Now in ninth grade, Warren drove a classmate into the ground on one tackle, skinning his face. The boy — the superintendent's son — complained to his father, who promptly marched toward Warren and jerked him up by the ears. Warren's feelings were severely damaged by the superintendent's harsh reaction. The next morning Warren let the school bus pass. Richard found his son on a horse-drawn hay rake, perhaps sitting in silent frustration.[30]

"You go to school," Richard ordered. "You got to go to school tomorrow."

The elder Brown wasn't a man to be ignored. Then again, neither was his youngest son. The next morning Richard made sure he watched his son board the school bus. Warren rode the bus six miles into Lingle, where he exited the bus wearing two pants and two shirts. He walked to the nearby highway, flagged an approaching motorist, and hitched a ride into Mitchell, Nebraska, thirty-two miles away. By nightfall, the disgruntled teenager landed a job picking potatoes.[32]

Warren earned as much as two dollars a day in exchange for back-breaking work that began before 8 a.m. and ended at nightfall. The teenager and nine other workers were assigned to a row in the field and required to briskly pick potatoes. The spuds were placed in baskets, sacked, and later sorted. At the end of the day, the sacks were counted to determine how each worker fared.[33]

Mexicans served the bulk of the Depression-era workforce in Mitchell because few others were willing to endure the grueling conditions in a potato field. Even Warren wondered how long he could last but remained loyal to his convictions. He stubbornly determined he would not return to school.[34]

Warren realized that selling his parents on his decision would be difficult at best, especially his father. Richard Brown displayed no tolerance for rude behavior or defiance under his roof. Warren once remembered his father's stern stance on hats. "My dad would have give me a whuppin' if he'd ever caught me out in the sun without my hat on," he remembered. "And he'da give me another if he ever caught me in the house with it on."[35] In retrospect, Warren appreciated that lesson on manners.

At fourteen, however, Warren knew much greater consequences would be attached to his decision to drop out of school. Yet he was willing to face whatever the consequences. Right or wrong, he concluded he would stand by his decision like a man. He also wrote his parents a letter after two weeks in Mitchell to express his desire to return home. He only had one stipulation: No more school.[36]

Warren waited for a response. Finally, he received a letter from his parents, telling him they had plenty of work for him at home on the farm. Warren gathered his scant belongings and returned to Goshen County. He did so nervously, but also resolutely.[37]

Somewhere between Mitchell, Nebraska, and Lingle, Wyoming, Warren entered a new phase of his life. He became an adult, if in no other way than in his mind. The only question that remained was whether his parents would ultimately respect his desire. He returned home one evening to find his family seated around the dining room table eating.[38]

Richard Brown looked up at his road-weary son as he entered the room. He then reminded his son of the greatest act of all when he simply said, "You're late for supper."[39]

Chapter Three
Freckles

"Anything you say, Freckles."

— **A dairyman upon meeting Warren Granger Brown**

The notion of destiny can be hard to corral. Are the events of one's life preordained by a higher power, or as random as rolling dice in a game of chance? Or some mixture? Regardless, by 1935, circumstances in the Wyoming home of the Browns and across the United States triggered a chain of events that would send Warren on a fateful journey — one that would later appear guided by Providence.

Although the widespread pain of the Great Depression surely masked any sense of nature's force or a divine hand for the spirited teenager. So too would the family's deep concern for Lucretia Brown's health. Warren's fifty-four-year-old mother struggled with arthritis for numerous years. Warren once told veteran rodeo writer Willard H. Porter that the family spent several winters in Arizona's arid climate due to his mother's ailments.[1]

Finally, Richard made the decision in 1935 to permanently move to Arizona. Lucretia's heath may have declined rapidly by then as Warren would describe his mother as an "invalid."[2] Richard sought the refuge of the Sonoran Desert for his wife in the growing city of Tucson, once a dusty, adobe village sixty miles from the Mexican border. Tucson residents then numbered more than 32,500 people, and the city served as a major transportation terminus for the state's southern region. The Browns loaded their furniture, clothing, and other belongings into two cars and a trailer for the 1,088-mile trip from tiny Lingle, Wyoming, to Tucson. Bryson pulled the trailer with his car, while Warren drove his parents' vehicle. He was fourteen years old.[3]

No record of the route taken by the family exists, although they likely traveled over some newly constructed highways built by Public Works Administration (PWA) laborers. The PWA — part of President Franklin Delano Roosevelt's New Deal — began construction of new roadways in August 1933. Over the next two years of the PWA's existence, workers created 27,055 miles of new highways nationwide — just one sign of a nation fighting to shake the worst economic depression in the country's history.

Nobody had any money. Or, at least, nobody Warren knew had any money. In 1935, 20.1 percent of America's civilian work force remained unemployed — a drop from the staggering 24.9 percent unemployment rate at the height of the Great Depression in 1933. Naturally, Tucson residents were not immune to the sting.

Warren and his family drove into Tucson when transients camped in "hobo jungles" near the city's railroad yard. The scene offered a grim glimpse of the hard times that plagued the country. Special agent C.L. Meyers of the Southern Pacific Railroad Company reported an average of 250 tramps arriving in Tucson daily on trains during the winter of 1931-1932. Meyers recalled the time he arrested some thirty railroad trespassers. He promptly turned them over to

Tucson police. A magistrate sentenced the violators to twenty days in jail, but they only served two days. On the third day Tucson Police Chief John Dyer marched the prisoners back down to the railroad yard and ordered them shipped out of town. Meyers protested. Dyer retorted, "You brought them into town, and you will take them out of town if it takes the whole force of Tucson to see that they go."[4]

Railroad officials promptly shuttled the transients out of Tucson in boxcars.

Townspeople treated transients slightly more humanely by the time the Browns arrived in Tucson. By then, the city had become known as a "one-meal town." Tucson Organized Charities began feeding vagrants a meal in exchange for one hour of labor at the city's rock pile. Afterward, the transient was expected to catch the first train out of town.[5] Those who tempted the city's generosity quickly faced the wrath of local law enforcement. One man who testified before the U.S. Senate's LaFollette-Costigan Committee on federal unemployment relief said that the "general rule" of Tucson police was "to visit the jungles and shelters each morning and escort to the city limits those who show a tendency to stay longer than a day."[6]

Desperate tramps were therefore often spotted walking the desert roads outside Tucson — a sight likely seen by Warren and his family as they drove the final miles to their new home at 509 South 6th Street.[7]

Tucson offered desirable attributes for the Browns despite the economic hardships that hammered at everyone's soul. Weather was naturally a major draw. Tucson's *1935 Classified Directory* declared its city's climate to be the "FINEST IN

AMERICA," with weather comparable to that of "lower Egypt." Boastful comparisons to the Nile River Valley aside, Tucson's reputation for sunny, mild weather was legitimate. Four decades of U.S. Weather Bureau statistics declared so. Tucson received an average of 309 days of sunshine annually.[8]

The city — affectionately known as the "Old Pueblo" — also grew from a frontier pedigree amid enchanting beauty. The rugged, yet alluring Santa Catalina Mountains and its sprawling foothills framed Tucson's skyline to the north and northeast for eighteen miles. A series of canyons with names such as Rattlesnake, Esperero, Bird, and Bear extended into the mountains like crooked fingers. The most magnificent of those was Sabino Canyon, long a magnet for those who sought the recreational pleasures of a picnic or a day hike.

Sabino Creek carved the canyon over thousands of years, beginning at the elevation of nearly 9,000 feet on the shady slopes of Mt. Lemmon and spilling 6,000 feet and ten miles away into the desert oasis below in the Catalina foothills. There, a majestic saguaro forest greeted visitors who wanted a respite from Tucson for a few hours or days. Despite the sparsity of annual rainfall, dormant wildflowers burst into full bloom each spring, sprinkling a rainbow of colors amid the vibrant shades of green presented by a variety of cacti.

The mighty saguaro — some reaching heights of fifty feet — had long been the showpiece of the land, rising from the desert floor like prickly sentinels with barrel limbs that reach skyward. Below, amid a maze of prickly pear, fishhook barrel, and hedge cacti, was a landscape teaming with wildlife. Coyotes, rattlesnakes, eastern collared lizards, quail, roadrunners, and mountain lions were among the mammals, reptiles, and birds found in the canyon and surrounding foothills.

By the time the Browns arrived, Emergency Relief Administration (ERA) workers — many of them homeless transients — were already building a roadway up the canyon. Planners designed the road to cross a series of new, stone bridges and ascend to the newly constructed Sabino Canyon Dam and Recreation Area, which would feature lakeside cabins. Crews began blasting roadbeds in November 1934, and quickly made progress. A rush by the public to secure one of the new cabins ensued. But the dam project ultimately died two years later from a lack of money. Critics bemoaned the canyon's "road to nowhere," although the work was not in vain. Crews left behind a roadway and campgrounds for countless visitors who previously did not have access to one of Tucson's greatest treasures in Sabino Canyon.[9]

Warren probably frequented Sabino Canyon during this period. He would have done so riding horses along the canyon's numerous trails for a local man he credited with teaching him how to wrangle broncs.

Tucson's arid, desert climate also became a refuge for those struggling with their health, such as Warren's mother. Novelist Harold Bell Wright championed Tucson as a haven for those suffering from tuberculosis. He did so with a 1924 article that appeared in *American Magazine* entitled, "Why I Did Not Die." Wright described how he contracted the disease in the winter of 1915 while camping in the Catalina Mountains, and how he dodged death thanks to the care he received at St. Mary's Hospital in Tucson. Wright later worked tirelessly through charitable endeavors to ensure similar healthcare was available for the poor stricken by tuberculosis. By then, his writings had already placed a national spotlight in Tucson as a health resort.[11]

Ultimately, Tucson is where Warren learned to survive.

Jobs were as scarce as rain in Tucson and the surrounding region. He spent the next few years hopping from one job to the next, often for nothing more than room and board. His father listed his employment as "rancher," although it's doubtful he earned more than enough to subsist given the scarcity of money.

Warren chipped into the family coffer wherever he could. He briefly returned to school, but still worked nights to help pay for his mother's medical expenses.[12] Eventually, he dropped out of school permanently. His first job in Tucson might have been secured by his brother-in-law, James "Shorty" Gordon. He delivered milk for a dairy company, and was married to Warren's elder sister, Ella. He was a short, round Dutchman with a balding head, a drawer full of toupees, and an addiction to humor.[13]

The nimble Warren rode with Shorty daily. He ran bottles of milk to the front porch of each home on their route. Together, Warren and Shorty were comedic trouble, and probably spent more time laughing than working. They quickly developed a tight bond. Years later, they would sit for hours and cackle about all the angry dogs Warren dodged daily to deliver milk. Their reminiscing always led to the time Shorty gave Warren special instructions at a certain house. On that occasion, the ornery Shorty told Warren to set the milk just inside the door, instead of on the porch. He then reminded Warren to grab the empty bottles inside the house before the youngster exited the truck.[14]

Warren did as Shorty instructed. He cracked open the door, set the milk down and walked into the house to retrieve the empty bottles. Warren then heard a woman's voice call from a hallway.

"Milk man," the woman called, "can you come scrub my back?"[15]

A curious Warren crept further down the hall to where the voice emanated. Suddenly, Warren peered into the bathroom and saw a naked woman soaking in a tub. The woman screamed, water splashed, and the startled teenager sprinted out the house as Shorty laughed until he nearly cried.[16]

The memory, like the laughter, never grew old for the two men.

Warren's whereabouts during this period are at times difficult to determine. He constantly moved from one job to the next, chasing a dollar wherever one could be found. If not entirely lost to history, the names of his employers and workplaces are sometimes jumbled, quilted together from interviews given throughout his lifetime. Ironically, even the origin story of his famed nickname — "Freckles" — remains shrouded by conflicting or incomplete details.

The story can be traced to "a dairy six miles from Tucson," where Warren recalled in his own handwriting how the owner gave him his legendary nickname.[17] As the story goes, Warren's new boss asked him his name. The diminutive, freckle-faced teenager replied, "Warren Granger Brown."[18]

Hesitating for a moment, the dairyman looked at Warren and wryly responded, "Anything you say, Freckles."[19]

Warren's freckles eventually disappeared. The nickname

never did.

The dairyman who delivered the famous line might have been a man Freckles identified simply as "Mr. St. Denis" to famed sportswriter W.C. Heinz for his 1979 book, *Once They Heard the Cheers*. By Freckles' account, St. Denis operated a dairy in or near Tucson, and pastured cattle in mountains "twenty miles from Tucson" — probably somewhere in the Santa Catalina Mountains.[20]

St. Denis doesn't appear in city directories or census records from that period, although that doesn't mean he didn't exist. He could have owned any of Tucson's seventeen dairies in 1935. Heinz might have also misspelled or misunderstood the dairyman's name during his interview with Freckles. Regardless, Freckles said St. Denis paid him ten dollars a month to milk cows. Freckles earned every penny. He and two other colleagues milked sixty cows twice a day, cleaned the barn, and scrubbed the equipment. His hands swelled so badly at the end of each workday, he had to soak them nightly in a bucket of cold water.[21]

The hardships didn't deter Freckles from dreaming. He never surrendered the idea of someday becoming a cowboy. Whether St. Denis knew of his young employee's ambitions is unknown, but the dairy owner may have also given Freckles his first job as a cow hand. St. Denis sent Freckles to a remote line-camp in the mountains outside Tucson where he grazed a herd of cattle in the vicinity of a natural spring. Freckles job required him to ensure the cattle had water, and to clean the spring whenever the cattle trampled through it with sand.[22]

For two and a half months, Freckles lived in a crude, tin-roofed shack on a mountain populated with deer, turkey, cottontail rabbits, foxes, and mountain lions. He enjoyed other company as well. His companions in the shack included a nine-year-old boy with intellectual disabilities and a dog. The boy never strayed far from Freckles, mostly because the dog scared him immensely.[23]

The rugged, solemn life didn't faze Freckles. He supplemented the beans and flour they were provided by shooting an occasional cottontail rabbit. He mostly cooked rabbit and made frybread over a heavy skillet. The threesome drank from the nearby spring where Freckles hauled wooden barrels of water with a mule-driven wagon.[24]

Freckles learned to find amusement in everyday life at an early age, even in that remote locale. One day he drove the wagon to the spring to fill two barrels with water. The boy sat by his side on the buckboard. The route to the spring followed a ravine atop a steep cliff. Freckles dozed off at some point, and when he awoke, realized the boy was walking behind the creaking wagon.

"What are you doin' back there?" Freckles asked in bewilderment.[25]

The boy answered matter-of-factly: "I thought you was asleep and that the mules might drive you over the edge, and I'd get your boots."[26]

Freckles smiled at the boy's honesty. Decades later, he remained amused by the moment. "Hell," Freckles said, "you couldn't have driven them mules over that edge, but he liked my boots."[27]

For an aspiring cowboy, there was arguably no better place to be than southern Arizona. The region offered an abundance of mild weather, natural water sources, and vast ranges for major ranchers. Col. Henry C. Hooker founded the first permanent ranch in Arizona Territory in 1872. Hooker built his Sierra Bonita Ranch atop the ruins of a Spanish colonial estate in the spring-fed Sulphur Springs Valley between the Galiuro and Pinaleno mountains, some 100 miles northeast of Tucson. Hooker realized once the Apache wars ended the cattle industry would flourish in the region.[28]

Peace arrived at a heavy price. The wars scarred both a territorial population weary of Chiricahua Apache depredations, as well as the confederation of Apache bands which were either forced onto reservations or rounded up as prisoners of war. The hostilities ended in September 1886 when Geronimo and his small band of loyalists surrendered in Skeleton Canyon near the territorial boundary with New Mexico. By then, railroads were already making inroads into Arizona Territory — a development that opened outside markets to cattle ranchers. Prior to the 1880s, most commerce clustered around military outposts and along emigrant routes due to the threat of Apache war parties.[29]

Ranches flourished in the decades that ensued. By the dawn of the 1920s, Arizonans — and more specifically southern Arizona ranchers — realized there was also big money in tourism. Ranchers big and small began selling their western heritage. Dude ranches popped up throughout the region, prompting the founding of The Dude Ranchers Association in 1924. Ranchers catered to wealthy easterners who wanted to trade their bitter winters for the invigorating air of a "Wild West" beneath sunny skies. More than 115 dude ranches called southern Arizona home by the 1930s, and Tucson served as railroad terminus for both their supplies and paying guests.[30]

Ranch culture emanated throughout the region, including in the heart of Tucson where the Arizona Polo Association sponsored the annual rodeo *Fiesta de los Vaqueros*. Locals debuted the rodeo in 1924 to promote their Western ethos, and the yearly event quickly became a rousing success.[31] Rodeos were a staple of entertainment in and around Tucson. In the El Montevideo neighborhood, the elegant El Conquistador Hotel served as a staging ground for regular rodeos run by local rancher Stanley "Buck" Fletcher.[32]

The Texas-born Fletcher first moved to Tucson in 1935 — the fateful year of Freckles' arrival. He was born eight miles south of the Red River on November 15, 1901, in Quanah, Texas, then a railroad pit stop between Fort Worth and Denver. In Tucson, Fletcher quickly became a prominent cattleman and rancher, eventually amassing more than 70,000 acres south of the city. His appetite for success held no bounds. Fletcher became one of thousands of stockmen nationwide who bred and sold horses to the U.S. Army as part of the Remount Service program. He additionally supplied stock for area rodeos and later opened his own rodeo arena eight miles east of downtown Tucson on Benson Highway. By 1940, he and his brother, Lloyd, were also cashing in on Hollywood's desire to film in Arizona. The brothers provided cattle, horses, and oxen for Columbia Pictures in May 1940, for a film appropriately titled *Arizona*. Columbia Pictures released the film to theatres seven months later, starring Jean Arthur and William Holden.[33]

Fletcher and Freckles crossed paths at some point in 1935, perhaps at one of the El Conquistador Hotel's regular rodeos.

The cattleman hired the eager youngster as a hand to work on his growing spread, or perhaps to even help transport his rodeo stock. Freckles' employment might have also been restricted to roundups since steady work remained elusive. He never elaborated on his time at Fletcher's ranch, although he clearly made an impression with his attitude and work ethic.

The influential Fletcher gave Freckles a personal letter of recommendation should he ever need one. Freckles proudly tucked the letter away for such a day.[34]

Fateful encounters continued to occur for the aspiring cowpuncher. As the calendar flipped to 1936 and Freckles turned fifteen, he found work with another horse dealer, John Hulon McMinn. Folks simply called McMinn "Mac" — a horse whisperer of sorts who was born February 3, 1908, in Ranger, Texas, and later grew up 114 miles south in Coryell County, Texas. He too bred and sold horses in the Remount Service but ran a much smaller operation than the ambitious Fletcher — a fellow rancher he undoubtedly knew.[35]

McMinn's employment of Freckles appeared to be destined.

McMinn possessed a gift for training horses, and generously shared his knowledge with his curious, young cowboy. Freckles eagerly soaked up McMinn's wisdom. He later credited the native Texan as the one who truly taught him how to wrangle horses.

"I worked some on and off for Mr. Hulon McMinn, helpin' him break horses," Freckles recalled four decades later. "He really taught me — how to put a hackamore on, and how to pull one's head around and when to leave 'em alone and when to keep on makin' them do something right, and how to teach 'em to turn and to come to the run."[36]

Horses had long been a passion of McMinn, who first arrived in Tucson by train as a teenager with a shipment of mules. His older brothers — Weston and Ray — had already established a family homestead on Mount Lemmon, the highest peak in the Santa Catalina Mountains. They traveled ahead of their younger brother, making the 900-mile journey from Texas on horseback. Hulon and Weston operated riding stables on Mount Lemmon, and that's where Hulon first met his future wife, Harriet Huntington Miller. She showed up one day to enjoy a trail ride. Instead, she found a husband.[37]

Hulon and Harriet married November 8, 1931, in Pima County, and owned a home in the unincorporated, ranching community of Tanque Verde, twelve miles northeast of Tucson. By 1936, the couple had moved into the Tucson Auto Inn, perhaps the result of a foreclosed home. Hulon and Weston were then ranching together, probably on land Weston claimed from an abandoned homestead near Tucson in 1932.[38]

Freckles rode broncs on their ranch for room and board.[39]

The education he received from McMinn later proved priceless, although at the time it didn't help pay his mother's medical bills. Desperation led Freckles to seek a bolder course of action. He went to his brother Bryson for advice. Bryson — his elder by eight years — recommended the risky venture of "riding the rails" to search for work.[40]

Danger shadowed those nomads who jumped aboard trains during the Great Depression. And many were willing to take their chances. Dangers be damned. An estimated

250,000 teenage hoboes roamed the nation at the height of the Depression, and their motivations to leave home were as varied as their names. Many sought to alleviate the burden on their families of another mouth to feed. The dreamers entertained visions of finding work and sending money back home. Some fled the shame of poverty in a broken home, while others simply sought a grand adventure. Some had the blessings of their parents. Others didn't.

Nearly all of them hoped to find jobs that simply didn't exist.[41]

Freckles clearly turned to the railroads as means to help his family. Bryson taught his younger brother how to jump on a train by running as fast as possible and catching "the ladder at the front end of the boxcar." Freckles caught his first train in this manner in Tucson. He later jumped aboard another train leaving in El Paso, Texas, only to discover he had joined 200 other men. He guessed about thirty of them were, as he put it, "professional bums." The rest were desperate job seekers like himself.[42]

The train carried Freckles into Tucumcari, New Mexico, where he caught another freight to Denver.[43] Each time Freckles latched onto a moving train, he risked his life. Nor did the risk subside once he safely secured himself on the ladder of a boxcar.

Tragic stories were common among those "riding the rails" during the Great Depression. Gene Wadsworth told one such story from those days. He was seventeen years old, and riding freights between California and Arizona when he teamed with another youngster he knew only as Jim. The boys were riding back-to-back on the ladders between boxcars one freezing night. "All of a sudden the train gave a jerk," Wadsworth recalled. "I heard Jim let out a muffled moan as he fell. I whipped round and made a grab for him. I got his cap and a handful of blonde hair. Jim was gone. Disappeared beneath the wheels. I felt so sick I had to climb up and lie on the catwalk. From then on, I was a loner."[44]

Freckles would have also had to steer clear of notorious railroad bulls like Texas Slim, who was known to treat transients violently at the Longview, Texas, yards. Denver Bob was another railroad bull reputed for shoving trespassers beneath the wheels of a moving train.[45]

Denver, meanwhile, is where Freckles hopped off the train in the summer of 1936. He trekked or hitchhiked eight miles south to Englewood and found two months of employment on a dairy and wheat farm for thirty dollars a month, plus room and board. During his stay, Freckles received a letter from McMinn, informing him that he had a new batch of horses and work for the winter.[46]

McMinn's offer called Freckles back to Tucson. By then, the horse trainer and his wife might have already moved into their new home in the Tanque Verde Valley — home of the famed Tanque Verde Ranch. Don Emilio Carrillo established the ranch in 1868. Bands of roving Apache warriors once preyed on the ranches in the valley, prompting the government to supply civilians with guns and ammunition. Back then cavalry units from nearby Fort Lowell patrolled the valley. And while the Apache had long since disappeared, remnants of the old days remained. Wild cattle — missed by various roundups — could still be found in 1936 high on the slopes of the Rincon Mountains to the east, as untamed as wild deer. [47]

Freckles undoubtedly rode through this legendary valley — as well as the canyons of the Santa Catalina Mountains — while training McMinn's horses. In the end, however, Freckles was forced to leave McMinn once again because "there just wasn't any money." He left with a strong sense of gratitude for the knowledge McMinn graciously bestowed upon him.[48]

The Depression continued to knock Freckles to his knees, but he never let it keep him down. Or steal his spirit. Through it all, he remained undeterred in his pursuit of that next opportunity. He found it in 1937 at a ranch on the outskirts of Willcox, Arizona — the "Cattle Capitol of the Nation."[49]

Willcox sat in the middle of the Sulphur Springs Valley in the far southeastern corner of the state. The *Arizona Star* first referred to the burgeoning new town in August 1880 as Maley, located eighty-three miles east of Tucson. The town's name was later changed to Willcox in honor of General O.B. Willcox, noted for his dogged military operations against the raids of Chiricahua Apache warriors. The general also rode the first train that pulled into the town's new depot.[50]

The valley that surrounds Willcox is essentially a bowl of flat, vast grassland, encircled by a chain of mountain ranges. The Winchester and Galiuro mountains imprint the skyline to the northwest; the Pinaleno Mountains in the northeast; the Dragoon Mountains in the southwest; and the Dos Cabezas Mountains to the east, extending southward to Apache Pass and the gateway to old Fort Bowie. Beyond the pass to the south are the mighty Chiricahua Mountains, once a refuge for Geronimo and his band of Chiricahua Apache when they fled into Mexico in 1882. During that fateful flight, Geronimo and his followers made a long night march to outdistance a superior force of U.S. troops and reach the safety of the mountains. One follower claimed to have witnessed Geronimo's spiritual powers during that desperate flight: "So [he] sang, and the night remained for two or three hours longer. I saw this myself."[51]

Geronimo's band successfully reached their mountain refuge and carried on their resistance another four years. Or so the legend has been told.

For the valley's pioneer cattle ranchers—brave trailblazers like Hooker — such news factored into their survival. So did water. The Sulphur Springs Valley has long offered a unique, geographical phenomena with an endorheic basin named the Willcox Playa, located adjacent to the Willcox to the south. The valley traditionally received its heaviest rainfall between July and September and collected all the drainage from the neighboring mountains. The Willcox Playa —an eight-mile-wide and ten-mile-long dry lake — is therefore generally full for two months, and as one observer noted, "hard and smooth as a billiard table" the remainder of the year.[52]

Hooker, for one, proved cattle ranchers could thrive in the valley. He diverted the runoff of seasonal flood waters from the mountains with hand-dug ditches, improving thousands of acres of grassland. His diligent commitment to the distribution of water additionally created new areas of perennial sacaton grass, a native grass that flourishes in arid climates. Hooker also impounded water with dirt embankments and planted sorghum and corn in irrigated fields from storm-water reservoirs. The crops, while not extensive, trapped water in the roots and could be plowed for forage in times of drought for famished cattle.⁵³

By the close of 1936, cattle prices were rapidly climbing, and shipments had increased dramatically. Ranchers shipped a total of 12,460 head from Willcox in November of that year, compared to the 10,000 head loaded onto trains that same month two years earlier. The *Arizona Range News* delivered the good tidings in December:

> *Willcox has long been acknowledged as the leading cattle shipping point in Arizona and the Southwest. According to Mr. [J. Frank] Wootan, a United States Inspector who recently visited this point, says it is now the leading shipping point in the entire United States for shipping cattle direct from the range.*⁵⁵

All signs pointed to an economic upturn for the region's cattlemen, which likely brought Freckles to the valley in 1937. The sixteen-year-old cow hand landed a job eighty miles to the east of Tucson on a ranch outside Willcox in Cochise County. By then, he had already traveled more than most folks much older than him. Whether he traveled by car or courtesy of the Southern Pacific Railroad, the trip to Willcox would have been memorable. The railroad paralleled U.S. Highway 80 and would have carried him past the cattle town of Benson on the San Pedro River. By vehicle, U.S. Highway 80 peeled southward toward Bisbee and the Mexico border, while State Highway 81 — a graded road — swung northward for another thirty-five miles into Willcox. The railroad followed the same path.⁵⁶

The highway weaves through Texas Canyon, along a route dominated by piles of gigantic, granite boulders and scenic vistas. Travelers eventually reached the hamlet of Dragoon on the northern edge of the Dragoon Mountains. Suddenly, the wide, sweeping grasslands of the Sulphur Springs Valley come into view.[57]

If Freckles didn't feel a sense of awe by the vastness of the valley, he most assuredly felt a sense of hope. Ranches dotted the sixty-one-mile-long valley, and a job meant one more day with food in his belly. He left no record of which ranch he worked near Willcox, although the historic Seventy-Six Ranch and the Page and Misenhimer Cattle Company are two prime candidates.

The Seventy-Six Ranch dated back to its founding in 1876 and was nestled at the base of Mount Graham some thirty-five miles northwest of Willcox. In 1900, W.T. and Claire Webb acquired ownership of the ranch, an expansive, 65,000-acre spread that stretched 100 square miles across the flat lands of the valley and up the canyons and mountains to the east. By 1937, the Seventy-Six Ranch also catered to tourists as a dude ranch.[58]

Gordon Winfield "Boozer" Page and his brother-in-law, J.L. "Tab" Misenhimer, owned the old Roberts Ranch. The ranch extended from the Willcox town limits eastward to the peak of the Dos Cabezas Mountains, and south to the northern tip of Willcox's famed dry lake. Page and Misenhimer were major players in the region's cattle industry. In fact, they bought, sold, and brokered most of the cattle shipped by rail from Willcox, and additionally owned cattle in seven states.[59]

Page, most noteworthy, also staged rodeos on his ranch three-quarters of a mile outside of town. The forty-eight-year-old Page earned a reputation in regional rodeo circles for his matched team roping events with his partner, Fred

Darnell. Together, they became local legends.[60]

Beyond his love of rodeo, locals considered Page an unforgettable character. He loved to tell stories. Born the youngest of six children in Abilene, Texas, his family moved to Tombstone, Arizona, when he was four. Eight years later the family moved to Willcox, where his father served as a justice of the peace. He grew up hearing tall tales of outlaws and renegades.[61]

One of Page's favorite stories involved the valley's notoriously harsh winds. As the story went, Page described how he was riding into town one day during a windstorm — presumably aboard his trusty horse, *Honey*. He then rode up on a black hat sitting on the sand. He dismounted, and picked up the hat, only to reveal the top of a man's head. Page frantically dug until he exposed the man's nose and mouth. Shockingly, the man was still alive. The man then said, "Son, you better go home and get a shovel. I'm on horseback."[62]

Page's wit made him a natural showman, and his tall tales were a constant source of entertainment at ranches and rodeos throughout the valley. Whether Freckles worked for Page and Misenhimer is unknown, although he most assuredly encountered Page when he promoted a two-day rodeo on his ranch June 26 and 27, 1937, — the only rodeo held in Willcox that year.[63]

Fate again seemed at play.

A fellow cowpuncher told Freckles one day about how he won some money at a local rodeo. For the first time in his life, Freckles seriously contemplated entering a rodeo. A few extra dollars from a winning ride appealed to the game teenager. So much so he rode a horse "into town" on Saturday, June 26, and his fellow ranch hand paid his entrance fees.⁶⁴

Rodeos in Willcox traced back to as early as April 1919 when H.A. Johnson — *aka* "Hackberry Slim" — entertained large crowds with a two-day extravaganza. The rodeo boss promised an event that was "Too wild for the Wild West and too swift for the movies."⁶⁵ In a town that promoted itself as "Where the West is Still West and the Cowboys are Real," rodeos were hailed as a celebration of a heritage stained with blood, sweat, and tears.⁶⁶

In short, Freckles discovered far more than a rodeo that fateful day. He found a party. Tickets sold rapidly in the weeks prior to the rodeo at The Tavern in town for twenty-five cents, and later at the gate.

Cowboys were treated as honored guests. S.W. Clark, a former Willcox barber and rodeo performer, served as announcer. Clark's voice boomed from a new Electrolux loudspeaker as he announced the names and times of each event, from bull riding and calf roping to pony races and team roping. "Novelty" events were also planned.⁶⁷

Spectators, meanwhile, guzzled cold beer and soda pop as they roamed the dusty grounds. They talked about the highly anticipated competition. A buzz ultimately prevailed concerning the featured attraction — a matched team roping event between Pierre Getzwiller and Claud Gardner versus Al Rix and the charismatic promoter himself, "Boozer" Page.⁶⁸

Later that night a public dance would be staged at the new Willcox Community Center, featuring the music by the Stafford Nite Hawks.⁶⁹

Freckles boldly entered the bull riding competition.

The daredevil in him knew a winning ride would mean a whopping $25 purse. For the first time, Freckles heard his name announced at a rodeo as he lowered himself onto the back of a bull. With the Dos Cabezas Mountains silhouetted behind him to the east, the chute's gate swung open, and Freckles hung on for the most memorable ride of his young life.[70]

"I rode my first bull and didn't win anything," Freckles recalled, "but I was real tickled I didn't fall off."[71]

Freckles departed Willcox far more than tickled. He was hooked on rodeo. The atmosphere, the people, the cheers, and the ultimate challenge of man-versus-beast appealed to his soul. Afterward, he competed in a handful of dude ranch rodeos, although bronc riding and roping were the only events offered.[72]

The Depression soon dashed any visions of rodeo glory.

A year later Freckles again found himself unemployed and back in Tucson. Bruised and battered by circumstances out of his control, Freckles remained unfazed by the hardships and even hopeful. Perhaps it was the naivete of youth blinding him to the reality that stared back at him. Or an internal fortitude than stubbornly refused to crack. Or both. Quitting wasn't an option. He desperately needed work.

Rodeo had to wait. Hope didn't.

Now seventeen, Freckles pondered his options. He surely thought of all the people he had worked for, and the places he had visited since moving to Arizona. One name kept coming back to him — Simon Snyder. The prominent Wyoming rancher spent his winters in Arizona, often visiting the border town of Nogales, sixty-six miles south of Tucson. Like

Fletcher and McMinn — two ranchers he might have known — Snyder also trained and sold horses to the government.

Snyder met Freckles one day in the winter of 1937, although the circumstances of their meeting have long fallen through the cracks of time. Snyder told the teenager about his ranch in the remote Sunlight Basin north of Cody, Wyoming, and if he ever found his way back to Wyoming, he would give him a try at breaking horses.[73]

Freckles filed Snyder's kind offer away in his satchel of hope, along with Fletcher's letter of recommendation.

Bryson, meanwhile, persuaded his brother to consider another option — one that could benefit them both. He reminded Freckles of how he found work sewing sacks on a wheat harvest in Walla Walla, Washington, one season. Bryson suggested they "ride the rails" together to the Pacific Northwest and take their chances.[74]

Frankly, the brothers had no better idea.

So, on a July day in 1938, the brothers packed all their clothes in one suitcase and hopped a freight at the Tucson railroad yard traveling north. They pooled their money — a grand total of fifteen bucks. The money quickly vanished with the food they ate.[75]

Unlike the money, the hunger returned. And the hardships mounted. From town to town on their journey, they knocked on doors and asked to chop wood or mow lawns for a meal. They possessed one bar of soap and cleaned in cattle troughs. At night, they wrapped themselves in packing paper from crates found in empty boxcars at various railroad yards.[76]

Sometimes they turned to hitchhiking. In La Grande, Oregon, they had no choice. A railroad bull ran them out of the yard. The enforcer threatened to sentence them to thirty days for vagrancy. The brothers reluctantly returned to the highway, in search of a ride. Only no cars stopped.

Bryson offered a plan. He concluded a driver might be reluctant to give two young men a ride.

"We'll split," he said. "You're a lot younger lookin' than I am, and somebody will probably pick you up."[77]

Once Freckles secured a ride, he would then tell the driver his brother was just down the road. The plan sounded fail proof. Or so Bryson thought.

Bryson grabbed the suitcase and walked ahead. He waited around a bend in the road. Soon, two elderly ladies stopped in "a long, expensive car" to give Freckles a ride. The two women were engaged in a conversation as they pulled away, driving slowly around the curve. Bryson came into view, his thumb extended in the air as the car approached.

"That's my brother Bryson there," Freckles said, "and we're travelin' together."[78]

The women never heard. Freckles helplessly looked out the window as the car passed his brother, who stood with his thumb still extended with a pained expression.

Freckles eventually traveled fifty miles north to Pendleton, Oregon, where the brothers vowed to reunite at the city park should they be separated. For three days Freckles roamed Pendleton in search of food. He knocked on one door after another, begging to work for a meal. The closed doors hurt as much as the hunger pains. If he wasn't huddled beneath newspapers at the city park at night, he was sleeping at the railroad yard, laying between two railroad ties on a bed of hay.[79]

Bryson never showed up. A feeling washed over the frustrated youngster. He realized something had happened. His brother wasn't coming.

Weary and starving, Freckles sat in the park. He sat alone. Despair waited at the doorstep of his thoughts. At that moment he reached into his pocket. He unfolded "Buck" Fletcher's letter of recommendation and began to read. He then thought of Simon Snyder's ranch in Wyoming's Sunlight Basin, and his offer of a tryout as a wrangler.

The survivor within Freckles rose to his feet, exhausted but not beaten. He began walking to the railroad yard. He had a train to catch to Wyoming.[80]

Chapter Four
Sunlight Ranch

"Where did you find that pun'kin roller?"

— Don Snyder, son of Sunlight Ranch owner Simon Snyder

Simon Snyder never saw a more pathetic looking cowboy. A short youngster stood before the seasoned rancher that summer morning in 1938, covered in soot from head to toe. The blackened shirt he wore barely hung on his shoulders; tattered and accentuated by a gaping rip that streamed down the front of the garment. He wore no hat — let alone a cowboy hat — or even cowboy boots. Instead, he stood in a pair of scuffed and blackened brogans. And his dirty, brown hair looked as disheveled as his clothes in the splash of sunlight painting the basin.[1]

For a moment, Snyder carefully studied the teenager outside the main house of his Sunlight Ranch.[2] A face of the Great Depression stared back. Snyder recognized him only as Freckles. The kid he met in Arizona. Freckles handed him the letter of recommendation from Stanley "Buck" Fletcher, and asked in a quiet, respectful tone if he could try his hand at breaking horses.

Freckles probably would have stood with his hat in hand, only he had no hat. Nor did he have a saddle. Or money. He only had determination.

Snyder was a no-nonsense man, steeped in a strict work

Simon Snyder became a ranching legend in the Bighorn Basin. *(Courtesy Sally Holberg and Sue LaFever)*

ethic and self-reliance. No other type of man would survive in the Sunlight Basin, an enchanting, yet remote setting amid northern Wyoming's majestic Absaroka Mountains. The basin's beauty was matched only by the harshness of its winters when roads were impassable. Each day therefore held a purpose. Snyder didn't tolerate slackers, and was fond of often saying, "Never hire a man who smoked or wears high-laced shoes; he has no time for working because he is either rolling a smoke or lacing his shoes."[3]

The fifty-three-year-old rancher glanced at Fletcher's letter. He looked back at his young visitor, who hitchhiked the final fifty miles of his journey to the ranch from Cody, Wyoming. Freckles' unexpected presence at the ranch alone proved shocking to the senses, as did his haggard appearance. Only Snyder knew there was much more to the youngster's story. Perhaps something even heroic.[4]

The obvious question followed: What happened between Arizona and Sunlight Ranch?

Freckles recounted his nomadic steps, leading to his separation from his elder brother and those desperate nights in Pendleton, Oregon. As it turned out, he successfully

Simon and Ora Snyder's ranch house in the Sunlight Basin. (*Courtesy of Sally Holberg and Sue LaFever*)

jumped a train in Pendleton and rode atop a tender — or coal-car — the entire 740 miles east into Cody. The whole time he ate the black fumes spewing from the coal-burning engine's smokestack.[5]

Lastly, Freckles explained the hardships he encountered in Tucson which led to his departure from Arizona.

Satisfied, Snyder turned to one of his cowboys. He told the cowhand to find Freckles a bed in the bunkhouse, a long, log structure not far from the ranch's network of corrals. He then directed him to outfit Freckles with a new shirt and jeans from the ranch store, where they sold groceries, clothing, candy, fishing tackle, and American Indian-made curios brought back from Arizona, New Mexico, and Old Mexico for their guests. Snyder, who once broke horses for William F. "Buffalo Bill" Cody, ran both a working cattle and horse ranch, and dude ranch. Finally, before putting Freckles to work, he wanted him fed a late breakfast — the first real meal the weary youngster had eaten in days, if not weeks.⁶

Moments later Freckles sat at a table with a spread of food laid out before him. A stack off hotcakes . . . butter . . . syrup . . . eggs . . . bacon . . . freshly squeezed orange juice . . . or as he remembered, "anything you could eat."⁷ He feasted like a king, or more accurately, like a starving teenager.

Void of hunger pains for the first time in recent memory, Freckles walked to the corrals to begin working with the horses. His eyes couldn't help but dart around at the grandeur of his surroundings. Mountains towered on the north and south sides of the ranch, along a valley floor plush with native grass and alfalfa hay meadows beyond the corrals. The steady flow of the Sunlight Creek ran parallel to the valley, and nestled against the creek was a long recreational hall — site of some high-stomping, square dances on summer nights.

Log buildings were clustered in a neat row, facing the corrals, while several pine-slabbed, guest cabins were located behind the Snyder's main ranch house. The cabins — while off limits to the cowboys — were tastefully decorated in a chic, western style, and featured Thomas Molesworth's iconic, rustic furniture he built at his shop in Cody. Molesworth's creations were heavily accented by branches, logs, and cowhides.⁸

Everywhere Freckles looked, he could see a portrait of efficiency. Neat stacks of wood were placed at various locations to feed the ranch's many stoves and fireplaces. A "chore boy" — an elderly man, actually — tended to a large garden, fed the chickens, cleaned coops, and milked the cows.⁹

Large strips of jerky — cut fresh from elk, deer, and moose hunted in the adjacent mountains — hung in large quantities in a cool room next to the sawdust-packed ice house. Workers cut the ice for the ice house during the winter in Sunlight Creek and packed the slabs in sawdust from the cut firewood. A pine-slabbed, rectangular building served as the ranch's root cellar — a true marvel of engineering in Sunlight Basin. To enter, one had to open a deadlock attached to two, heavy wooden doors. Inside, the cellar revealed itself to be a partial dugout. Two rows of concrete ran parallel to one another, divided by giant logs. Sawdust was strewn between the logs. At the back of the cellar were three large, sand-filled bins — each for storing potatoes, carrots, and onions. Nearby, crocks were filled with eggs submerged in a pickling lime and water solution for preservation and rows of shelves packed with canned corn, beets, and peas.[10]

Finally, Freckles gazed upon the ranch's extensive corrals. Cowboys worked the horses in essentially three round corrals enclosed by stout, uniformly cut pine poles. Each corral opened to the larger one — the last of which was oblong and large enough to hold hundreds of horses at one time. And sometimes did. Broncs were often ridden for the first time in the smallest, while colts were generally ridden first in the second, slightly

The corrals where Freckles initially proved his skills as a wrangler to Simon Snyder. (*Courtesy of Sally Holberg and Sue LaFever*)

Simon Snyder (standing) and his wife, Ora, take a family picture with their son, Don, daughter-in-law, Faye, and granddaughter, Sally, circa 1939. (*Courtesy of Sally Holberg and Sue LaFever*)

larger corral. At night, the horses were released into the hay meadows along Sunlight Creek and then rounded up again each morning.[11]

A blacksmith shop sat next to the oblong corral, complete with a coal-burning hearth, anvils, and kegs of horseshoes. The shop buzzed with activity throughout the year, especially in the spring when horses were shod for summer riding and during haying season to keep mowers, rakes, and baling stackers in shape.[12]

Freckles thought he had stepped into a dream. Years later, he would call Sunlight Ranch, "The most beautiful ranch I had ever seen."[13]

Whether Freckles remained on Sunlight Ranch rested on

his ability to break horses.

Upon Simon Snyder's direction, one cowboy cut a bay mare out from the herd. Freckles approached, talking to the horse, and calmly slid a hackamore over her head. He then led her around and turned her. No one said a word.[14]

One by one, cowhands continued to bring Freckles a new horse. He rode them all.[15]

A few hours later Snyder's twenty-seven-year-old son, Don, rode into the ranch. He had been leading a string of guests — commonly referred to as "dudes" — on a morning trail ride. They had been clamoring to see a real cowboy in action, riding untamed horses at the corrals. As the guests rode through the ranch's main gate, Don noticed a new man breaking horses at the corrals. At first, he was pleased. The previous wrangler — Chuck King — had recently underwent a hernia operation and was out of commission at an inopportune time. Don's father had therefore searched for weeks to replace King with a hand who could help break a bunch of four- and five-year-old geldings, some of which would be sold to the U.S. Army as part of the Remount Service. The government paid $150 for every sound, broke gelding that could walk, trot, and gallop, and business had been "poor" at the ranch since the Depression hit.[16]

Don's relief soon turned to angst. Then disappointment. He glanced briefly through the pine rails of the corral as he helped guests unsaddle their horses. He noticed the new hand had no hat or boots, and if that wasn't bad enough, he was even using one of the ranch saddles.

"I hated to admit to our guests that a guy who looked so unlike a cowboy was to be our new horse-breaker," Don recalled years later, "for there had been a lot of talk about breaking horses and our guests were looking forward to watching the operation from the top rail of the corral."[17]

The idea of a greenhorn breaking horses infuriated the young rancher. He couldn't wait to question his father about the new hand, but the inquiry had to wait. The family always sat down to dinner — meaning lunch on a western ranch — with the guests at the main dining table.

After a short time, the dudes dispersed, and Don found himself alone with his father. He could hardly contain his frustration.

"Where did you find that punk'in roller?" Don asked sharply, tagging Freckles with the derogatory term for a farmer. The line smacked with more than a little ranch snobbery.

"Doesn't he have any hat or boots?" Don continued. "Where's his saddle?"[18]

Simon Snyder didn't appreciate his son's quick condemnation of Freckles. Or his son's disrespectful tone.

"His name is Freckles," the elder Snyder replied. "I don't know his last name. I met him in Arizona last winter and told him I would give him a try at breaking horses if he came up here this spring. He rode the rods up to Cody and hitchhiked a ride out here this morning."[19]

"How old is he?" asked Don, his words increasingly laced with frustration. "He looks like a punk kid."[20]

Shoveling food onto his plate, Don failed to realize he had ventured too far with his harsh words and apparent lack of empathy. By the time he looked up at his father, it was too late. The elder Snyder — a hardened pioneer who was not to be trifled with — unleashed a verbal barrage on his beloved son.

"He's seventeen," Simon snapped. "He doesn't have any boots, hat, or saddle because he has been going to school and working nights to support his invalid mother. Does that answer your ill-mannered questions? And you better watch him work for a while before you go shooting off your mouth about his being a punk'in roller!"[21]

Don instantly knew he was wrong. His father seldom raised his voice, but when he did, his children nearly always knew they had it coming. After dinner, Don ventured to the corrals to watch Freckles work. Sitting on the top rail of the corral, he did so with a humble heart and open mind. He immediately observed a catching technique he had never seen before. Instead of "front-footing the green colt," he crowded them into the small corral so tightly they could hardly move. Freckles then walked among the horses, talking, and petting them until he slid a halter on his chosen colt.[22]

Simon Snyder looks over his herd of horses. He broke horses for years and sold them to the U.S. Army's Remount Service. (*Courtesy of Sally Holberg and Sue LaFever*)

The stream of conversation never ceased. If Don had closed his eyes, he would have thought Freckles was talking to another person.

By noon, Freckles already had four colts tied to the fence — a productive half day for anyone, and he didn't even show up at the ranch until after nine that morning.

"How many are you going to tie up at once?" Don asked.[23]

"Oh, three or four more, I guess," Freckles answered. "Looks like there are three or four more good posts to tie to."[24]

"You think you can handle that many at once?" Don continued.[25]

Flashing a disarming, crooked grin, Freckles replied, "I reckon."[26]

Suddenly, unexpectedly, Don found himself fascinated by Freckles. Work pulled him away, as was life on the ranch. Several dude horses needed to be shod. He grabbed a couple of halters, caught two horses, and led them to the blacksmith shop. As he fitted the horses with horseshoes, he found himself amused by the constant conversation coming from the corrals by the lone voice of their new hand.

Once the first two horses were shod, he emerged from the blacksmith shop to retrieve more horses. The sight of dudes perched on the top rail of the corral "like crows on a dead limb" surprised him greatly. They were spellbound by Freckles and his interaction with the horses, and if they spoke, they did so in whispers so not to interrupt the show.[27]

Somewhere in Arizona's Tanque Verde Valley, Hulon McMinn would have been proud of his protege.

Freckles continued to work through supper. The ranch guests once again gathered around the corrals, happily sitting along the top rail. By then, Freckles had turned all his broncs

Freckles and a taller, unidentified ranch hand proudly pose after cooking. (*Courtesy of Sally Holberg and Sue LaFever*)

loose in the pasture except one — a little brown horse he was now riding bareback around the corral.

Don stood at the corral gate and asked, "Can I help you turn him loose?"[28]

"No," Freckles said. "Your dad said I could keep him in the barn and feed him oats. Come on in. I want to introduce you to *Little Brown Jug*. He's so smart that if he was a girl and could cook, I'd marry him."[29]

Laughter erupted all along the top rail. Freckles appeared to be a keeper.[30]

For the next several weeks, Freckles rode every horse placed in front of him. Simon Snyder proved to be a tough taskmaster — physically and morally. Snyder didn't drink or smoke. And he unabashedly didn't care for folks of low character. Once, in 1930, Ernest Hemingway and his wife,

Pauline, sought the isolation and beauty of Sunlight Ranch. The famed author didn't impress Snyder, who curtly asked him to leave after a few days.[31]

Snyder didn't appreciate the way Hemingway had treated his own wife.[32]

As for Freckles, he came to realize he was an impressionable youngster. The elder Snyder influenced him in many positive ways and inspired him to be the best person and wrangler possible. Whether the rancher knew it or not.

Freckles never wanted to disappoint his new boss.

"I was ridin' those colts and they were buckin' me off, but I was getting' back on," Freckles recalled. "There were some bad horses, too, but I wasn't afraid of hittin' the ground, only that when they bucked me off that made them much worse."[33]

Hitting the ground was nothing new for Freckles. Neither was standing up. Snyder rewarded his resilient new hand by paying him sixty dollars a month, plus room and board. The wages made Freckles, in his own words, "the tickledest kid you ever seen."[34]

Ranch guests were also tickled by Freckles.

For two weeks he trained *Little Brown Jug*. Then, one evening after supper, Freckles put on a memorable show for the ranch hands and guests. He led *Little Brown Jug* into the middle of a corral with everyone gathered around. On Freckles' command, the horse rolled over like a dog, shook hands, laid down and played dead, and even stood with all four hooves on a nail keg. Don later quipped that the horse did everything he asked, "except talk."[35]

Freckles quickly became entrenched at the ranch as a

On the back of this blurry photograph, someone wrote, "Freckles (on horse to the far left), Johnny and Slim acting up. Mable (Brown) taking a picture." (*Courtesy of Sally Holberg and Sue LaFever*)

A teenage Freckles holds a colt steady, while Don Snyder places his firstborn child, Sally, on the animal for a picture. (*Courtesy of Sally Holberg and Sue LaFever*)

reliable hand — even beloved. The feelings were mutual. So was the respect. Frankly, the Snyders were hard not to respect. Their family saga revealed the kind of grit and character that carved settlements out of the wilderness. And they did.

Cyrus R. Snyder — Simon's father — planted the family's roots in Wyoming in the spring of 1898 after being "droughted out" of Nebraska. Known as "Pap" to his family, he heard "Buffalo Bill" Cody was building a canal in northwestern Wyoming and traveled west to scout out prospective homesteads. He leased land twelve miles west of what would become the town of Cody and built a log cabin on Marquette Creek near the South Fork of the Shoshone River.[36]

Once he completed the cabin, Cyrus sent word for his wife and children to join him in Wyoming. He met them one hundred miles north at the train station in Billings, Montana. The giant, German redhead struck an imposing pose wherever he went and wasn't one to easily flinch. He also enjoyed a hardy laugh.[37]

The family always enjoyed talking about the day Cyrus met his wife and children at the train station in Billings. A young, wide-eyed cowboy sat on his horse nearby watching the train pull into the station with its smokestack belching steam and black fumes. Bells were ringing and whistles were blowing. The train's engineer leaned out his window and hollered at the young cowpoke, "Look out there, kid! I'm gonna turn this thing around!"[38]

The cowboy, clearly gazing at a train for the first time, instantly wheeled his horse around, spurring it one hundred yards away in the pasture until he felt he was safe. The engineer laughed, but not as much as the giant redhead.

Cyrus roared with laughter on the platform.[39]

Cyrus soon loaded his wife, Mary Catherine, and his six boys — Simon, Roy, Perry, Loyd, Merrill, and Glen — into a covered wagon to begin the trip to their new homestead. On the second night of their journey, on the Crow Indian Reservation, they hobbled their horses and turned them loose for the night to graze. By sunrise, the horses were gone. Two Crow tribal members appeared later that afternoon, and Cyrus asked if they had seen their horses.

"No," one simply answered.[40]

Then the other man added, "Two dolla, maybe we see 'um."[41]

Cyrus instantly understood the two men were exacting a toll for having trekked across Crow land — an inconvenient, yet common practice at the time. The towering German agreed to pay once his horses were returned. A short time later, the two men appeared, driving the horses into the family's camp. Mary Snyder even fed the men some baking-powder biscuits left over from breakfast, and the family soon returned to the trail.[42]

The Snyders traveled eight days to their new homestead on Marquette Creek, although the stay was brief. Cyrus soon moved his family a short distance away at the confluence of the North and South forks of the Shoshone River. But the government confiscated that land to build the world's largest arch dam in a canyon west of Cody, creating the Shoshone Reservoir. By then, capital to construct the Shoshone Irrigation Company's Cody Canal had already bled dry.[43]

Undeterred, Cyrus relocated his family one last time to a homestead thirty miles up the South Fork of the Shoshone

The majestic Sunlight Basin today from atop Dead Indian Pass. *(Author's Collection)*

River. Cyrus and his wife later added two more children to their clan, Harold and Gladys. Cyrus guided hunting parties in those early days, pastured sheep, and dabbled in mining in the Shoshone Mining District along the South Fork of the Shoshone River.[44]

Simon, the eldest of the eight children, certainly inherited his father's rugged nature and bold spirit. As a child, he remembered standing on the street corner in the infant town of Cody, watching the construction of Buffalo Bill's grand Irma Hotel. He later broke horses at the celebrated buffalo hunter and showman's TE Ranch thirty miles from Cody and owned a small dude ranch thirty-eight miles west of Cody on the South Fork of the Shoshone River near Valley. The ranch — known as the Triangle Bar Ranch — served as a staging point for the guests whom he escorted on camping and hunting trips until 1920. His reputation as a hunter and trapper became renown throughout the Big Horn Basin.[45]

Simon also worked for the United States Forest Service between 1908 and 1910, marrying Ora Pettys of North

Dakota, June 23, 1909, in Cody. The couple homesteaded in a sod house above the ranger station at the time their firstborn, Don, was born March 10, 1911. Two children soon followed — Catherine and Jack. Understanding the rugged country in which they lived, Simon knew the critical importance of horsemanship. He therefore strictly required his children to ride horses bareback until they became expert riders. Only then were they permitted to use saddles.[46]

Life changed profoundly for the Snyder family in 1922. Simon had been dickering over the Painter Ranch in Sunlight Basin, and finally struck a deal with Mary Painter and her estranged husband, William, for $800. The two parties formally signed the deed August 28, 1923, for the 400-acre spread at the Park County courthouse in Cody, but Simon had already hauled lumber and supplies into the basin to transform the Painter Ranch into his new dude ranch.[47]

The move into Sunlight Basin became a monumental undertaking.

Access into the basin from the supply hub of Cody meant traversing Dead Indian Mountain — a notoriously treacherous pass at an elevation of 8,071 feet. The earliest pioneers descended the steep pass into the basin by locking their back wagon wheels with a chain so they wouldn't turn. The trunk-end of a felled pine tree was then chained — branches and all — to the back of their horse-drawn wagons to prevent losing control of their rigs and tragedy. Piles of cut trees remained clustered at the foot of the mountain when Simon made his first trips into the basin with his freight. He did so with a wagon and team of four horses. By then, the U.S. Forest Service had graded a dirt road that featured seven switchbacks. But the road's steep, 2,000-foot drop still presented numerous challenges and dangers.[48] One old-timer remembered the pass with a queer fondness:

> *At times we have cursed the road, and no wonder, as we choked on its dust, skidded on the icy pitches, shoveled ourselves out of drifts, and sank over the hubs in thick red mud. That road has shaken our vehicles apart on the dry washboards, overheated our engines, blown our tires, and we've overturned, been hung up on trees, sailed out into space, and with a fair amount of regularity, have been forced to head for the nearest shelter on foot. But never when traveling on the road to Sunlight have I been bored!*[49]

Unflinchingly, Simon endured the rigors of the Dead Indian Mountain pass repeatedly to transform the Painter Ranch into the Sunlight Ranch he envisioned. The final act involved moving his wife and three children into Sunlight Basin for the celebrated opening of their new dude ranch.

The memorable occasion nearly turned tragic.

Simon and his family departed Cody on a sunny spring day in their Model T Ford and drove seventeen miles to the expansive Two Dot Ranch, where they traded their vehicle for horses and a buggy. The family continued their journey several more miles before staying overnight at Mary Say's place — a popular destination between Sunlight Basin and Cody. The family began its final push the next morning on horseback.[50]

Rain suddenly tumbled from the sky during their ascent to the summit of Dead Indian Mountain. Simon and Mary slipped raincoats on their three children — Don, twelve; Catherine, eleven; and Jack, five — before resuming their trek. Only the rain turned to snow. Then the snow turned into a flurry. Jack, sharing a horse with his sister, started to shiver.[51]

Mary placed her youngest boy on her horse, announcing, "He can have my coat and I'll walk."[52]

Dutifully, Mary continued to travel on foot. But Simon, Don, and Catherine had to continuously holler because the flurries became so blinding, she couldn't see the horse ahead of her. Finally, the family reached the summit and dismounted, breathless and freezing. Simon desperately tried to start a fire but failed to maintain a flame in the harsh conditions. The snow fell mercilessly. Simon suddenly realized their perilous situation.[53]

If they hunkered down, they might die. They had to keep moving.[54]

Simon urgently pressed forward, carefully guiding his family down the increasingly slick mountain road. By then, his ranch hands had already went in search of the family, worried when they never arrived. They encountered the weary and frozen band halfway up the mountain road, and quickly loaded them into a wagon. The children suffered from hypothermia. The men carried the family down the mountain to the nearest homestead, a place owned by the Sanzenbackers who lived below Sunlight Ranch on Elk Creek. The couple fed the family hot soup, rubbed their legs in snow — then an accepted treatment for frostbite — and kept them huddled near the fire throughout the night. And none of them ever forgot how they narrowly escaped tragedy that day.[55]

In time, on trails and sitting around campfires, Freckles

became intimately familiar with the family's inspirational, origin story. He not only respected what they had built at the Sunlight Ranch, but how they did so with grit, ingenuity, and determination. The respect flowed both ways. Freckles more than earned his keep, growing into a top-flight wrangler. Even more so, he grew into a top-flight young man. He used his wages in the coming months to purchase a cowboy hat and boots, a saddle, an eiderdown sleeping bag, and even a 1936 Chevy. And he never forgot about his aging and impoverished parents. He sent money home every month to help with their expenses, such as his mother's medicine.[56]

Freckles had left home only a few months earlier in a fog of economic despair, desperate but still hopeful. The world tested his resolve. Dropped him to his knees. Time after time he rose to his feet. Fate now seemingly landed him in the right place at the right moment in time.

Warren Granger Brown could now call himself a cowboy. Hardships be damned.

Life suddenly felt full of possibilities. And, for perhaps the first time in his life, even the dreams he never dared to dream — or had yet imagined — now felt within reach.

Chapter Five
Legendary Journey

"I was a real honest-to-goodness bull rider."

— Warren Granger "Freckles" Brown

The legend appeared as old as the Sunlight Basin itself. Old-timers repeated the tale so many times from generation to generation, folks accepted the origin of the basin's name as readily as they did the valley's enchanting beauty.

Long ago the storytellers traced the legend back to the early nineteenth century when a group of prospectors — or fur trappers — were pinned down in the remote valley by a dense fog. Eventually, the sun pierced through the fog, flooding the entire basin with sunlight. One of the men supposedly remarked, "the only thing that can get into this valley most of the year is sunlight."

Freckles would have found great symbolism in that legend.

Life in the Sunlight Basin exceeded anything he imagined when he first arrived three years earlier in the summer of 1938. Back then he rode the rails and choked down soot in a desperate flight to outrun hopelessness. Since that fateful time, he had been living his dream as "a real" cowboy.

The sunlight in the basin did indeed chase away his darkness.

Freckles reveled in the freedom of life in the Sunlight

Basin, a place with a lush range still unspoiled by modern machinery. All the horses were range-raised, and once the mares were bred, turned loose to graze. The horses formed their own bands and gathered at different points throughout the basin, from Russell Creek north of Sunlight Creek to White Mountain and its adjoining draws. Each pasture offered fresh water and an abundance of native grass. The cowboys would later round up the horses as the seasons dictated.[1]

Those fond experiences would last him a lifetime. He drove cattle over the precipitous Dead Indian Mountain pass, guided wealthy dudes on trail rides throughout the valley, cooked over open campfires where few men had ever walked, and hunted in the rugged Absaroka Mountains where grizzlies still roamed. Freckles also enjoyed riding high-bucking broncs in corrals now as familiar as old friends.

And he never went hungry.

Simon Snyder fostered a familial environment at his Sunlight Ranch, where he playfully advertised, "the prairie dogs bark at strangers."[2] Only nobody ever felt like a stranger at the ranch. Snyder and his son often gave the ranch cook a break on Sundays. They would load their families and staff on horses and wagons that day, treating everyone to a bountiful picnic or fish fry.[3]

No, no one ever went hungry. Or bored.

The cowboy life allowed Freckles to also entertain his inner daredevil, whether on a nasty bronc in the corrals or on the open pastures of the basin. Once he rode a large, stout colt named *Tiger* to trail horses to the winter range. *Tiger* had a nasty reputation as a fierce, bucking horse, having led Chuck King on memorable romps before his medical departure. As

Freckles waited for Don Snyder to drive him and his saddle back to the ranch, he got a wild notion.

Freckles removed his saddle from *Tiger*. He then remounted him bareback. Don pulled up in his vehicle to see Freckles sitting bareback on *Tiger*, holding the unpredictable horse by the mane.

"Do you think he'd buck, Don?" Freckles asked curiously.[4]

Don replied, "Well, I don't know."[5]

Freckles slowly slid the bridle off *Tiger*, and then stuck his shoes into *Tiger's* neck. The big, gray colt exploded, jerking Freckles loose from the mane and bucking him skyward. Freckles landed on the ground, cracking his head on a rock. He rose to his feet and walked a few paces, although he was essentially knocked out on his feet.[6]

A few days later he emerged from the fog in his head while pitching hay from a wagon. That's when he remembered what had happened.[7] The episode was reminiscent of a couple of childhood experiences in London Flats. He clearly still loved chasing thrills. Testing *Tiger* provided a higher level of adrenaline rush, something more akin to what he experienced in 1937 when he rode his first bull at a Willcox, Arizona.

Riding bulls and bucking broncs in rodeos simply appealed to his wild side. Whether he considered rodeos a viable endeavor is unknown. Nevertheless, the seed had been planted, and the idea grew like the roots of a mighty oak. Unbeknownst to Freckles, events were transpiring a world away that would present him with an enticing opportunity—one that would change his life forever. And in more ways than one.

War in Europe at the time continued to have a rippling effect in the United States, and when France fell to Adolph Hitler's Nazi Germany in June of 1940, an uneasiness swept across the nation. American leaders began to worry that Great Britain wouldn't be able to defeat Germany. The worries festered.

As a result, President Franklin Delano Roosevelt signed the *Selective Training and Service Act* into law September 16, 1940. The law required all men between the ages of twenty-one and forty-five to register for the draft — the first in the nation's history during peacetime. Those selected in a draft lottery were then required to serve one year in the armed forces.

The prospect of war beckoned.

The draft soon touched every corner of the United States, including the far reaches of Wyoming's relatively tranquil Big Horn Basin where Yellowstone National Park officials joyfully predicted a heavy tourist season.[8] News of the draft, meanwhile, trickled out until it became an unpleasant reality. *The Cody Enterprise* delivered one such dose of cold truth in the April 23, 1941, edition of its weekly newspaper: FORTY-EIGHT PARK COUNTY BOYS TO LEAVE FRIDAY FOR INDUCTION IN ARMY AT WARREN. John Ward Kencke. . . Harold Edward Pearson . . . Charles Benard Isom . . . Ernest William Schmitt . . . the list of Park County draftees went on. The young men represented towns such as Cody, Powell, Meeteetse, and Pitchfork, sending a message of change to nearly every ranch, neighborhood, and community in the basin.[9]

A week later *The Cody Enterprise* reported news far less

foreboding. The board of the Cody Stampede — the town's highly celebrated annual rodeo — announced it had "broke from tradition" and would allow all riders of the Big Horn Basin and its tributaries to compete. For championship cups and buckles and all. The article read in part:

Rules are being relaxed somewhat and encouragement is being offered to young fellows who are experienced in corral and range bronc handling, but never before have appeared in rodeos, as well as men who in recent years have taken a back seat because of age.[10]

Bill Durnen, the Cody Stampede Association president, added that officials made the decision after they noticed many of the previous year's competitors now served in the U.S. Army.[11]

Word of the Cody Stampede's "relaxed" entry requirements undoubtedly reached every ranch and cowhand in the vast Big Horn Basin, including Freckles at Sunlight Ranch. In truth, Simon Snyder's daredevil wrangler didn't need much enticement to rodeo. For Freckles, his decision to compete only made sense. The twenty-year-old asked his boss for permission to participate in Cody's three-day rodeo, from July 3 - 5. He planned to ride the fifty miles into Cody on horseback — a grinding trip by anyone's standards.

Simon enjoyed rodeos, and even once staged a joint event in 1929 for local bronc busters with fellow Sunlight Basin dude rancher Dewey Riddle. Simon readily gave his blessing to Freckles with one caveat: He had to ride a big, wild sorrel cowboys "used to let get away on purpose" into Cody.[12]

Freckles never flinched.

Soon, Freckles would again hear the cheers of the crowd and feel the adrenaline rush of riding a raging bull in a rodeo. And not just any rodeo. The Cody Stampede — a rodeo so steeped in heritage it operated independent of the Rodeo Association of America.[13]

Like most things in the town of Cody, the trail almost always led back to its famous namesake. William F. "Buffalo Bill" Cody had already left a monumental footprint on the town by the time of his death January 10, 1917. He was not only instrumental in founding the town in 1895, but also began publishing *The Park County Enterprise* (later *The Cody Enterprise*) newspaper in 1899, built the Irma Hotel — a frontier palace named for his daughter — in 1902, and even held tryouts for his world-renown Buffalo Bill's Wild West shows downtown.

Buffalo Bill's death cast a mammoth shadow on the town. Then, on the evening of April 20, 1920, six of Cody's most prominent citizens gathered to brainstorm an annual event that would be so spectacular, it would reverberate far beyond the town limits. They held their meeting at the home of Caroline Lockhart, a national bestselling novelist with a flair for publicity.

Lockhart, unmarried and pushing fifty, wielded influence in Cody despite being a controversial figure in various quarters. She openly drank alcohol in a town that overwhelmingly voted for Prohibition in 1919, owned *The Park County Enterprise*, and was known to juggle several boyfriends at once. Her striking blonde hair and voluptuous figure made her desirable to multiple townsman — single and married. Or so the rumors flourished. Lockhart also knew how to get things done and possessed the passion and money to back up her talk.[14]

The group met in Lockhart's living room, which alone evoked the spirit of Cody's charismatic founder. Frontier mementos decorated the room, a bearskin rug covered the floor, and a tamed wildcat prowled the premises. Each representative found inspiration in the town's three-day Entrance Celebration held the previous June. The event — anchored by the pageantry of a rodeo — celebrated the opening of the eastern entrance to Yellowstone National Park and blossomed into a rousing success.[15]

Lockhart and the other five members wanted to ride the momentum of the 1919 event. Their goals included several objectives. Honor "Buffalo Bill," keep the Wild West legacy alive, and capitalize on the tourists who flocked to Yellowstone each summer through Cody. They eagerly agreed to stage an annual Fourth of July rodeo and created the Cody Stampede Association. Finally, they voted Lockhart as the association's first president — a wise, if not obvious choice. An article in Lockhart's newspaper soon proclaimed: "For the purpose of keeping alive the spirit of the west and perpetuating the memory of our late honored townsman, Col. W.F. Cody ("Buffalo Bill") a stock association has been formed for putting on an annual event to be known as 'The Cody Stampede.'"[16]

Thus, a legendary rodeo was born.

The 1941 Cody Stampede marked the rodeo's twenty-second anniversary, and as had become customary, promoters were again predicting the largest crowds in the event's history. The predictions weren't all bluster. Rodeo officials installed extra bleachers in 1939 and 1940 to accommodate the throngs of people who increasingly flocked to town for the three-day extravaganza.[17]

Organizers once again promised a spectacular show, including the return of Crow elder Al Holds-the-Enemy who had performed the previous two years with other tribal dancers. Holds-the-Enemy was a respected elder from the Crow Indian Agency in Montana, and renowned for his talents as a war dancer. He signed "a treaty" with the Cody Stampede Association two years earlier on the banks of the Shoshone River to perform each night for the crowds. That year he brought twenty Crow dancers dressed in full battle regalia, twenty-five of their finest horses, and vowed, "You people will see every day the biggest war dance we have put on in years."[18]

The 1941 festivities began in earnest June 25, with Cody's Pup Rodeo — a nightly, amateur-only affair that debuted in 1938. The event was the brainchild of the energetic Carl Downing, a trusted protégé of the late "Buffalo Bill" Cody and former Wild West performer.[19] By then, townspeople were gearing up for what promised to be "three turbulent days of wild west, bucking horses, roaring six-shooters and jangling spurs."[20]

A week later Freckles joined the throng. As promised, Freckles left the Sunlight Ranch aboard a big, unruly sorrel Simon wanted tamed. Reddish in color and more than a touch stubborn, the horse served as his only companion in what he later remembered being a legendary fifty-mile journey into Cody.

Freckles likely left the ranch before sunrise on Wednesday, July 2 — a day before the Cody Stampede's opening night. He followed Sunlight Creek in an easterly direction, skirting the distinctive Steamboat Mountain to his right as he crossed Elk Creek and then Dead Indian Creek at the base of the notorious Dead Indian Mountain.

Darkness still blanketed Sunlight Basin when he and the sorrel began their steep ascent toward the mountain summit. If he couldn't see the piles of dead pine trees at the bottom of the mountain, he knew they were there, hidden at least until sunrise. The graded, dirt road was a familiar one to Freckles but still considered dangerous, especially given the unpredictability of his hefty mount. Midway up the mountain he would have passed through a drift fence — a barrier intended to prevent cattle from drifting out of the basin.[21]

Freckles maneuvered the seven switchbacks up the mountainside until he reached the elevation of 8,071 feet at the summit, where Simon and his family could have perished eighteen years earlier during that devastating snowstorm. The summit always marked an important milestone for those traveling to and from Cody, and it never failed to inspire awe for those who gazed upon the Sunlight Basin below.

"To me the view from the top of Dead Indian Pass looking into Sunlight Basin is one of the most beautiful sights in the world," one old-timer once wrote. "It never fails to catch me off guard; to treat me with something new. Here the sky becomes our element; we are touched by heaven."[22]

On this morning, with the basin probably still flooded by darkness, Freckles might have indeed felt as though he could touch Heaven. Or at least the moon as it dangled brightly in a canopy of stars.

By the time Freckles reached Mary Say's old place, the sun's rays were already beating down on the rugged terrain. Say and her brother, Alfred M. Walters, routinely accommodated travelers for years on the original wagon road in what became known as "Walter's Inn." The family expanded its accommodations by erecting a two-story log building which rested perpendicular on the side of a ravine above the dry fork of Pat O'Hara Creek. A barn sat to the south of the two-story structure and was large enough to hold a dozen teams of horses. Nearby, large corrals were installed for large herds of horses or cattle being driven on the trail.[23]

In July 1941, the structures were still standing as Freckles rode past, but the property was now part of the vast Two-Dot Ranch.[24] The once-popular inn would have been just another landmark for Freckles, at most a place to water his horse at the old water pump. But, unlike countless travelers before him, there would be no overnight stay or break.

Freckles kept riding. He had a date with a rodeo. The trip from Sunlight Basin to Cody generally took folks three days by horseback. The Snyder ranch hand planned to make the trip in less than one.

A profound sense of solitude surely overwhelmed him as he rode through the ocean of open countryside. He would have heard only the sound of his horse's hooves striking the trail. Or his own whistling or conversation with his horse. Or his own breathing. Stunning mountain plateaus stood like monuments far in the horizon. Everywhere he looked he saw immense swaths of range land, separated occasionally by a small draw or trickling stream. And the sky was as blue and as clear as his own eyes.

The American West had long been declared officially closed by 1941. Freckles would have found that declaration amusing. He never felt so free. Nor had he felt such a sense of adventure. Years later he would speak of the journey in simple language, but words laced with nostalgia. One might suspect he knew then he would never travel that road again, on horseback, breathing freedom, and dreaming once unimaginable dreams.

Freckles triumphantly reached his destination when he passed through Cody's railroad station on a bluff overlooking the town. He descended the bluff along a narrow, graveled road and crossed the Shoshone River over a metal truss bridge, riding until he reached Main Street. He covered the fifty-mile journey in nine hours. What's even more impressive is that he "felt good" after all those hours in the saddle.[25]

Downtown Cody buzzed with a festive atmosphere of banners, flags, and music. Dude ranch guests mingled with Indians and cowboys, reminiscent of Buffalo Bill's Wild West shows. Merchants enjoyed the flow of traffic and money. Shopkeepers even vowed to close their doors each day and reopen after the rodeo's final event to help with ticket sales.[26]

The Cody Trading Company, meanwhile, proudly displayed a new line of trophies for the winner of each event. The company bypassed the usual engraved cups and trophies for castings of saddled horses, mounted on shiny, bronze ashtrays.[27]

Amid the celebration, Freckles surely heard the sobering news of twenty-six-year-old cowboy Sam Osborne of Cody.

Osborne, an employee of the TE Ranch, lay unconscious at a local hospital after sustaining critical injuries during the steer wrestling competition at the Pup Rodeo four days earlier. Witnesses said as Osborne left his saddle, the steer fell, and the cowboy crashed to the ground. Simultaneously, his horse toppled over the steer and landed on top of him. The accident served as a harsh reminder of the real danger inherent in every rodeo event, although the prospect of danger is what drew crowds to the grandstands.[28]

The irony never seemed more clear than what appeared in *The Cody Enterprise* the day Freckles arrived in town. An article reporting on the critically injured Osborne shared the front page with another story that praised stock contractor John Weinz of Hyattville, Wyoming. The article boasted:

> *Johnnie makes a business of furnishing bad horses for rodeos and when his horses come out of the chute the spectators will see some of the orneriest critters that ever spilled a cowboy. His brahmas, as mean as they are active, not only cause the cowpokes plenty of trouble to ride but will give them a chase to the nearest fence.*[29]

Of course, neither Freckles — nor any cowboy — would have been fazed by the prospect of danger in riding a bucking bronc or raging bull. If there weren't a challenge to the endeavor, what would be the point? And wasn't life itself a risk? Freckles risked his life every time he jumped on a moving train in the quest for a job.

Riding broncs and bulls made him feel alive. And Freckles was dying to live.

Crowds lined Main Street the next day — Thursday, July 3, — to watch the big parade. A high school band from Powell led

The cover of the official Cody Stampede 1941 program. *(Author's Collection)*

the colorful procession with flags waving and music playing. Al Holds-the-Enemy wore a decorative war bonnet aboard his newly purchased racehorse, while his fellow Crow dancers rode with him in full ceremonial regalia on their finest ponies. Somewhere in the procession — riding among cowboys from other Big Horn Basin ranches — Freckles rode Snyder's old *Sorrel* down Main Street, most assuredly grinning and waving at the cheering spectators.[30]

The procession marched to the Cody Stampede grounds, a fenced, oval arena with wooden grandstands on one side and chutes on the other. Tall, wooden beams supported a pitched metal roof, which protected spectators from the glaring sun. In addition, a few Crow teepees also stood erect across the dusty arena, in full view of the paying customers. Organizers understood the value of Wild West theatrics.[31]

Freckles, meanwhile, understood the value of opportunity. He wanted to make the most of his, entering three events — bull riding, bareback riding, and saddle bronc riding. He certainly didn't ride fifty miles on horseback to sit around and watch life pass by. He came to chase every thrill possible.

A yellow, billfold-sized rodeo program indicated he had

The official 1941 Cody Stampede program, showing "No. 21 Freckles Brown" matched with the bull "Salt Peter." *(Author's Collection)*

drawn a bull named *Salt Peter*. Naturally, Freckles didn't know anything about the bull, let alone its tendencies once it exploded from the chute. But if the name meant anything, *Salt Peter* promised to be as explosive as gunpowder.

As it turned out, so was Freckles. The game, Snyder Ranch hand placed in all three of his events the first day, taking first in saddle bronc riding, second in the bull riding aboard *Salt Peter*, and third in the bareback riding.[32]

Freckles rode the momentum into day two. He turned in the winning ride on another of Weinz's Brahman bulls to outpoint three other cowboys. Suddenly, Freckles realized he was one good, eight-second ride away from his first trophy. Claude Thompson remained his closest competition, having placed third on day one and splitting a second-place finish on day two.[33]

Death shockingly marred day two. Holds-the-Enemy fractured his skull after tumbling from his racehorse, casting an eerie pall over the rodeo grounds as the show continued. The forty-seven-year-old Crow leader died ten hours later.[34]

Heavy rains greeted competitors before the final rounds. Thompson responded on the muddy dirt with a first-place ride, but Freckles sealed the overall title with a second-place ride in front of packed grandstands of cheering spectators. Freckles displayed the grit and determination he showed when his stomach ached from hunger pains a few years earlier, or when the only warmth he could find at night was beneath packing crate paper in a railroad yard.[35]

Each time he rose to the occasion with a strong heart and unshakable will. Frankly, it was becoming a habit. The last bull even gave Freckles a parting gift by stepping on his right leg. Freckles didn't care. He now clutched more than $200 in cash earnings and his championship trophy — a small, saddled horse mounted on a bronze ashtray. The trophy was rather modest, not much larger than his hand, and even a bit odd for a bull riding title. Alas, that tiny piece of hardware held a monumental symbolism. Freckles Brown had just won the 1941 Cody Stampede bull riding championship — an achievement that would forever change the course of his life.[36]

The next morning the young cowboy faced another challenge as he prepared to leave Cody for the return trip

The first rodeo trophy ever won by Freckles. He earned this one for placing first in bull riding at the 1941 Cody Stampede in Wyoming while working at Simon Snyder's ranch in the Sunlight Basin. (*Author's Collection*)

to Sunlight Basin. His right leg had swollen so badly from being stepped on by the bull, he couldn't place his foot in the stirrup. He rode the fifty miles back to Sunlight Ranch with his right leg sticking out as straight as a Winchester rifle.[37]

"Rode all the way back like that, but I didn't care 'cause I had me a fine trophy," Freckles fondly recalled decades later. "I was a real honest-to-goodness bull rider."[38]

The pride of Sunlight Ranch returned home more than slightly hobbled, but victorious. Naturally, he received more than a few handshakes and back slaps. He also told and retold the story of his first rodeo title, probably in the bunkhouse, at the corrals, and dinner table. The stories would have ended with his cherished showpiece — the trophy. *The Cody Enterprise* delivered another first for Freckles the following week. The newspaper reported the rodeo's final results, and there on the front page, he read his name in bold, black print: "Freckles Brown, a wrangler at the Simon Snyder ranch in Sunlight, took the brahma bull riding championship . . ."[39]

If Willcox, Arizona, hooked him on rodeo in 1937, the Cody Stampede left him undeniably obsessed. The need to rodeo now flowed through his veins.

A month later Freckles traveled to another rodeo in Casper, Wyoming, 260 miles from the Sunlight Ranch. He arguably turned in a more memorable performance with a single saddle bronc ride. Moments before the chute opened, the bronc's halter slipped off, leaving Freckles with nothing to grab. The horse bolted from the chute. Freckles rode his bucking mount with sheer balance and willpower, enough to complete the ride and win the day money.[40]

Again, Freckles entertained visions of rodeo glory. And, again, events out of his control dashed those dreams.

Four months after his amazing ride in Casper, on December 7, news swept through the country of Japan's surprise attacked on Pearl Harbor in the Hawaiian Islands. The first news reports filtered into Wyoming at 12:30 p.m. on CBS Radio. Citizens were shocked and outraged. Later, details of the attack spread. Four U.S. battleships sunk . . . 188 aircraft destroyed . . . thousands of sailors dead . . . the total loss of life eventually climbed to 2,335 American souls.

The next day President Roosevelt delivered a brief address to Congress that lasted six minutes and thirty seconds. Simon Snyder, his family, and staff huddled around radios at the Sunlight Ranch, just as millions of fellow Americans did on that memorable day. The president's words awoke a sleeping giant:

> Yesterday, December 7, 1941 — a date which will live in infamy — the United States of America was suddenly and deliberately attacked by naval and air forces of the Empire of Japan. The United States was at peace with that Nation and, at the solicitation of Japan, was still in conversation with its Government and its Emperor looking toward the

maintenance of peace in the Pacific. Indeed, one hour after Japanese air squadrons had commenced bombing in the American Island of Oahu, the Japanese Ambassador to the United States and his colleague delivered to our Secretary of State a formal reply to a recent American message. And while this reply stated that it seemed useless to continue the existing diplomatic negotiations, it contained no threat or hint of war or of armed attack.

Talk of war instantly filtered through every home and workplace in the nation. Young men enlisted in droves. Women stepped up immediately to do their part on the home front. Tears flowed for those marching off to war; many of whom never returned.

By February, Freckles had waited long enough. Now, twenty-one, he decided to enlist. Simon Snyder pulled his top wrangler aside one day, and said, "The government is allowin' me one man, and you'll be it if you want to stay out of the war."[41]

Freckles thanked his kind boss for everything he had done for him, shook his hand firmly, and drove out of Sunlight Basin in his 1936 Chevy.

"I felt awful bad leavin' him," Freckles said later, "but I'd of felt awful guilty if I hadn't been in."[42]

Freckles drove to Cheyenne, Wyoming, sold his car for $200, and enlisted in the U.S. Army on February 16, 1942. The decision was an easy one. His country called.[43]

Chapter Six
Love and War

"They asked me if I'd be afraid to bail out of an airplane, and I told them I didn't know. I'd never been on one."

— Freckles Brown

Sergeant Warren Granger "Freckles" Brown became quite a letter writer during World War II. He often wrote a letter a day, and occasionally multiple letters a day. He spent idle hours writing, even when he chose to remain alone with his thoughts while his buddies hit the town on a Saturday night. Sometimes, he'd wake up in the middle of the night and craft a missive in his bunk, beneath a dim light in a darkened barracks.

Freckles wrote with misspelled words and run-on sentences and improper punctuation, but he always wrote with an honest heart.

The letters revealed something about the man, as did the war that controlled his world. The words that flowed from his pen exposed Freckles to be a hopeless romantic — about one woman and all rodeos.

Edith Gregory — the lone object of his undying affections — and his obsession with rodeo crowded out most other topics that occupied his mind during his four years of war-time service. His extreme love of both became evident shortly after his arrival at Fort Sill, the historic home of

Freckles' descendants still cherish the stacks of letters he wrote to Edith during World War II. Note the ashtray that was the first award Freckles won in rodeo. *(Author's Collection)*

the United States Army Field Artillery School in Lawton, Oklahoma. Freckles breezed through basic training, and shortly thereafter was identified as a soldier who possessed a special skill with horses. The horse-drawn artillery units of World War I were already being replaced by trucks, although horses, mules, and even oxen would be needed to maneuver through remote, rugged terrain scattered throughout the Pacific Theatre. Hence, skilled horsemen such as Freckles were still valuable assets.

For Freckles, duty was duty. Edith and rodeo were his love and passion.

The depths of that love and passion were never more apparent than in the sweltering August days of 1943 — fifteen months after he first stepped off the bus at Fort Sill, April

Edith Brown as she appeared during World War II. *(Courtesy of the Harrison-Brown Family)*

10, 1942. He met Edith shortly after his arrival. An army buddy and his wife arranged a blind date with "a pretty, black-haired gal" who worked as a cashier at TG&Y, a popular dime store in downtown Lawton. "Edith had laryngitis and couldn't talk," Freckles was fond of recalling. "So we went to a dance and had a high 'ol time."[1]

Words were not needed that night to light the flame.

Freckles and Edith became inseparable until that summer day in 1943 when she boarded a bus in Cheyenne, Oklahoma, bound for a relative's home in Flagstaff, Arizona. The separation stung mightily, although the intensity of that pain continued to plague them for the next few years as the war lurched onward. On August 9, Freckles wrote a letter to Edith from his post at Fort Sill, unable, or unwilling, to mask the pain. "My Sweetheart," he wrote. "Well sweet how are you getting along and how do you like Ariz. by now? I can't hardly stand this place without you here . . ."[2]

Committing those words to paper might have been too jarring in the moment, and he quickly transitioned to another love — rodeo. "I think I won Bronc riding last night," he continued upon more joyful footing. "I rode old *Flying High* . . . I went to the show last night and caught hell for it today. The whole Battery is restricted now. But I am going to try and sneak in this afternoon to ride My bull . . ."[3]

The words smacked of obsession. His need to rodeo and love Edith were already addictions that would become increasingly intertwined in his heart and soul. And the risk-taker within didn't flinch when it came to either. "If something happened so you didn't come back, I don't believe I could ever get with another girl," he wrote. "I really love you Darling and it is either you or nobody with me sweet."[4]

The next day Freckles remained true to another promise. He escaped the post to rodeo.

"I slipped off yesterday and went in and rode my bull," he confessed to Edith in another letter. "I rode him to the whistle, and he bucked me off on the back of my neck and then stepped on my head."[5]

The bull easily could have killed Freckles. Instead, the beast knocked him out. Wayne Louks, an army buddy who also rodeoed, reveled in the adventure. He too defied orders that night and snuck away to ride horses. Louks carried his groggy pal back to the post before any of their superiors noticed they had been gone. He sat with Freckles until his head cleared, and when it did, the Wyoming cowboy was staring at a check for winning the bull riding.[6]

The two comrades must have shared a hardy laugh that night.

A similar story circulated forty years later. Whether the two versions are of the same rodeo may never be known. The later story highlighted how the army put "a cramp" on Freckles' rodeo schedule. In that tale, which made the rodeo

Freckles pictured (L to R) with an unidentified soldier, Tony (last name unknown), Wayne Louks and Freckles in 1942 at Fort Sill near Lawton, Oklahoma. *(Courtesy of the Harrison-Brown Family)*

circuit, Freckles looked at his battery's roster to see if he was on duty. He was on call, but liberally took that as a sign he was safe to leave. He soon departed for the nearest rodeo. Only Freckles was called into duty that day, and when he was nowhere to be found, news quickly reached his sergeant. His irate commander severely reprimanded Freckles. The sergeant told him the next time he needed a weekend pass, to simply ask for one. Never just leave. Freckles promised.[7]

A week later, and much to the sergeant's astonishment, Freckles asked for a weekend pass so he could attend a "very important" rodeo. The sergeant honored his word and issued the pass. Later, when asked to confirm rumors that he "borrowed" the army's horses to ride in those rodeos, Freckles only grinned.[8]

The earliest known record of Freckles competing during the war can be traced to October 1942, at the Arkansas Live Stock Show in Little Rock. Freckles entered bareback riding and bull riding events, finishing as high as second place on the third day of bull riding. The results were published in *Hoofs and Horns* — a magazine Freckles read religiously whenever he could get his hands on an issue.[9]

By March, Freckles used his leave to travel back home to Tucson. He stayed with his parents for a night, telling Edith, "My mother is getting worse but she tries not to let anybody see it."[10] The next day he left to enter the Phoenix World's Championship Rodeo. He earned $200 for working stock from 8 a.m. to midnight, taking the entry fees out of his wages. The twenty-two-year-old private took breaks from his job to place first on his last bull and fourth on his first bareback ride.[11]

Legendary rodeo photographer DeVere Helfrich of Klamath Falls, Oregon, may have captured the first rodeo image of Freckles at that Phoenix show. Helfrich snapped a shot of Freckles riding in a photo titled: "P.F.C. Freckles Brown on *Ace in the Hole*." DeVere also took a picture of Freckles aboard the horse *Five Minutes to Midnight*, although fellow photographer Ralph R. Doubleday shot the same ride from a different angle. Doubleday, however, caught Freckles at the dramatic moment his horse bucked him high into the air as he desperately tried to hang on to the bronc rein.[12]

Through it all, Edith remained at the forefront of Freckles' deepest thoughts and desires. The intensity of his love, like the pain of their separation, only increased with time. By August, the physical distance between them began to toy

Freckles Brown in Phoenix leaving *Five Minutes to Midnight*. Ralph R. Doubleday, circa 1940, photographic print. (*Gene Lamb Collection, Dickinson Research Center, National Cowboy & Western Heritage Museum. 1990.016.035.*)

with his psyche. On August 18, 1943, with Edith still in Flagstaff, the pain spilled from his heart as he wrote:

I love everything about you. There hasn't anything seemed right since you got on that bus that night at Cheyenne (Oklahoma). I never did feel more like crying than I did that night. If I had been somewhere by myself I might have even done that. Remember darling that I will always love you . . .

All My Love,
Brownie

P.S. I am not crazy. I am just crazy about you.[13]

Three days later, Freckles returned to his barracks after

a march with Battery "D" of the 26th Battalion, 6th Training Regiment. Freckles drove a four-horse team with the horse-drawn artillery unit and rode the rowdiest horses. He also thought non-stop about Edith, and everyone around him knew it, too. Even his stable sergeant. So as soon as Freckles returned from the march, the sergeant handed him a letter from Edith. Freckles ripped open the letter and began to read.[14]

A pen soon glided across the pages of a return letter from Freckles when he heard Helen O'Connell crooning her latest hit, *Never a Day Goes By*, on the radio. O'Connell sings:

> *Never a day goes by, not a night that I*
> *Could live my life without you*
> *Never a day goes by, there's no time when I*
> *Can ever forget what you mean to me*

Freckles shared the romantic moment with his love 820 miles away in Arizona, writing, "The radio is playing *Never a Day Goes By*. I think it is so pretty. It makes me think of you honey. All I do is think of you. I love you so much sweet." He closed his letter with what would become his signature phrase: "All My Love, Brownie."[15]

The next day Freckles received another letter from Edith. He again wasted no time responding with his own letter. He wrote:

> *I got your letter today. Just makes me so happy to hear from you. I sure do love your letters honey. The only thing I would like better would be for you to be here yourself. The print of your lips on that letter was so sweet honey. Gee but I would like to Kiss and hug you again. I love you darling . . .*[16]

Freckles penned another letter to Edith thirteen days later, unable to control his feelings. "I do miss you sweet," he wrote, adding that he planned to compete in a three-day rodeo in nearby Chickasha, Oklahoma. "Gosh Darling but I wish you were here to go with me," he continued. "I am so darn lonesome for you." He then added a postscript: "I LOVE YOU!!!!!! Hurry and come home honey. Please!!"[17]

Edith did come home. Long enough to marry Freckles. Rumors of Freckles being shipped to another military post in November left them leery about her potentially remaining in Lawton alone. But there was another reason for Edith to eventually leave. She was pregnant. Freckles convinced his newlywed to stay with his family in Tucson, assuring her upon her arrival, "I know you will get along fine darling as they cannot help but like you."[18]

"I guess you will get to see all my brothers and sisters as they are all there . . . they will probably ask you a lot of questions about how mean and ornery I am," he added playfully. "So don't make me out to be bad sweet."[19]

The reality of Edith's absence set in less than twenty-four hours later when Freckles wrote, "I lay in bed this morning and didn't go to breakfast just thinking about you . . . Your Loving Husband, Brownie."[20]

Two weeks passed without a letter from Edith. The hours and days passed bitterly, until angst consumed his thoughts. Finally, on November 24, he wrote another letter laced with desperate words:

> *Honey I can't figure out why you haven't heard from me. If I am not mistaken this is the eighth letter I have written you ... I usually get your letter four days after you write*

them. I hate for you to think I could ever forget you for even a minute, sweet you are the only thing I ever think of . . . I love you so much.[21]

As it turned out, Edith was fine. She was also now five months pregnant, and in new surroundings.

Change soon arrived in waves for Freckles and Edith as the calendar flipped to 1944. On March 6, the couple welcomed the arrival of a baby girl, Donna Lucretia Brown, in Lawton.

Nine days later, Lucretia Brown wrote a letter from her hospital bed in Tucson to express her joy over the new grandchild. The sixty-three-year-old grandmother had been suffering from blood clots in the brain. "Well how is daddy Warren and family?" she asked, never referring to her health. She ended her letter with a loving reference to her tiny namesake: "Kiss Donna Lucretia for me. Mother."[22]

Lucretia Brown died two months later after a twenty-day stay at St. Mary's Hospital in Tucson. A medical examiner determined her cause of death on May 17, to be cerebral venous sinus thrombosis, which occurs when blood clots form in the brain's venous sinuses. The condition can lead to swelling and bleeding in the brain.[23]

Lucretia's passing, coupled with Donna's birth, highlighted the cycle of life for the Brown family. The birth of a new life and the finality of death did offer much to reflect upon, although in Lucretia's case, death probably felt mostly merciful. The woman suffered from major health issues for at least the last decade of her life, and yet was never known to complain.

If Freckles inherited any of his mother's qualities, it was her stoicism. Freckles grew up watching her endure pain and hardships without complaint.

Now, as a newly christened father, he would ante up and follow her lead.

Once again life changed beneath his feet in a world on fire. As Allied forces plowed through Europe after the landings at Normandy, France, June 6, 1944, the army shipped Freckles to Cavalry School at Fort Riley, Kansas, where he was placed in the post horseshoeing school. Freckles, who learned how to shoe horses from Hulon McMinn in Arizona, found the school to be a bit tedious. For one week he sat at a desk and dissected the feet of horses and mules preserved in formaldehyde, which as he distinctly remembered, "stunk like hell." He spent another two weeks learning how to use a blacksmith forge before even being allowed to touch an animal — necessary for some, but elementary for a cowboy from Wyoming's Sunlight Basin.[24]

The results showed. Freckles graduated with the highest marks ever recorded at the post's horseshoeing school.[25] On the day of graduation — December 14, 1944 — Freckles posed for a class photograph with twenty-seven other classmates, sitting front and center in the first row, smiling.[26]

Unsurprisingly, Freckles made the most of his weekend passes during his time at Fort Riley. Fellow classmate Stanley H. Kosinski remembered Freckles using his weekends "to go to rodeos and ride animals to earn extra cash."[27]

By March, two officers with the Office of Strategic Services (OSS) arrived at Fort Riley to interview several soldiers for clandestine missions in China. Freckles name cropped up, undoubtedly because of his exceptional skills with horses and pack mules.

President Roosevelt created the OSS with an executive order he signed on June 13, 1942. The OSS — a predecessor to the Central Intelligence Agency — had one mission: Gather intelligence to sabotage military operations of enemy nations. Agents of the OSS fought a dangerous, convert war, often behind enemy lines. If the agency sounded a bit Hollywood, its commander certainly fit the role.

Maj. Gen. William Joseph Donovan – nicknamed "Wild Bill" — was the agency's first director. The former Wall Street attorney became a World War I hero who received the Medal of Honor for his actions October 14 and 15, 1918, in a battle with German forces at Landres-et-St. Georges, France. During the battle, Donovan received machine-gunfire that smashed one knee and a tibia. He refused to evacuate, and instead insisted on being carried forward. He rallied his troops for the next five hours despite being dizzy from the pain and loss of blood, ultimately blunting the German's counterattack.

The press fawned over the old war hero as an intelligence director during World War II. *The New York Times* described the silver-haired Donovan as "suave," and even referred to him by his nickname, "Wild Bill."[28] Beyond the hype, Donovan earned his steely and colorful reputation. On D-Day, he landed on the beaches of Normandy along with Col. David K.E. Bruce, commander of his covert operations in Europe. A German plane fired at the pair as they made their way to the American front lines, where they encountered heavy machine-gun fire from a German nest. Both dove to the ground.

"David, we mustn't be captured," Donovan told Bruce. "We know too much."[29]

Donovan told Bruce he had two suicide pills if needed, only to realize he had forgotten or lost them.

"I must shoot first," Donovan said boldly.[30]

"Yes, sir," Bruce replied, "but can we do much against machine guns with our pistols?"[31]

"Oh, you don't understand," Donovan shot back. "I mean, if we are about to be captured, I'll shoot you first. After all, I am your commanding officer."[32]

If Freckles didn't know about "Wild Bill" Donovan or the dangers associated with the OSS missions, he would soon learn. Capt. W.R. Moore told Freckles he would train to be a paratrooper, and eventually jump into Mongolia where OSS soldiers would use Mongolian mustangs for cavalry units and train Chinese soldiers to fight the Japanese. Later, he learned the OSS planned to fly over the Himalayas from India with supplies, train Chinese paratroopers, and then jump with them behind enemy lines.[33]

"They asked me if I'd be afraid to bail out of an airplane, and I told them I didn't know," Freckles once recalled. "I'd never been in one."[34]

Freckles later reflected on his humorous, yet honest answer.

"That was the truth," Freckles said. "How could I know? It's like when I was growin' up, my dad taught me things like that. He would point and say, 'What's that over there?' If I said, 'That's a cow,' he would say, 'I believe that's a cow. Don't make it a fact unless you're sure.'"[35]

In the end, OSS officers approved of Freckles. They immediately processed paperwork to transfer him to Fort George G. Meade in Maryland, where he would be given a two-month, crash course in the Chinese language. His "INTENDED ASSIGNMENT" designated him for the China-Burma-India Theatre. Once there, he would "train and operate cavalry units in China." Freckles never saw the classified paperwork.[36]

Freckles arrived March 30, in Washington, D.C.[37] He and the other OSS recruits were housed fifteen miles outside the nation's capital at an "old colonial estate" on the Potomac River. Naturally, his thoughts drifted back to Edith, who was again living in Lawton. He sent Edith a postcard the day he arrived. The next night he lay tired in bed and wrote Edith a letter.

"Well, I have been all over Wash. D.C.," Freckles wrote. "Sweet it is very beautiful the cherry roses are just a mass of blossoms. You couldn't believe it the place we are staying. It is an old colonial estate and really pretty . . . I am the only one up here who hasn't been to college."[38]

In that moment, Freckles — the soldier who never made it past the eighth grade — displayed a trait that appeared to be a natural gift. He not only recalled the opulence of his temporary home, but he did so in detail. He noted to Edith how the stairways were "the old circular type" . . . and how there were venetian blinds and flowerpots in every window . . . the beauty of the hardwood floors . . . and the grand, circular driveway out front. His attention to details — big and small — would someday serve him well. "We start in Monday learning to talk Chinese," he concluded. "All my love Warren."[39]

Five days later Freckles reported back to Edith about his attempt to learn Chinese, as well as his aching heart. He wrote:

> *I am trying to learn Chinese, and it is a hell of a job. The only thing that makes me feel better is that I am doing as good as the rest of them and better than some . . . I had better close. I get so damn lonesome sometimes. This is a lot worse than when I first came into the Army. I love you so much Sweet!!! All my love, Brownie.*
>
> *P.S. Take good care of Brownie's Little Chicken (Donna). Kiss her for me huh?*[40]

Of course, his other love never strayed too far behind. Chinese language or not, Freckles informed Edith a short time later that he "went into town last night and entered the rodeo," adding that he only wished he had his "bareback rigging."[41] He promised to send the money home if he won.

Freckles remained committed to his passions.

Then, on May 2, Freckles and his OSS comrades heard the news that shocked the world. The headline in *Stars and Stripes* said it all in big, bold, black type: HITLER DEAD.[42] Adolph Hitler shot himself in a bunker in Berlin with enemy Russian forces only a few blocks away. The German Third Reich signed an unconditional surrender on May 7, essentially snuffing out the Axis powers and the war in Europe.

Three days later Freckles boarded an airplane with other OSS troops at New York's LaGuardia Airport. They were bound for the China-Burma-India Theatre in hopes of ending the war once and for all with Japan. The journey carried them first to Egypt and then India before they made the final hop to China.[43]

Many of the sights and sounds of the foreign countries

he saw didn't impress Freckles. In Egypt, he complained, "This is some country, everything is sand."[44] Although he did concede, as a good cowboy would, that the Egyptians had "a lot of good horses."[45]

India brought out a crankier side of Freckles with its smothering heat and shocking, cultural differences. Nor did he find comfort in the "damn war" which prolonged his forced exile from his bride and daughter. His deepest, most intimate feelings poured out in a five-page letter to Edith on a day in late May:

> *Well honey I am still in India and don't like it any Better. And it's still just as hot and getting hotter. But I miss you Sweet that is all I do just think of you and the more I think of you the more lonesome I get for you. It is going to be hell living away from you so long. I was sure sick the last couple days I was here. But feel pretty good now. I dreamed of you last night sweetheart ... I wake up at night and just lay there awake and think of all your little sweet and loving ways. I love you so much Baby and want to hold you in my arms and hold you and love you. I will always be true to you honey. I never have any desire to be with anyone else . . .*
>
> *All My Love, Brownie*[46]

A few days later Freckles expressed his disdain for India's repressive heat, as well as bewilderment over the dress, cleanliness, and habits of some of the Indian men. "I believe I would go nuts if I had to live in this country long," he told his wife. "These people wear the darndest clothes. Some of them have a rag tied around their head what looks like an old dirty mosquito bar around them. The men squat to pee like a woman and they are apt to do it anywhere they don't care if anyone is looking or not."[47]

A restless energy appeared to overtake Freckles when he sat down to write Edith a letter on June 1, perhaps sensing — or knowing — his unit would make the final push over the Himalayas and into China. The reality of an encounter with Japanese forces suddenly became more imminent. "The general opinion here of most of the boys is that the war will be over in from 9 months to a year," he wrote. "But I think that is wishful thinking. I wish to God it would end tomorrow."[48]

Official records from the United States War Department indicate Freckles was in China by June 10, 1945.[49] Freckles harkened back to his interview at Fort Riley upon landing in China, and whether he would be afraid to bail out of an airplane. He later mused, "Over there in China, I found out I'd whole lot rather bail out of one then to land in it."[50]

The commitment to training Chinese soldiers clearly became more focused since the surrender of the German Third Reich a month earlier. As late as October 1944, the strength of the OSS in China amounted to a paltry 106 agents. The final push to end the war was now at hand. By July 1945, the OSS had reached its peak of 1,891 agents in China.[51]

Freckles and his OSS comrades would be part of that push as members of the Strategic Services Unit — a predecessor to the Army's 1st Special Forces Group.[52] They landed in Kunming, the capital of the Yunnan Province and now the site of OSS headquarters. The city benefited long ago from its place on the ancient caravan roads through India, Tibet, and southeast Asia. As far as U.S. brass were concerned, Kunming held a key position as the northern and easternmost terminus in the supply chain into China.

Kunming would also serve as one staging point in a larger plan to invade territory held by the Japanese with Chinese troops.[53]

Several American paratroop instructors began training Freckles and other OSS recruits in Kunming, along with 120 Chinese counterparts. Freckles adapted to jumping from airplanes like he did riding bulls.

"There wasn't nothin' scary about the whole thing," he said later. "I just figured that, if them other fellas could do it, I could do it. That opening shock shakes the hell out of you, but from then on you wish it was ten thousand feet because it's the most beautiful feeling."[54]

Kunming, meanwhile, remained within reach of Japanese bombers.

Yet the daily routines of life were as present as the threat of a Japanese bombing raid. American soldiers still flocked to town on Saturday nights, and Freckles still longed to be with his love a world away in Oklahoma. "This thing of seeing a lot of country is a lot of hell," Freckles wrote Edith one night in late June. "The only country I want to see is where you are."[55]

The hours between training were sometimes filled with daydreams of his return home. "Are you getting cowboy minded?" Freckles asked Edith in one letter. "I hope so. I hope you get to like Rodeo and horses and things."[56] He would later spell out his vision of the future in simple, yet heartfelt language: "Honey when I get home all I want to do is Rodeo and have horses. And I want you with me all the time . . . Every day away from you is a wasted day Sweet."[57]

Edith and rodeo shadowed his thoughts wherever he went.

Ironically, if not an omen, the rodeo came to him one day in Kunming. He walked into a café run by the Red Cross and read a hand-written poster announcing an upcoming rodeo. The Red Cross sponsored the show, while the Army's mule pack promised to provide mules and native cattle. The rodeo would feature four events — saddle mule riding, bareback mule riding, steer riding, and steer roping.[58]

Freckles eagerly signed up for all three of the four of the events at $2.50 apiece.[59]

The cowboy paratrooper could hardly contain his excitement. He even sat down and braided a new rope to use in the competition, calling it the "best I believe I have ever made."[60] He then shared his joy with Edith:

My Darling,

They are having a rodeo near here next Sunday (July 28). I have entered bareback bronc, mule and steer riding. I don't know how much the purse will be. Not to much I don't think ... this coming rodeo will be quite a thing here. I don't imagine the Chinese have ever saw anything like it ... Remember I love you all the time Sweet and think of you and wish to be with you so bad.

All My Love, Brownie[61]

The American GIs and local Chinese flocked to the rodeo. Freckles placed first in bareback mule riding, second in saddle mule riding, and first in the all-around. His success came with a pile of Chinese money, which didn't amount to much when converted to American dollars. He recalled decades later, "I think I won forty-six dollars."⁶²

Freckles didn't care. The rodeo brought him joy. He even reunited with his friend Chuck King, Simon Snyder's former wrangler at his Sunlight Ranch. King won the steer riding event, and they later took pictures for posterity in the pouring rain.⁶³

The two Wyoming cowboys might have enjoyed more success at the Kunming rodeo if not for a sudden deluge of rain. One of the events — "steer roping from a Jeep" — was, in King's words, "monsooned out."⁶⁴

"Boy, those Chinese didn't know what to make of it," Freckles once told a writer. "At first, half of them were just dumbfounded. And the other half were laughing so hard I thought we'd need ambulances for them. It was fun and, heck, how many other cowboys can say they were 'Bareback Mule Riding Champion of China?'"⁶⁵

Freckles and his pal Chuck King at the Capital Hill Rodeo in Oklahoma City in 1943. Both worked as wranglers for Simon Snyder at his ranch in Wyoming's Sunlight Basin before the war. *(Courtesy of the Harrison-Brown Family)*

China's "first rodeo" temporarily relieved the stress of an impending invasion of Japanese territory. Freckles knew the day was coming when he would be parachuting behind enemy lines with newly trained Chinese paratroopers.

Something miraculous then happened. Nine days after the Kunming rodeo, at 8:15 a.m. on August 6, the American B-29 *Enola Gay* dropped the world's first atomic bomb on the Japanese city of Hiroshima. Between 70,000 and 126,000 people were killed by the bombing, which sent shock waves across the globe.

Then, three days later, the American B-29 *Bockscar* dropped another atomic bomb on the Japanese city of Nagasaki. The death toll from that bomb hovered between 60,000 and 80,000 souls.

The Empire of Japan, which vowed to never surrender, officially did so September 2.

Suddenly, the barrier between Freckles and his greatest passions in life had vanished. He would soon be free to love Edith in all the ways he desired and to rodeo in all the ways he dreamed.

By October, Freckles returned to the United States where his plane touched down at New York's LaGuardia Airport. He received a Bronze Campaign Star for his service in the China Offensive Campaign. Before leaving China he even posed in a group photo with Maj. Gen. William "Wild Bill" Donovan himself in Kunming, although his thoughts were already a world away in Oklahoma.[66]

"I am not sure what I want to do when I get back," Freckles wrote Edith in one of his final letters from China. "I know I want to shoe horses and rodeo. But we need someplace to call home . . . nothing really matters anymore except to be with you and Donna."[67]

Freckles now sought to win his own peace.

Chapter Seven
Living the Dream

"He's as rugged as a piece of harness leather ..."
— **Newspaper columnist Ernie Deane describing Freckles Brown**

Jim Shoulders couldn't remember the year he pulled into Pond Creek, Oklahoma, after nightfall for a rodeo and a moment he would never forget — "about '46 or '47," he once recalled. The town's lone motel had no vacancies. So, the slender, slim-hipped teenager from Tulsa crashed in the backseat of his car at the rodeo grounds.[1]

Shoulders awoke early the next morning to "a racket" and sat up, dusting off the sleep. A gray wash still covered the eastern sky. He peered out his windows and saw a diminutive cowboy busily shoeing a horse. Shoulders closed his eyes and fell back to sleep. The next time he awoke, he saw the cowboy shoeing another horse. The man never stopped moving. The moment passed as quickly as it took for Shoulders to crank the starter, and drive to town for breakfast.

A short time later Shoulders returned to compete in the rodeo, where he again saw the cowboy "winning all the events."[2] He noticed the cowboy yet again later that night at a dance. The cowboy hit the dance floor every time the band started playing a new tune. Shoulders marveled at the cowboy's endless well of energy, "I said right there I knew he was made right because he was shoeing horses before six that morning and at 2:30 a.m. when they closed the dance, he was still goin' strong."³

Shoulders quickly discovered the name of the energetic cowboy — Freckles Brown. And he would never forget the name, or more importantly, the man he eventually called friend.

Few, if any, would.

True to his word, Freckles began rodeoing full-time in the spring of 1946. He received his honorable discharge October 27, 1945, and eagerly embraced his post-war life with Edith and Donna.⁴ Upon his return to Lawton, he thought about his travels throughout southwest Oklahoma while stationed at Fort Sill. He harbored fond memories of his many visits to the Wichita Mountains Wildlife Refuge, a 60,000-acre federal reserve of prairie and stunning, granite mountains that bordered the military post. A wild buffalo herd — one that began with fifteen bison brought by railroad from the New York Zoological Park in 1907 — roamed the refuge during his visits, as did herds of majestic elk.⁵

"We went back in that wildlife refuge in the Wichita Mountains, and I thought, 'Gee . . . this is the prettiest country I ever seen — a great cattle country,'" Freckles recalled. "Timber and grass and water. And I got to know a lot of the native people around here, and they was good ranchers and good people."⁶

Freckles became enchanted by the region's land. He dreamed of rodeoing and owning a ranch, and relentlessly worked to make both a reality. The industrious cowboy broke horses for local ranchers and shod horses, and even found a job as a janitor for a Lawton taxi company.⁷

The whole time Freckles searched for a patch of prairie

he could call his own. Eventually, he found acreage east of Lawton with an old, dilapidated house that resembled something closer to a shack. The unpainted, wooden structure sat on rocks with a collapsing floor and no windows.[8]

Freckles bravely envisioned a three-bedroom home. He first enclosed the porch, converting that space into a small room for Donna. He fixed the floor, installed windows, and then built a barn and outhouse. Andy Jordan — the taxi company's owner — also loaned Freckles $2,000 "with no note or nothin' " to purchase his first twenty-five head of cattle. He repaid the loan within a year.[9]

Life offered another path as well.

Shortly after the war, Freckles received an opportunity of a different sort from a familiar voice in his not-so-distant past. Don Snyder, who now owned Sunlight Ranch, reached out to his old friend with a letter a few days before Christmas. The letter encapsulated their mutual love and respect with a language both men understood, stout and playful sarcasm:

> We got your Christmas card and also letter addressed [to] Dad. Mother and Dad are in Arizona, and I was very anxious [to] find out whether or not you were still alive.
>
> So you have been para-trooping. Why don't you pick out a rough job. I think I would be pretty much like they said about the Italian para-troopers. They said they carried a crew of 14 men and one para-trooper in each plane; one pilot, one co-pilot, and 12 men to throw the Para-trooper out.[10]

Snyder and his wife, Faye, bought out his parents who wanted to retire in Cody. They closed the deal November 26, 1945, and Donald desperately needed help he could trust.[11]

The letter continued:

> Anyhow, <u>I want you to come up here in the spring as soon as you can and break horses for me and I won't take no for an answer.</u> I am so short of horses, I don't know what I am going to do and I don't know of any other two men I would rather have than you. I'll give you $150 a month and board and room for yourself and family, and if that ain't enough I'll give you more. In fact I'll pay you better than you are getting now whatever it is. Your wife can work or not as she likes. You can imagine how scarce help is up here when I have to write a letter like this to a bum like you, Ha ha.[12]

Snyder closed the letter the way Freckles might have expected. "Give our best to your wife who we are very anxious to meet," he wrote, concluding, "and I'll bet my two little girls can whip your one any day! Sincerely, Donald Snyder."[13]

Freckles never accepted Snyder's generous offer, although he tucked away the letter as a keepsake from an old friend and possibly as a reminder of a place and time that forever changed his life. The two men would remain lifelong friends. Freckles, meanwhile, chose another path. The only path for him, really. His dreams led him down the rugged, adventurous road of rodeo's "Suicide Circuit," where Freckles became one of the hardest working cowboys in the business.

The ambitious cowboy always maintained a rigorous schedule. As soon as he arrived at a new town, Freckles placed his name on the rodeo's labor list. He helped work stock and shod horses for extra cash, in addition to riding the bulls and broncs he drew with an inner fire that burned white hot.[14]

Freckles did enough to make a living, and more than enough to be noticed. He won the all-around cowboy title at the Black Hills Roundup in Belle Fourche, South Dakota, in 1947 . . . won another all-around title at Omaha, Nebraska, in 1948 . . . and placed second in bull riding in 1949 on his first trip to Madison Square Garden in New York — then the site of rodeo's glamorous world championships. He joined over 200 cowboys and Indians at the 24th Annual World Championship Rodeo in New York that year, including the "Singing Cowboy" himself, Gene Autry.[15]

In 1949, for posterity, Freckles also sat for a portrait with legendary western photographer James Cathey of Fort Worth. Seated, Freckles leaned into Cathey's camera with his right elbow on his leg. He wore a pristine cowboy hat, white plaid western shirt, neck scarf that dangled to one side, and he flashed an authentic, warm smile accentuated by his puffy round cheeks. Freckles could have easily passed for one of Hollywood's cowboy stars — an image that seemed a lifetime removed from the soot-covered lad who appeared at Simon Snyder's ranch eleven years earlier.[16]

Freckles posed for a portrait with noted Texas photographer James Cathey in 1949 in Lawton, Oklahoma. *(Courtesy of the Harrison-Brown Family)*

Freckles was living his

dream.

Edith shared in the adventure in those early years, often making a few extra bucks herself as a timekeeper at various rodeos. She grew fond of the energy and rumble of the wooden bleachers beneath her when fans cheered and stomped, just as she did for the families traveling the rodeo circuit with them.[17]

"In some parts of the country, we'd have afternoon rodeos," she once said, "and afterward we would get food and all go down to the river and cook."[18]

Traveling America's highways and backroads created its own collection of special memories.

Once Freckles and Edith drove from town to town with a friend who rarely won as consistently as he entered rodeos. But his fortunes changed one day. He won both the bareback and saddle bronc riding at one rodeo. Suddenly, the cowboy had a pocket full of cash. As they rumbled down the road to the next rodeo, the friend removed his cowboy hat — a fine hat, Freckles recalled — and studied it carefully.

"I ride better than that," scoffed the cowboy confidently as he flung the hat out the window. He promptly bought a new cowboy hat at the next stop with his winnings.

Much to their amusement, the story ended just as the Browns suspected it might. The cowboy had to borrow money two weeks later for entry fees at a rodeo.[19]

The Browns often retold that story with great delight.

As for Freckles, he never wasted a dollar or an opportunity. He always signed up to work on a rodeo's labor list to pay for his entry fees and other expenses. He once estimated he cleared about half of his winnings each year after he deducted the costs for entry fees, gas, motel rooms, meals, clothing, boots, medical bills, and so on.[20]

Winning ultimately paid the bills. So, Freckles entered every event he could manage. Bull riding, bareback riding, saddle bronc riding, and even steer wrestling. He competed in them all as often as possible. At 5-foot-7, 150 pounds, Freckles wasn't considered hefty enough to toss a steer, but he was always game enough. Rodeo writer Willard H. Porter recalled one such time when Freckles displayed his true grit while grappling a steer.

"The fastest steer he ever dropped was at Carlsbad, New Mexico, in 1950," Porter wrote. "On Slim Whaley's noted grulla gelding, *Little Blue*, he made the stopwatch sing 4.2 seconds."[21]

Winning also meant a better life. He once told Edith if he could ride his next bull at Madison Square Garden, he'd make enough money to drill a well, install an electric pump, and plumb in an indoor bathroom. If he failed to ride the bull, he promised to put a door on the outhouse.

Freckles rode his bull — a ride that earned him $1,300. And Edith got her bathroom.[22]

Injuries, naturally, were unavoidable. Broken bones were commonplace through the years, as were concussions for the game cowboy. Freckles remembered being knocked out at least three times after he started rodeoing full-time. Once, in Odessa, Texas, he awoke in a hospital with no memory of his ride. "When the nurses came in the morning, I said, 'What the hell am I doin' in this hospital?'" Freckles recalled. "They said, 'Don't move.'"[23]

On another occasion Freckles was knocked unconscious

for an hour in Lawton. Then, in Chickasha, Oklahoma, a bull knocked him out before he was supposed to compete in a wild horse race. Someone doused his head with water, and he rode in the race. He placed second. Later that night, while sitting at a café forty-seven miles away in Lawton, Freckles snapped out of his foggy mind. He said matter-of-factly, "I didn't remember that race."[24]

Ironically, the greatest scare of Freckles' life occurred on his ranch in Lawton in April of 1952. He planned to harrow a field with his tractor when he crossed a ditch. The tractor flipped over backwards, breaking his leg, and pinning him to the ground. The exhaust pipe stabbed the red dirt, killing the engine and causing gasoline and battery fluid to pour over him as he lay trapped.

A hundred yards away, Edith visited with their neighbor, Mabel Dobbins, while Mabel tended to her laundry in her garage. Carlina, Mabel's four-year-old daughter, kept running in and out of the garage, saying, "Come see what Brown is doin'. Come look at Brown, and see what Brown is doin'."[25]

Finally, Edith and Mabel stepped outside to see what the child was talking about. Edith instantly saw the overturned tractor and took off sprinting, literally running out of her shoes as she frantically reached her husband with her feet bloody from the stubble in the field.

"Go find somebody to come with a jack," Freckles said.[26]

By the time Edith returned, Freckles had worked himself free and crawled away from the tractor. He later called it "the most painful break I ever had," which is saying something for a man who rode raging bulls for a living.[27]

Yet a worst pain overtook Freckles in the aftermath of the accident. A sense of helplessness overwhelmed him. He needed to plant his sweet feed but couldn't find anyone he could hire to operate the tractor. The frustration mounted until one morning he awoke to loud noises stirring outside. He stepped from the house on his crutches to see twenty-eight large tractors rumbling through his pasture. Neighboring women were also there, bringing bowls of food — meatloaves . . . chicken . . . vegetables . . . enough for a grand feast.[28]

"Those tractors started at 8 a.m.," Freckles fondly recalled, "and some of them worked until dark."[29]

Freckles never forgot the kindness of his neighbors or the gift of life.

Kindness certainly wasn't a lesson Freckles needed to learn. In rodeo circles, he was universally beloved for his own brand of humanity and generosity, as well as respected for his hard-earned riding skills and unfailing determination. By 1959, he even entered the season with a new intensity. He became fixated with qualifying for the first National Finals Rodeo in Dallas, but due to a broken leg he sustained in Syracuse, New York, couldn't rodeo until April.

Once healthy, Freckles competed with a renewed fury. He also began flying to rodeos in private airplanes that year with his traveling companions, enabling him to sometimes make two rodeos in one day. In one two-day period — in 1959 perhaps — Freckles supposedly rode forty-one bucking horses and once mounted as many as twenty bulls in a day. Such feats were improbable. Despite the tall tales, Freckles picked up his pace dramatically in 1959. He qualified for his first National Finals Rodeo, doing so in bull riding — his best event. By the time the dust settled in Dallas, he finished fourteenth in the world in that event.[30]

And Freckles now offered a relentless appetite for more.

Momentum carried Freckles into 1960 as he turned thirty-nine years old. By then, most considered him something of an old sage, a cowboy from a bygone era.

"He's 39 now and past the age, he said, when most professional cowboys quit risking their bones in the ring," wrote Ernie Deane, an Arkansas columnist. "He's as rugged as a piece of harness leather, stands something around six inches over five feet, and weighs only 155 pounds."[31]

Yet Freckles showed no signs of slowing down. Not even close.

Legendary saddle bronc rider Casey Tibbs recognized a world-class competitor when he saw one, and he saw that rare quality in Freckles.

"He's like an old hound dog," Tibbs once said of Freckles. "You pen him up and take the others out huntin', and he'll howl himself to death."[32]

Tibbs ushered in rodeo's "Golden Age" when he won his first saddle bronc riding world championship at age nineteen in 1949. The youngster who was dubbed "Kid Wonder" eventually won a total of nine world titles, six in saddle bronc riding, one bareback riding and two all-around, between 1949 and 1959. Born on the eve of the Great Depression on March 5, 1929, Tibbs emerged from a remote horse ranch in central South Dakota, a place on a dirt trail called Mission Ridge. John Tibbs, Casey's father, plowed a few acres for watermelons and sweet corn, but mostly raised horses with his wife and ten children. [33]

From these humble roots, Tibbs stormed the rodeo world with his free-swinging riding style and flamboyance.

"Casey was fun-loving, flamboyant, wild and reckless, and he was everybody's hero," said Deb Copenhaver, who broke Tibbs' string of four consecutive world championships in saddle bronc riding in 1955. "He came along right after the war — and everybody was looking for a new hero. With his charisma, everybody loved him."[34]

Tibbs gave the fans what they craved, cashing in on his success in the arena with his handsome looks and shockingly, glitzy flair in public. He dressed in a bold ensemble of purple clothing — shirts, chaps, neckties — and even drove his trademark lavender Cadillac. His celebrity also carried him to Hollywood for a time.

In the arena, Tibbs proved just as gifted as he was glamorous. In 1951, the native South Dakotan claimed both the Rodeo Cowboy Association's saddle bronc and all-around world titles. During one surreal stretch, he rode 274 of 280 horses he mounted to the whistle. His fame even landed him on the cover of *Life* magazine — a first for a rodeo cowboy.[35]

Some rodeo historians would later credit Tibbs with single-hand-

Casey Tibbs on the cover of *Life*.

edly launching the sport in the nation's popular consciousness. Although other cowboys were not nearly as flashy as Tibbs, he had company in an era that also produced two other all-time greats in Jim Shoulders and Harry Tompkins.

Shoulders, in truth, arose to become the greatest of them all. Born May 13, 1928, in Tulsa, Oklahoma, he shocked the rodeo world in 1949, when at age twenty-one, he became the youngest cowboy to win the all-around world championship. The title marked only his third year as a professional.[36]

The first time Tibbs saw Shoulders ride, he turned to a fellow cowboy and remarked, "You know, that guy looks like he could go forever."[37]

And he did. Shoulders stormed the rodeo world. He eventually collected what was then a record sixteen world championships — seven bull riding; five all-around; and four bareback riding. He won six straight world titles in bull

Jim Shoulders won six consecutive world bull riding championships from 1954 to 1959. In this 1958 picture, he's enjoying a wild ride on a bull named Levi. *(DeVere Helfrich Rodeo Photographs, Dickinson Research Center, National Cowboy & Western Heritage Museum. 81.023.13615)*

riding from 1954 to 1959 before Harry Tompkins broke his streak by claiming the top prize in 1960.[38]

Shoulders also accomplished the unimaginable. He grabbed rodeo's "triple crown" in 1956, capturing world titles in the all-around, bareback riding, and bull riding. He then duplicated the feat in each of the next two years.[39]

Tompkins, himself an eight-time world titleholder, routinely paid Shoulders a great compliment whenever he introduced himself to groups. "You may not know me," he would say of his old traveling buddy, "but I'm the guy who kept Shoulders from winning twenty-two world titles."

Tompkins might have been the most improbable legend of this era. Born October 5, 1927, in Furnace Woods, New York., he grew up three miles away in Peekskill, across the Hudson River from the U.S. Military Academy at West Point. No one in his family had ever ridden a horse, but Tompkins gravitated to horses. He went from working at a riding stable to a dude ranch, and then at nineteen, experienced his first rodeo at Madison Square Garden as a representative of New York's Cimarron Ranch. He entered the bareback and bull riding events, winning $316 in bull riding.[40]

Jim Shoulders was the youngest cowboy to win the all-around championship at the age of twenty-one and for decades was recognized as the greatest all-around cowboy in rodeo. *(ProRodeo Sports News)*

Two years later in 1948, at age twenty-one, he won his first of three consecutive world championship bull riding titles. He won his last two world championships twelve years later in 1960, arguably the greatest year of his career. That year he won world titles in the all-around and bull riding.[41]

A year later Tompkins injured his elbow and never competed again.[42]

Harry Tompkins became an unlikely rodeo legend growing up in upstate New York and never seeing a bucking bull until the day he climbed aboard one. (*Photo courtesy of Ferrell Butler*)

Tibbs essentially retired in 1964, although he attempted a brief comeback in 1967. Shoulders, meanwhile, continued to compete until hanging up his spurs in 1970, although he never captured another world title after 1959.[43]

Shoulders, Tibbs, and Tompkins reigned supreme during rodeo's "Golden Era," collectively capturing thirty-two world championships between 1948 and 1960 — a period that coincided with Freckles' arrival on the scene in 1946. Shoulders and Tompkins alone won twelve of thirteen world bull riding titles from 1948 to 1960.

Miraculously, Freckles outlasted them all.

"Freckles was unique," Shoulders once said, "he really came into his own when everybody else was quitting."[44]

Freckles never stopped grinding. Throughout the 1960 season, Freckles continued to climb the money standings with quality performances. His ascent was no mistake.

A cub reporter with the *Colorado Springs Gazette-Telegraph* observed Freckles at the Pikes Peak or Bust Rodeo that year, limping around the corral where the bulls were penned several hours before the opening rounds. He wore a sweat-stained elastic bandage haphazardly around his jeans to support an aching knee. Atop his head sat a "bedraggled straw hat, its crown layered with sweat," and his starched jeans were tucked into tall, tawny boots. The reporter also noted Freckles' heavy spurs, "glistening in the last gasp of sunlight."[45]

Every few steps Freckles stopped like a statue to stare between the corral's wooden boards.[46]

Finally, the young scribe approached sheepishly.

"They tell me you're Freckles Brown, the bull rider," he mumbled with his pencil and notebook in hand. "May I ask you some questions?"[47]

"Shore," replied Freckles, never breaking his stare into the corral. "Shore. Go to 'er."[48]

"Do you bull riders always hang around the bulls' corral, right before a rodeo?"[49]

"Naw," Freckles answered with a drawl. "Not as a rule. But do ya see that bull yonder, the one with the ugly, crooked horn? And I'm hopin' I can draw a turn on him."[50]

Freckles gestured toward an immense bull that was snorting back at him.

The reporter looked at the bull — "as gray as a battleship bound for combat" — and asked, "Why?"[51]

"Well, two months ago, that bull throwed me off down in Texas," Freckles drawled. "They claim it dislocated my shoulder. A year ago, he throwed me off in Wyoming . . .

put a click in my wrist that's still there. You see, I figure that bull needs another dose of me on his back to teach him more gentlemanly ways."⁵²

Translation: The veteran bull rider was studying his nemesis and details mattered.

Freckles finished sixth in the final bull riding standings that year, $6,219 behind Tompkins who claimed the world title. Freckles also finished seventh in the final standings of the all-around, which Tompkins won as well. Yet both were personal bests for the aging cowpoke.

Still, despite a storied career, one thing remained elusive for Freckles — a world championship.

Time certainly wasn't on Freckles' side. Freckles turned forty as the 1961 season loomed, and yet he continued to defy the odds. He steadily climbed the money standings in both bull riding and all-around, and when he showed up the National Finals Rodeo in Dallas, he still had a shot to win the bull riding title.

Twenty-four-year-old Ronnie Rossen of Broadus, Montana, entered the Finals in the lead, but had to perform well to secure the championship. Both Bob Wegner of Ponca City, Oklahoma, and Freckles challenged close behind.

On the final night, the championship remained up for grabs.

Rossen was as tough a cowboy as could be found on the circuit. In 1959, he broke his jaw at the Finals. Doctors wired his jaw shut, and he continued to compete.⁵³

Now he was one ride away from wrapping up his first world championship. He drew Harry Knight's bull *No Doze*, only to get bucked off. The bull turned toward Rossen.

Bullfighter Wick Peth tried to save Rossen by climbing on the bull's neck but was instead flipped into the air. The bull then plowed over Rossen, who somehow avoided breaking any bones.[54]

Rossen would later spend three nights in a Dallas hospital, but not after watching the fate of his slim lead from behind the chutes.[55]

Wegner didn't fare any better against a bull appearing in its first National Finals Rodeo. *Tornado* — a 1,700-pound Hereford-Brahman crossbreed — hailed from the ranch of Jim Shoulders. The bull was unbeaten, but relatively unknown outside of Texas and Oklahoma. Regardless, Wegner proved no match for the bull and Freckles was now an eight-second ride away from claiming his first world championship.[56]

Fans inside the Dallas State Fair Coliseum left no doubt as to who they were rooting for in that fateful moment as Freckles lowered down on Harry Knight's bull *Nitro*.

Ronnie Rossen won world bull riding titles in 1961 and 1966. His career spanned four decades until 1991 when he died from injuries suffered riding bulls at a National Old Timers Rodeo event at the age of fifty-four. (*Photo courtesy of Ferrell Butler*)

"Freckles brought something out in rodeo, which is harder to produce than blood out of a rock, and that's sentiment," one writer noted. "There were more people pulling for him to win the championship than has ever happened before."[57]

Rossen and Wegner were even seen cheering Freckles

on as the chute opened.[58]

Seven seconds later, the crowd saw Freckles bucked skyward. Freckles would later remember how he was "still in the air when the whistle blew."[59]

Rossen clung to his lead to be crowned world champion, finishing ahead of Wegner by a mere $418 and Freckles by $542. Freckles also finished fifth in the all-around standings, completing the best season of his illustrious career.

"And this is no place for anyone not in top shape, young and healthy," one writer stated. "But Freck stayed with them and walking sounder than most when it was over."[60]

A bittersweet feeling hung in the air that night in Dallas. Freckles rode off with unfinished business. Would he be able to win that elusive world title? Or would that one second forever haunt him?

Chapter Eight
Black Smoke

"If sentiment was a contributing factor, Freckles Brown, the ageless veteran from Lawton, Okla., already would be World Champion."

— The Rodeo Sports News, August 15, 1962

Writers were running out of words to describe the storied career of Freckles Brown as 1962 dawned. As one exasperated rodeo scribe playfully put it, "There's not much you can say about Freck that hasn't been dang near worn out."[1]

Articles about Freckles commonly retold the colorful highlights of his legend, harkening back to his first rodeo in Willcox, Arizona, at sixteen in 1937 — only a year after the release of Margaret Mitchell's bestselling novel *Gone with the Wind*. Freckles riding native steer and army mules in China's "first rodeo" during the war also made for entertaining copy, although it was ultimately his grit, skills, and tireless determination in the arena that summed up his career best.

Freckles gamely competed in all three roughstock events and bulldogging since he started rodeoing. He experienced success at many of the sport's most iconic venues, from the historic Pendleton Round-Up in Oregon to the world championships at Madison Square Garden in New York. Along the way he collected more than his share of honors and prized hardware. Trophies, belt buckles, engraved saddles, plaques, loving cups, and certificates crowded his humble ranch house in Lawton. Collectively, they were a testament to his skill and longevity.

Simply stated, Freckles had been one of the best rodeo hands in the business since he started rodeoing full-time in 1946. He was also one of the most popular. Cheers and adulation shadowed "the old man" wherever he competed, whether at the Cheyenne Frontier Days in his native Wyoming or at the Cow Palace in Daly City, California.[2] Fans loved the wily veteran cowboy.

Freckles works his rope before another ride at the Cheyenne Frontier Days during his championship campaign of 1962. *(DeVere Helfrich Rodeo Photographs, Dickinson Research Center, National Cowboy & Western Heritage Museum. 81.023.20478-01)*

Still, despite all the success and love, one thing remained missing from his illustrious resume — a world championship.

Now, at forty-one, the rodeo world sensed the hourglass draining on the beloved cowboy. Even Freckles seemed to realize he was on the clock. After all, riding bulls for a living came with no guarantees of a tomorrow. No one — not even Freckles — knew how long he realistically had to compete for a world title.

Freckles lingered between fourth and fifth place in the RCA bull riding standings through the first three months of

In a rare moment, Freckles is found resting during his 1962 season. Freckles was always in motion. *(DeVere Helfrich Rodeo Photographs, Dickinson Research Center, National Cowboy & Western Heritage Museum. 81.023.20625-08)*

the 1962 season. By July 15, he had climbed into second place behind Amarillo's durable Bill Rinestine. Only $406 separated the two cowboys when they entered the historic Cheyenne Frontier Days — "The Daddy of Them All" — to close July. Freckles left Cheyenne in second place behind seasoned bull rider Pete Crump of Green Acres, Washington.[3]

The hard-riding Freckles also departed Cheyenne convinced he had to drop saddle bronc and bareback riding events from his schedule. He had only won a combined $1,808 in the two events, certainly not enough to justify the wear and tear on his body. Since rodeoing full-time, Freckles maintained one of the most rigorous schedules on the circuit, often competing in three or four events per show. The workload undoubtedly took its toll.

Now, after missing a world title by one second, another world championship again dangled within reach. Would it be his last opportunity? Freckles wasn't going to let the moment pass without a fight. He decided to focus solely on bull riding for the remainder of the regular season, scheduled to conclude November 4. The National Finals Rodeo would then be staged December 4-9 in Los Angeles, perhaps with the title again up for grabs.

Crump traded blows with Freckles in the opening days of August. But his lead quickly vanished. With the use of a private airplane, Freckles competed at three overlapping rodeos during the first week of August. He hauled in a combined $1,200.

Freckles made his biggest statement at Deadwood, South Dakota. He claimed victories in the first and third go-rounds, as well as the average to collect $467. He also won at Great Falls, Montana, and posted a third-place finish at Casper, Wyoming. The bull riding standings posted on August 15 reflected his torrent of success. Freckles suddenly stood atop the heap with a total of $11,579, ahead of Crump ($10,461) and Rinestine ($9,035).[4]

Hoof and Horns now referred to Freckles appropriately as the "41-year-old Iron Man" from Lawton, Oklahoma.[5]

"If sentiment was a contributing factor, Freckles Brown, the ageless veteran from Lawton, Oklahoma, already would be world champion," *Rodeo Sports News* declared. "The happy, little Oklahoman, 41, is having his greatest rodeo season."[6]

Freckles aggressively rode the momentum through September, increasing his lead by finishing in the money at successive rodeos in Pendleton, Oregon; Albuquerque, New Mexico; Dallas, Texas; Omaha, Nebraska; Oklahoma City; and Pine Bluff, Arkansas. He entered the final go-round at the Pacific International Rodeo in Portland, Oregon, on October 21, with a nearly $6,000 lead on Rinestine.[7]

The respected outfit Christensen Brothers of Eugene, Oregon, supplied the stock for the event, including a large, muley Brangus named *Black Smoke*. The bull weighed between 1,800 and 2,000 pounds, possessed great length, and a reputation for being rank. *Black Smoke* was no stranger to Freckles, who successfully rode the animal two years earlier at the Cow Palace.[8]

Freckles again drew *Black Smoke* in Portland's Sunday matinee event that promised some explosive action.

Ominously, rodeo officials nearly canceled the entire show. A massive storm swept in from the Pacific and pounded Portland, October 12, on the eve of the event with 116-miles per hour winds. The storm struck with the ferocity of a Category 3 hurricane, killing dozens in the process, and leaving a wake of destruction. The next day the rodeo opened with sparse attendance. By day seven, fans began to appear in greater numbers, perhaps as a distraction from the devastating storm.[9]

Fans cheered enthusiastically for the beloved Freckles as he lowered down onto *Black Smoke*. Moments later, *Black Smoke* exploded from the chute with four straight jumps and spectacularly high kicks.[10]

"Then he lunged and turned back to the left and jerked

Freckles rode *Black Smoke* to the whistle before the large, muley Brangus nearly ended his life in 1962. *(DeVere Helfrich Rodeo Photographs, Dickinson Research Center, National Cowboy & Western Heritage Museum. 81.023.20940)*

the rope out of my hand," Freckles later remembered. "I was just riding him with the tail of my rope. I was jumping over to the left every time he came around."[11]

Suddenly, Freckles found himself too far to the left — on the edge of "the well" — when the whistle sounded. In that moment, *Black Smoke* caught the cowboy with his head and viciously flipped him into the air. Freckles landed with a deadening thud, his face planted in the dirt, unable to move.[12]

Freckles lay conscious but paralyzed.[13]

"I couldn't move anything," Freckles recalled. "I thought my back was broke..."[14]

A hush descended upon the crowd as medics rushed into the arena with a stretcher. They carried Freckles into the bowels of the complex and placed him in a first-aid room where a doctor tugged on his head. Feeling instantly returned to his right side and left foot.[15]

An ambulance rushed Freckles to Portland's Emmanuel Hospital, where a team of doctors greeted the rodeo star upon his arrival at the emergency room. Ensuing X-rays revealed Freckles had broken his neck, having mashed his fifth and sixth cervical vertebrae. A neurosurgeon informed Freckles he would require a pioneering front neck fusion that he had been studying. The operation required the removal of broken bones from his neck and the fusion of a piece of his hip bone to the vertebrae. The surgeon said he would likely recover, but two bone specialists argued strongly against the operation. They thought it was too risky.[16]

Both specialists then told Freckles he would never ride again.[17]

Freckles spoke up. He told the neurosurgeon to do the operation.[18]

Doctors placed Freckles in traction — an effective, but barbaric practice where sandbags weighed down a rope on a pulley, with the rope anchored to his head. Holes were first drilled into the top of his shaved head and into his skull, where tiny tongs attached to the rope were then clamped. Nurses later tilted Freckles to one side or the other every five hours. Freckles remained in this dreadful state of misery for the next thirty-four days.[19]

"One of my friends come to see me there," Freckles once said, "and he took one look and got so sick he had to run to the men's room and vomit."[20]

The *Rodeo Sports News* first delivered the devastating report to its readership in its November 1 issue. The headline hit as hard as *Black Smoke*: "Freckles Brown Badly Hurt In Bull Riding." The newspaper noted how "the cowboys' own favorite for championship honors lay in a Portland, Oregon, hospital with a broken neck."[21]

"Freckles is a tough little guy, now 41, and has won a total of $18,675 so far this year, giving him a $6,035 lead (over Rinestine) for the title," the article reported dutifully. "He may still win the championship even though out of action for the rest of the year."[22]

The article failed to question whether Freckles would ever ride again, although the thought was on everyone's mind.

Naturally, Edith didn't care. The stoic woman simply wanted her "Brownie" to walk again. Edith spent every day at the hospital with her husband, and at night, at Donna Madland's home in Portland. Madland, once a rodeo wife, insisted on Edith staying in her home while Freckles recovered. Madland's gracious hospitality was heartfelt and personal. Her husband Ken had died years earlier while riding a bull.[23]

The great Casey Tibbs witnessed his friend's death.

"It was a bull that got him, a high and nasty bucker that had tossed many a cowboy," Tibbs said. "When we got to him, Ken still had the rope in his hand and a back that was broken to pieces. It took him almost fifteen weeks to die after we finally got him to a San Bernardino hospital."[24]

Freckles, meanwhile, remained upbeat despite the torture of being stuck in traction. Letters and phone calls from friends and fans throughout the United States inundated the hospital in the weeks after the injury. All wished him a speedy recovery.[25]

Thirty-three days after nearly being killed by *Black Smoke* — on Thanksgiving Day — a medical team finally wheeled Freckles into surgery.[26] Once he emerged from the operating room, the staff helped him stand. The doctor proceeded to wrap his upper body in a cast, from his waist to the top of his forehead. Only his face, ears, and the top of his head were left uncovered.

The doctor stood on his toes as he finished wrapping the cast, quipping, "I'm glad you're not any taller than you are."[27]

Freckles smiled and tried to breathe.

"For about two days, until a cast cures out, it's real tight," Freckles later explained, "and when they were puttin' it on, I kept tryin' to keep a little air in my lungs and this nurse kept givin' me smelling salts."[28]

One rodeo writer reported, surely with tongue in cheek, noted how Freckles "tried out his new head-to-hip cast by dancing a little jig."[29] Writers found it too tempting to describe the seemingly ageless cowboy with Paul Bunyan-like language. Truthfully, Freckles felt as weak as ever.[30]

Shortly thereafter Freckles and Edith flew from Portland to Los Angeles, where he attended the National Finals Rodeo as a spectator — a strange, if not challenging time for a man who waited his whole life to be crowned a world champion. In typical fashion, Freckles spent his time making public appearances, shaking hands, and signing autographs. And as expected, Freckles' mammoth lead proved insurmountable. Officials declared him the 1962 world champion bull rider. His total of $18,675 was $4,633 more than second-place finisher Rinestine and even $5,283 more than Ronnie Rossen earned the previous year when he grabbed the world championship.³¹

"This tough, gay, ageless little feller is one of rodeo's immortals," one *Rodeo Sports News* writer declared. "At 41, he has won a championship that had eluded him since he began rodeoing over two decades ago. A championship in this, one of the world's most dangerous sports, is not easily won by a young man . . . it is even tougher for a man heading toward middle age . . . at least it would be for most men. It doesn't seem to bother Freckles a bit . . .

"Freckles came down to the National Finals, making publicity appearances and was on hand to receive his announcement as the Champion of the World. No cowboy ever deserved that title any more than Freckles Brown."³²

Such sentiment echoed through most of the rodeo fraternity.

Back in Lawton, Freckles struggled with his strength as he tried to maintain his cattle and horse ranch. He spent the winter trying to feed cattle while toting his bulky, fifteen-pound cast, but often had to sit

Flanked by Donna and Edith, Freckles still dons his bulky neck brace as he proudly accepts his 1962 World Championship saddle in Denver. *(DeVere Helfrich Rodeo Photographs, Dickinson Research Center, National Cowboy & Western Heritage Museum. 81.023.21409-08)*

down and rest. A neck brace replaced the cast on February 5, although he still felt listless and "pretty weak."[33]

Now, for the first time in his career, Freckles wondered if he could bounce back from an injury. Or, if he did, could he withstand a hard fall from another bull. Freckles mulled his fate daily. Wiley Harrison — then Donna's boyfriend and future husband — knew something about his father-in-law-to-be that would have shocked the rodeo world.

"He said he was done," Harrison recalled. "He had no plans to rodeo again."[34]

Freckles planned to retire.

Chapter Nine
A Phoenix Rising

*"I was worried more than anything else whether
I could stand a real hard fall . . ."*

— Freckles Brown

Doubts and questions choked Freckles during the first months of 1963 like the brace around his fused neck. Should he permanently hang up his spurs, and spend his final years quietly on the ranch of his dreams? Or should he return to the arena where his true passion resided? If so, could he survive a hard fall from another bad bull? Or would the next ride leave him paralyzed? Or dead?

Rank bulls didn't faze Freckles. Riding rank bulls after recovering from a broken neck was another matter entirely.

Publicly, Freckles said nothing of his planned retirement. Not a word. His silence may have spoken volumes about his shifting mindset. Perhaps, deep within, beyond the shadows of doubts and daunting odds, he knew he couldn't walk away from a life he loved — the life of a rodeo cowboy. And certainly not in this fashion, forced out by a broken neck and fear after being crowned a world champion.

Freckles stood at the top of his game at this critical juncture in his career.

Now only he could decide how his story would end. Edith certainly had no intention of telling her husband what to do. Such a gesture wasn't her style. A writer once asked her if she ever talked to him about retiring. "No," she replied simply. "That's up to Brown."[1]

And Brown alone.

May 11 marked a major milestone for Freckles. On that day, his doctor permitted him to finally remove his neck brace — a liberation he hadn't felt since *Black Smoke* mauled him nearly six months earlier in Portland.[2] By then, he was already contemplating a comeback. Freckles later told a rodeo reporter, "At first I couldn't do one push up; by July 4, I could do thirty-five or forty fairly easy."[3]

Privately, Freckles eyed "July or August" as a potential time for his return.[4] Behind the scenes he exercised as if his life depended on it, which of course it did. He ran, swam, and did pushups until he couldn't do anymore.[5]

"I learned that in the army," he once said of exercising. "If you messed up, if you took a wrong step in the dummy plane or didn't tumble right on the tower, the jump master would say, 'Give me fifty pushups.' We did a lot of runnin' and jumpin' and tumblin', too, and when I got out I just felt it was kind of foolish not to stay in shape."[6]

In this way, the forty-two-year-old Freckles proved to be an anomaly on the rodeo circuit. Few cowboys worked out, and even fewer ate the way he did. Fried foods were forbidden. He never served fried foods in his home. If chicken landed on the menu, it was either boiled or baked before it touched his lips. His healthy lifestyle had undoubtedly already added years to his extraordinarily long career.[7]

Time now lingered while Freckles contemplated his future. Refusing to sit still, he continued to make the time work for him by judging rodeos, exercising, and searching for his dream ranch. He longed to buy a bigger spread where he didn't feel so cramped. In Lawton, he often had to drive miles to feed and check his cattle on pastures leased from the Kiowa and Comanche tribes.[8]

One day his old friend Todd Whatley told Freckles about some prime land for sale near his Oklahoma home in Choctaw County, tucked in the southeast corner of the state against the Red River. Whatley — the first Rodeo Cowboys Association all-around world champion in 1947 — owned the T4 Ranch in the nearby town of Hugo.[9]

Whatley and Freckles first met while stationed at Fort Sill during World War II. Both broke horses for the army and ventured to rodeos together on weekend passes. Like Freckles, Whatley formally competed in his first rodeo in 1937, entering the bull riding event in the village of Battiest, Oklahoma. Ten years later he was crowned all-around world champion, hauling in a record $8,898 for a single rodeo at Madison Square Garden. The record stood until 1976. He was born the second of six children in 1920 in the unincorporated Oklahoma community of Rufe, which prior to statehood in 1907, sat in the heart of the Choctaw Nation in Indian Territory.[10]

Quiet by nature, Whatley later dropped out of school after the eighth grade to travel the rodeo circuit. His first taste of rodeo in Battiest left him hungry for more, and he quickly developed skills for bull riding, bareback riding, and bulldogging. By 1963, his legacy had already been cemented. In addition to his 1947 all-around world title, Whatley also won world championships in steer wrestling (1947) and bull riding (1953). The latter championship marked the only time during a fourteen-year period that someone other than Harry Tompkins or Jim Shoulders won the bull riding title.[11]

Whatley encouraged his friend to scout the land for himself, a 540-acre spread known as the Kelly Bend Ranch in Soper. The ranch, named for the Indian family that once owned it, offered an abundance of timber and plush pastures that extended into a horseshoe bend in the tea-colored Muddy Boggy Creek. Natural springs fed the creek which ran so deep it was unfordable by wagon or vehicle. Thick foliage blanketed the tree lines along the creek, regularly drawing turkey and deer. In October, wild plums grew so plentiful throughout the property, they could be picked and cooked into tasty jams.[12]

Freckles only needed one visit to become enchanted by the possibilities of owning the land. He immediately began to visit banks in search of a loan. All inquiries hit roadblocks.

Finally, Whatley offered to loan Freckles $32,000 — "on just his word," as Freckles once stated — to buy the ranch. The Farmers Home Administration agreed to finance the entirety of the loan, but after the land appraisal and closing costs were added, Freckles and Edith were still $12,000 short of finalizing the deal.[13]

Wiley Harrison remembered his father-in-law telling him that's when he gathered his rodeo gear and hit the road. He needed an extra $12,000 to secure the ranch.[14]

Although the notion of coming back clearly preceded the land deal.

Freckles traveled to Camdenton, Missouri, to judge a rodeo between June 29 and July 6. While in Camdenton, he determined he would return to rodeoing. Naturally, he shared his thoughts first with Edith.

"I told Edith for two cents I would just go to Coleman (Texas, July 10-13) and enter bronc and bull riding," Freckles recalled. "She didn't give me two cents, but said that was up to me: if I felt like it, fine, and if I didn't feel like it, to stay home."[15]

Edith never complicated matters. She also declined to accompany her husband to Texas, perhaps hesitant to encounter the fear of what might happen to her beloved "Brownie."

Coleman — the chosen site of Freckles' comeback — housed a modest population of 6,311 residents, located fifty-two miles southeast of Abilene. Farming, ranching, and oil were the standard economic staples of the community and surrounding region, which celebrated football and rodeo with equal enthusiasm.

The rodeo, like the town, offered a small enough stage for Freckles to test his strength and reflexes without any major distractions.

"I felt real good," Freckles recalled. "I knew I wasn't quite as strong as I needed to be. I also knew the only way to get stoutened up was to start rodeoing."[17]

Skipper Lofting, who worked for the RCA and rodeoed in the 1930s,

Wiley Harrison married Donna Brown September 3, 1966, in Apache, Oklahoma. Donna died February 10, 2019. *(Courtesy of the Harrison-Brown Family)*

remembered the tension around the chutes when Freckles mounted his first bull — Elra and Jiggs Beutler's explosive bull number *Seven*. Lofting would later recall, "When [Freckles] got on that bull in the chute and they announced his name, it was so quiet that you could hear cars a mile away on the highway."[18]

Number *Seven* busted out of the chute, spinning to the right in a tight circle, away from Freckles' left hand as it tightly gripped the rope. The bull then lunged, jarring him from his rope and bucked off the game champion on his next jump.[19]

Freckles crashed hard to the ground. Fans collectively held their breath.[20]

In that moment, the cowboy who survived the Great Depression and war and a raging bull named *Black Smoke*, rose like the mythological Phoenix from the caliche soil of the arena floor. He rose unharmed.[21]

Freckles' illustrious career spanned five decades, from 1937 to 1974 when he retired at the age of 53 – a biblical age for bull riders. *(DeVere Helfrich Rodeo Photographs, Dickinson Research Center, National Cowboy & Western Heritage Museum. 81.023.09590)*

A symphony of applause rose with him.

"I was worried more than anything else about whether I could stand a real hard fall ... and I took a pretty hard fall from number *Seven*, but it didn't hurt my neck," Freckles revealed. "I rode him about six or seven seconds . . .

"I felt I should have rode him. I wasn't jumping at him or using my feet like I should have been."[22]

Later, Freckles climbed aboard his second bull at Coleman, another of Beutler's noted stock simply named number 100. This time he took a more aggressive approach mentally, vowing to "beat him out of the chute . . . and not be sitting there asleep and let him jerk me off my rope."[23]

Number 100 kicked out of the chute and spun to the right, but Freckles remained centered. Freckles later described the bull as "real common" for the remaining six seconds as he rode him to the whistle. He added, "I got a good start with him, and it felt good all the way."[24]

Freckles knew then he was on the comeback trail, although he never harbored delusional thoughts about the work required to return to his top form. By October, he had ridden nine bulls. Seven of them bucked him off. He told the colorful Willard H. Porter that month, "My neck feels real good and I have felt good on my last three head . . . but I haven't rode enough stock to tell for sure yet."[25]

Ironically, the year didn't pass without another scare for Freckles. This one involved his good friend and traveling buddy, George "Tex" Martin. A big brindle tossed Martin at a rodeo in Sidney, Iowa, and then planted a hind foot into his chest. Freckles recalled the disturbing moment in detail:

> *He stepped plumb through Tex to the back of his rib cage, and when he brought that leg up, Tex was on it. It was like pullin' a cork, but there was a doctor right there, and he had the guys hold Tex out straight in the air and he just kept wrappin' the bandage around him.*

*I got into the ambulance with Tex, and he was hurtin'. On the way to the hospital in Hamburg (Iowa) he got to gaspin' and sayin', 'I can't breathe.' He said, 'It hurts.' I said, 'The hell it does. You sorry little bastard, keep breathin'.'*²⁶

Martin miraculously lived. ²⁷

During Martin's recovery, the ambulance driver approached him with a disturbed sense of curiosity about Freckles. "You know," the man told Martin, "I never heard anybody talk to a dyin' man like that friend of yours was talkin' to you."²⁸

The two friends later howled at the driver's shock.

By the end of 1963, Freckles estimated he had ridden between "1,800 and 2,000 bulls" since he began his career in Willcox, Arizona, in 1937.²⁹ No other active cowboy on the circuit — save for the great Jim Shoulders — had ridden more rank bulls than the Wyoming native.

Now, with the comeback in his rearview mirror, the legend of Freckles Brown only continued to grow. Sports writers soon began to pay homage to his undisputed grit

Freckles made the cover of the *1964 Rodeo Sports News Annual*, which recapped the 1963 season in pro rodeo.

and determination with a new nickname, one inspired by RMS *Titanic* survivor Molly Brown: "The Unsinkable Mister Brown."

During the 1964 and 1965 seasons, Freckles scaled back his rodeo schedule so he could build a new home on their newly acquired Kelly Bend Ranch. He and Edith sold their Lawton home in 1964 and finalized their loan for the Soper spread that summer. Freckles also repaid Whatley in full for his generous loan.[31]

The work consumed Freckles whom his daughter, Donna, often said could do the work of "four men."[32] Anyone who personally knew Freckles, wouldn't challenge that claim. Freckles cleared timber in the horseshoe bend portion of the ranch with a bulldozer, sprigged coastal bermudagrass, erected fences, and tended cattle before building a two-bedroom ranch house from native pine.[33]

During the construction of the house, the Browns lived in an old wooden shack with a red tin roof that already stood on the property. They also used an accompanying outhouse. Freckles finished the house in six months, framing the lower portion on the outside with native stone he hauled from the Kiamichi Mountains along the southeastern fringe of Oklahoma.[34]

Native stones were also used by Freckles to build a beautiful fireplace that featured a stout, wooden mantle. Several of his most prized trophies soon adorned the mantle, including his cherished first bull riding trophy from the 1941 Cody Stampede.[35]

Freckles, Edith, and Donna moved into their new home in January 1965 — just in time to celebrate Freckles' forty-

The shack Freckles and his family lived in while he built what would eventually become the family's home. *(Courtesy of the Harrison-Brown Family)*

fourth birthday.[36]

Soon, Freckles returned to the road, chasing rodeos and his destiny. As the life of a rodeo cowboy often revealed to him, the journey came with great pain and sacrifice. On one occasion in 1965, at Springdale, Arkansas, he pulled into town at three in the morning. He checked into a motel and asked the desk clerk to wake him in two hours. He wanted to take a quick shower and head the rodeo grounds.[37]

Freckles arrived at the arena cold and stiff, and just in time to mount his first bull — "a real arm-jerker."[38]

"He was really stout on that rope, and after the ride, I was puttin' up my rope when I noticed something lyin' like a big lump near my elbow," Freckles remembered. "There was just skin and bones above, and that was my bicep lyin' there."[39]

The tendon had snapped.

A doctor tied the tendon back together at his shoulder,

Edith, Donna, and Freckles pose for a picture, circa 1962. *(Courtesy of the Harrison-Brown Family)*

placing his arm in a sling for ten days. Freckles spent those days feverishly squeezing a rubber ball to regain strength as quickly as possible. Amazingly — or perhaps foolishly — he thought he could still win money by riding with his weaker right hand. He couldn't.

Later, he freely admitted with a touch of amusement how that plan "was a mistake."[40]

Freckles loved to laugh — sometimes at himself and sometimes at the world around him. Over time he became a seasoned storyteller, drawing from his hard and colorful life with an unabashed joy and wit.

Cowboys often jockeyed for a chance to travel with him on the road just to hear him speak.

"He was a great guy," recalled Ferrell Butler, a legendary rodeo photographer and friend. "He had a personality that didn't quit . . . He was so funny. He could tell stories, I swear, he'd just get down and roll. He was the best storyteller there

Ferrell Butler shows off one of the Rolleiflex T 75 mm cameras he used during his illustrious career as a rodeo photographer. This is the type of camera he used when he captured his iconic shots of Freckles on *Tornado*. *(Author's Collection)*

ever was. People fought to get him to ride with them to the next rodeo because Freckles would start out on a story when you left the rodeo arena or the motel. And that story wouldn't end until you got to the rodeo in the next town . . . I mean he could embellish a story like nobody else in the world . . . You'd die laughing or almost wreck the car. Freckles was so funny."[41]

Butler first met Freckles around 1958 at the newly minted Mesquite Championship Rodeo in his hometown of Mesquite, Texas. Rodeos in Mesquite dated back to 1946. In 1950, Dallas annexed the community of Pleasant Mound —site of the original rodeo grounds and where Butler resided — and refused to issue a special zoning permit for the rodeo. Shortly thereafter, the star-studded team of rodeo cowboys Neal Gay, Ira Akers, D.J. Gaudin, Bob Grant, Jim Shoulders, and Harry Tompkins purchased land on a hill nearby and built an open-air arena that opened in 1958. From this legendary ensemble, the Mesquite Championship Rodeo was born.

At that time, Butler had been trying his hand at calf roping. Born in Davidson, Oklahoma, his family later moved to Pleasant Mound where he did what every other youngster did — sling a rope. Butler roped goats and calves, but mostly cans. Tons of cans. "I wore them cans out roping," Butler said.

"I could rope, but I never did have a good enough horse."[42]

Butler's love of roping eventually brought him to Mesquite's rodeo grounds where, in 1960, he struggled to pay his ten-dollar entry fees. Gay, an old-school cowboy and savvy businessman, suggested that he to start taking pictures at the rodeo and sell them to pay his fees.[43]

No rodeo photographers were working in that section of Texas at the time. The market sat wide open like the vastness of the Texas Panhandle.[44]

Gay's advice took root. The twenty-four-year-old Butler began shooting regularly at the Mesquite rodeos. In the beginning, Shoulders helped the young cowboy photographer. He bought his pictures of the stock, often dropping ten or twenty dollars at a time — enough to initially keep Butler afloat with his film, chemicals, and paper.[45]

Shoulders possessed that kind of heart.

Soon, Butler's photography gig turned into a full-time venture. Everybody wanted to purchase his photographs, even the *Rodeo Sports News*. Gene Pruett, editor of the popular publication, told him, "Do more rodeos besides Mesquite."[46] So Butler sold his horse, ropes, and saddles to buy better cameras and equipment. He did all this

Bobby Berger competed in all three roughstock events and is one of only four cowboys to qualify for the National Finals Rodeo in all three. He won the world saddle bronc riding title in 1979 and inducted into the ProRodeo Hall of Fame in 1990. (*Photo courtesy of Ferrell Butler.*)

while holding down a full-time job with Dallas Power and Light as an engineering technician. Eventually, he hit the road on weekends and during vacations, traveling throughout Texas, Oklahoma, Arkansas, and Louisiana. He journeyed as far north as Burwell, Nebraska, and Cheyenne, Wyoming, where he captured images of Freckles and other top rodeo hands of that era at the historic Cheyenne Frontier Days.[47]

Butler traveled among rodeo's next generation of stars — cowboys like Bill Kornell, Bobby Berger, and Larry Mahan. Collectively, they represented a new breed of cowboy in the sport. Many were college educated like Berger, who graduated from California Polytechnic State University, San Luis Obispo with a bachelor's degree in animal science. Or they emerged from unlikely corners of the country like Kornell, an athletic youngster who grew up in Palm Springs, California, as the son of a corporate scientific writer.[48]

The debonair Mahan, meanwhile, would forever change the image of rodeo. The Brooks, Oregon, native didn't drink or smoke, worked out at gyms, flew his own airplane, and handed out business cards.[49]

All three would go on to become world champions. Mahan alone would win six all-around world championships before he retired, including five consecutive titles between 1966 and 1970. Kornell took the RCA by storm in 1963, claiming the world bull riding championship as a nineteen-year-old rookie from Clarksville, Texas. Berger claimed the world bronc riding championship in 1979, although the rodeo world took notice of him fourteen years earlier as a twenty-year-old college student. On July 4, 1965, Berger turned in one of the great performances in rodeo history when he became the first

Bobby Berger wrote and published *Bobby Berger's Basic Bullriding: A Fundamental Instruction Manual* in 1971. One of the only rodeo instructional manuals, until Larry Mahan published *Larry Mahan's Fundamentals of Rodeo Riding* in 1972.

cowboy to ride the great bucking palomino saddle bronc *Descent* at the Black Hills Roundup in Belle Fourche, South Dakota. [50]

Each cowboy also shared something else in common — a love and respect for the ageless wonder, Freckles Brown.

"He's just the most wonderful person you'd just ever want to meet," Berger said of Freckles. "I just thought so much of him, and he was everybody's hero. Everybody liked him. One of a kind."[51]

Once, Berger wrote a book titled *Bobby Berger's Basic Bullriding: A Fundamental Instruction Manual*. Berger proudly showed Freckles the book one day. "He said, 'Oh, I have to have one of those,'" Berger fondly recalled. "He bought one instantly — one of the first to buy one."[52]

Freckles occasionally flew with Berger to rodeos in his single-engine, low-wing Comanche airplane, nicknamed "The Bumble Bee" because of its bold black and yellow paint. The veteran cowboy traveled light with no frills.

"I liked to have him fly with me because I didn't have a real powerful plane, and I didn't like getting any weight in it," Berger noted. "And he had the smallest gear bag of any bull rider going on down the road. A little ol' army duffle bag and he just had a minimal amount of stuff in it.

"That's all you needed, and all he needed. And he'd just jump in and go."[53]

Stories of Freckles riding in airplanes became nearly as legendary as those of him riding on the back of raging bulls.

Kornell loved to tell of the time when Freckles and Myrtis Dightman — the first African American cowboy to qualify for the National Finals Rodeo in 1964 — were flying to a rodeo when the pilot passed out. The pilot had apparently indulged himself in alcohol the previous night. Without hesitation, Freckles jumped into the pilot's seat and began to fly the plane.

"I was told Dightman's eyes were as big as saucers," Kornell said with a laugh. "Fortunately, the pilot came to in time to land the plane."[54]

Mahan told an equally riveting story that involved Freckles. Mahan recalled the time Freckles rode in the back seat of his airplane as they soared over the Rocky Mountains.

"We were going from St. Paul, Oregon, to Calgary and I had to get up to 14,000 or 15,000 feet to get over the rock pile for about thirty minutes," Mahan said.[55]

Another passenger suddenly announced, "Freckles just died."[56]

"I didn't have any oxygen on the plane," Mahan said. "Man, I panicked. I said, 'See if he has a pulse. Feel his heart. Feel his wrist.'"[57]

The cowboy said, "I think I feel a heartbeat."[58]

"I just nose-dived it when we got over those clouds," Mahan continued. "We were around 9,000 feet and ol' Freckles just woke up. If I could have got in the back seat, I would have kissed him on the lips. It scared me to death."[59]

Such stories — whether slightly embellished or not — only added to Freckles' aura of invincibility.

In 1966, Freckles returned to the rodeo circuit full-time and again rode bulls exclusively. He entered the National Finals Rodeo in first place, only to falter in the Finals. He finished in third place overall.[60]

Fans and even some of his fellow cowboys now viewed him as a larger-than-life character. Reporters also frequently sought rodeo's elder statesman for his colorful stories and quotes. Freckles rarely, if ever, disappointed during an interview. Of course, scribes almost always asked him how he received his famous nickname. They usually noted curiously how Freckles didn't have, well, any freckles. He always responded with a standard, yet witty answer: "I don't have freckles anymore. I reckon all those bulls shook 'em off."[61]

Reporters loved the quote.

And whenever Edith's name came up, Freckles enjoyed launching into the story of their first date. Edith showed up that night with laryngitis. He would say, "She couldn't talk and I thought she was a fine girl."[62]

Freckles would then laugh at his own line. Oklahoma columnist Frank Boggs heard the line and mused, "He laughed at this joke I bet he's told a jillion times."[63]

Once Freckles explained what it took to be a good bull rider. His words were classic Freckles Brown.

"People ask me, 'What makes a good bull rider?'" he said. "All I can tell them is the good Lord just puts all your brains in your arms and legs."[64]

Yet beyond the down-home, country humor and colorful yarns existed a quintessential pro. A seasoned quintessential pro with twenty-nine years of experience. His contemporaries recognized it, and none more than the legendary Shoulders.

"Freckles and me, we done a lot of rodeos together," Shoulders once said of his long-time friend. "The man just don't know a thing 'bout pain. Or fear, either. He likes them bad bulls the best.

"It's kind of funny, when you've ridden as many bulls as I have, you get to where you don't always watch the other guys make their rides. But when ol' Freckles tells 'em to open the gate, I always watch. 'Cause it's gonna be spectacular."[65]

Freckles success didn't happen by chance. He always studied the bulls, taking notes of their strengths and tendencies. Details mattered to him, as much as seconds. He studied bulls he had already ridden and those he might someday draw.

One bull especially caught his eye — a 1,725-pound, Hereford-Brahman crossbreed that had been unridden since he burst onto the scene in 1960. Freckles had yet to draw the bull but anticipated that day might come. If so, he wanted to be ready.

The bull possessed a nasty disposition, a competitive streak, and an ominous name: *Tornado*.

Chapter Ten
Tornado

"He'd run over that barrel, and then he'd eat your lunch. If you fell off in front of him, you were gonna get a hookin' for sure."

— Ferrell Butler on Tornado

Thin and sickly, the red-haired bull with a distinctive white face first appeared publicly at a Bay City, Texas, auction barn in the spring of 1960. Several prospective buyers passed on the frail animal until rancher "Big" John Williams of nearby Garwood purchased the bull for $147.[1]

The gregarious Williams stood 6-foot-3, and possessed a large appetite for company, laughter, and training bucking bulls for rodeo contractors. Williams — known as "The Bull Man" — took a chance on the sickly bull and brought him to his sprawling 8,000-acre ranch in western Colorado County, Texas, between the towns of Sheridan and Rock Island. The ranch sat in a "transitional zone," divided by vast stretches of flat, rice fields on its eastern boundary and plush pastures to the west. The dividing point featured a slight undulation with post oak stands and oak motts scattered throughout the land, with various pastures plowed and planted with Bermuda grass for grazing.[2]

For a brief period, it looked as if the bull might not even make it to the pasture.

Williams carefully inspected the animal after his arrival at the ranch. The animal's frame was thinning daily, and his red hair had been falling from his neck. Brown Todd — a Louisiana rodeo stock contractor — passed on the bull, opting to buy a healthier looking one from "Big" John before departing Texas. Later, upon closer inspection, Williams discovered the bull was severely plagued by liver flukes — parasites that attacked the animal's bloodstream.[3]

A few doses of medicine promptly brought the bull back to life.[4]

From these shadows of uncertainty, and against all odds, emerged the greatest bucking bull to ever burst onto the rodeo scene. Handlers later gave the bull an ominous, yet appropriate name, *Tornado*.

In those early days, however, Williams simply named the bull "Number Four." As the Hereford-Brahman crossbreed gained strength, Williams soon began to see promise. The bull showed an ability to buck and a general dislike of people. He also seemed fated to be in the hands of Williams, who invented a new way to train bucking stock.

Williams made "bull dummies" from old, blue tarps and would cinch them to bulls like a saddle to simulate a

"Big" John Williams, the man who discovered the infamous bull, *Tornado*. *(Courtesy of Bill L. Owens)*

rider. He released the bull from a chute in an arena on his property. A tripping device then released the dummies as a reward for the bulls that bucked as he desired. The dummies were primitive and flat like an old pillow, but surprisingly effective.[5]

"He was the first one to ever do that sort of thing," recalled Marvin Paul Shoulders, the son of Jim Shoulders. "He put that dummy on a bull a couple times out to see if he had any athletic ability or if he wanted to play."[6]

Tornado quickly showed the signs of a born athlete. The animal's unlikely origin story showed the signs of a legend.

Foaled in 1957, *Tornado* was born on the Pierce Estate Ranch near Wharton, Texas, roughly sixty miles west of Houston. The site of his birth was on land owned by Clive Runnells, a mutual fund and cable television pioneer, and great-grandson of the cattle baron Abel Head "Shanghai" Pierce.[7]

The colorful Pierce — a larger-than-life Texas legend — received his famous nickname from friends in his native Rhode Island who thought he resembled a Shanghai rooster. In June 1854, at age twenty, Pierce stowed away on a schooner bound for Indianola, Texas. The ruse didn't last long. Discovered, the captain required him to work off his passage by handling cargo. Years later he began amassing a sizeable cattle herd. Eventually, he acquired 250,000 acres of land that stretched from Wharton County south into Matagorda County, all the way to Matagorda Bay.[8]

Pierce towered over most Texans in his time at six-foot-four, and possessed an unmistakable flair and wit that matched his height. Once he commissioned a gravesite statute of himself made years before his death so he could enjoy it while still alive. Another memorable story involved a cow discovered on his range with the brand "AHP is a SOB." Instead of being outraged, Pierce expressed amusement. He allowed the cow to roam his range for life, declaring the animal provided good advertisement.[9]

From these deep Texas roots, *Tornado* surfaced.

Destiny now appeared in play for a new Texas legend. Williams regularly hosted hunts for friends on his ranch, which teamed with an abundance of whitetail deer and quail. He developed extensive business ties and friendships throughout the rodeo community, such as those with two of the sport's icons, Jim Shoulders and Neal Gay. Both rodeo giants were frequent guests on those South Texas ranch hunts. In 1960, with the weekly Mesquite Championship Rodeo in Dallas County in full swing, Gay visited Williams in search of bulls.[10]

Jim Shoulders & Neal Gay
(DeVere Helfrich, 1965, safety film negative. DeVere Helfrich Rodeo Photographs, Dickinson Research Center, National Cowboy & Western Heritage Museum. 81.023.25921-08.)

The thirty-four-year-old Gay — who joined the Rodeo Cowboys Association in 1946 and competed in virtually every event — now served as managing director of the Mesquite rodeo. He purchased three bulls from Williams on that trip, paying $247 for "Number Four." The bull eventually ended up with

Shoulders, Gay's close friend and partner in the Mesquite Rodeo Company. By then, Shoulders had embarked into the world of stock contracting.[11]

Shoulders, who gave the bull his famous name, first received *Tornado* at his J Lazy S Ranch in Henryetta, Oklahoma, with "a batch" of other bulls.[12] He always bucked his stock to determine which ones would make the "rodeo truck," and *Tornado* easily made the cut because he could "buck like hell."

Shoulders provided stock for the Mesquite rodeo every Friday and Saturday nights from April to September, and in 1960, this is where *Tornado* made his rodeo debut.[13]

No one remembers the exact date, only the impact of his arrival.

Ferrell Butler caught his first glimpse of *Tornado* through the lens of his Rolleiflex T 75 mm camera. Standing within thirty feet from the chute — so his strobe could cast enough light on his subjects — the rookie bull first appeared to Butler, exploding from behind a heavy, wooden gate and into the dimly lit arena. Local cowboy Gene Cummings held on tightly as *Tornado* violently pounded the arena's rich, black soil with each buck.

Within a couple of seconds, *Tornado* crashed down on the clown barrel. The young bull went crazy, hooking and jumping and spinning in a desperate effort to break free of the barrel. Cummings hung on for an unforgettable ride — a moment Butler would never forget.

"Gene rode him the entire eight seconds," Butler recalled. "But it didn't count because *Tornado* got hung up in the barrel. Hell, for six seconds he had that barrel under him. He couldn't get the damn thing off of him . . . He hooked it and

Tornado earned a reputation as an "unrideable" bull and a crowd favorite by chasing bull fighters and blasting barrels as shown here in 1965. *(Bern Gregory Rodeo Photographs, Dickinson Research Center, National Cowboy & Western Heritage Museum.1999.025.0084.05)*

tried to jump it and kept landing on the damn thing.

"If *Tornado* hadn't gotten on that barrel, he'd have thrown Gene off."[14]

Butler is also convinced that one ride with Cummings forever changed *Tornado*.

"I think he really hated barrels after that," Butler theorized. "Boy, he loved to hook the clown barrel . . . If he bucked you off, he didn't just want to nail you right there, he'd take off and nail that barrel. He'd knock it plumb out of the arena. He'd run over that barrel, and then he'd eat your lunch. If you fell off in front of him, you were gonna get a hookin' for sure."[15]

Tornado also seemed to sense the spotlight. Once the bull flung a cowboy, he cratered into a barrel, chased a clown, and then sometimes stood in the middle of the arena as if waiting to hear the roar of the crowd.

Fans responded by lustily cheering with each new appearance by the explosive bull. Cowboy after cowboy mounted him, only to fail to reach the eight-second mark. Every bull rider in *Tornado's* path fell. And some fell hard.

Pat Scudder, a former Marine who served in the Pacific Theatre during World War II, had the misfortune of drawing *Tornado* on more than one occasion. Those rides always ended poorly for the Dewey, Oklahoma, cowboy.

"I remember every time Pat Scudder got on him, *Tornado* just more or less pancaked Pat," Butler said. "Pat would get on him, and it would be dadgum, here it goes. I think he even broke his nose one time."[16]

Tornado's unbeaten streak began to mount. So too did the anticipation over who would become the first cowboy to ride him. The Texas-bred bull soon became the Mesquite rodeo's main attraction. Gay stared at a promoter's dream and made sure *Tornado* was always the last bull of the night.

Crowds loved the build-up.

Occasionally, on a Saturday night, Shoulders heightened the excitement around *Tornado* by offering a $500 bonus to any cowboy who could ride his star bull. Cowboys initially flocked to the arena to put their name into a hat for a chance to win that much cash. But, in the end, everyone who mounted *Tornado* wound up unceremoniously bucked off.[17]

In time, the eagerness to ride *Tornado* faded. A few even did the unthinkable. They would "turn him out" if they drew him, rather than risk bodily harm trying to ride a bull many deemed "unrideable."[18]

Texan Myrtis Dightman, arguably the strongest bull rider on the circuit and the first African American to qualify for the

National Finals Rodeo in bull riding, boiled *Tornado's* success down to two factors: "He didn't want you on his back . . . and nobody wanted to ride that bull."[19]

Tornado's fierce reputation started to toy with the psyche of some cowboys.[20]

Ironically, *Tornado* never caused trouble for his handlers. Harold Leftwich, a young bull rider who worked for Beutler and Brothers in Elk City, Oklahoma, occasionally hauled *Tornado* to rodeos in a cattle truck for Shoulders. He witnessed a different side of the bull away from the bucking chutes.

"He was always easy to haul, a real athlete," Leftwich said. "Some bulls you have to hit with a lightening rod to move. Not *Tornado*. He was a real professional. But make no mistake, he was rank, and he was special.

"And he knew it, too."[21]

Tornado finished his rookie season at the National Finals Rodeo in Los Angeles, where he bucked off California's rugged Jim Charles and future world champion Bob Wegner (1964) of Washington. Cowboys voted *Tornado* the Finals Third Best Bull that first year — a sign of the greatness to come.[22]

Tornado would go on to be voted the "Best Bull of the Finals" for the next four years, beginning in 1962. During that period, and in the glare of the Finals' spotlight, *Tornado* bucked off some of the world's best cowboys. The list included Bob Robinson, Howard Carroll, Ken Stanton, Joel Sublette, Hank Abbie, David Glover, Carl Nafzger, Gid Garstad, Bob Sheppard, Charles, and Wegner. None of them survived the eight-second count.[23]

"This bull is real active," Shoulders said of *Tornado* in 1964. "He can jump higher and turn back quicker than bulls smaller than he is. *Tornado* weighs 1,700 pounds and the old bull is pretty cagey, too."[24]

Bobby Berger, another of the world's best bull riders of that era, thought *Tornado* possessed a lethal combination of skills.

"He bucked real hard and had a lot of drop," Berger said simply. "That's hard to overcome."[25]

Amazingly, Berger never experienced a ride on *Tornado* firsthand. The native Kansan simply never drew the bull.

Marvin Paul Shoulders poses in front of *Tornado's* mounted horns and the No. 2 chute used at the 1967 National Finals Rodeo. Marvin Paul was also a top bull rider, qualifying for the National Finals Rodeo four times during his career. Both the horn mount and gate are on display at the Henryetta (Oklahoma) Chamber of Commerce. *(Author's Collection)*

"Do I wish I had ever ridden him?" Berger said. "No, not really. To be real honest, at that time, I didn't think I could ride him. I didn't want him. I didn't want him because whoever else got him was gonna get bucked off.

"So, if I had a little easier bull, I had a better chance of winning."[26]

The reigning four-time Best Bull of the Finals had yet to be ridden, and many cowboys started to think like Berger — perhaps the bull can't be ridden.

Tornado's conquests

Painting of Jim Shoulder's *Tornado* by Orren Mixer. The painting was featured on the July 1967 cover of *Western Horseman*. *(Bern Gregory, 1966, safety film negative. Bern Gregory Rodeo Photographs, Dickinson Research Center, National Cowboy & Western Heritage Museum. 1999.025.3033.03.)*

reached mythical proportions — 100 cowboys . . . 200 cowboys . . . 220 cowboys. Yet no one — not even Shoulders — knew the real number of cowboys who had been bucked off *Tornado* since he burst onto the scene in 1960. Nor did it really matter.

Only one question seemed relevant: If *Tornado* were ridden, who would be the cowboy to stake that prestigious claim?

Legends are made on such historic rides.

Yet as the unbeaten streak mounted, so did security around *Tornado*. Jim Shoulders protected his prized bull by keeping him separated from other bulls and alone in a horse stall. Behind the scenes, and unbeknownst to most, Shoulders also had *Tornado* watched.[27]

Marvin Paul Shoulders — fifteen years old in 1966 — had been given the most important job of all by his father when workers loaded *Tornado* into the chutes. As the prospective rider tied his rope around the famous bull, his father instructed him to watch everyone intently. The young Shoulders remembered the tension of those days when he recalled, "My deal was to stand on the back of the chute and make sure nobody tried to give him a shot or drug him or something."[28]

The fame of being the first to ride *Tornado* would not come so cheaply. Or so easily.

Chapter Eleven
The Draw

"Is he a goodin'?"

— Former world champion calf roper Jim Bob Altizer to Freckles regarding his opening night draw at the National Finals Rodeo.

Opportunities are often fleeting — if they come at all. They can appear as if out of nowhere, and then disappear like a wisp of smoke.

Or, in Freckles' world, vanish in a second.

Freckles received news of a legacy-changing opportunity on the eve of the 1967 National Rodeo Finals (NFR) in Oklahoma City. Rodeo officials posted the opening night matchups at a tiny office on the Oklahoma State Fairgrounds five miles west of downtown. He learned that his first-round draw was bull No. 461 — *Tornado*.

Word of the draw in rodeo circles struck like a bolt of lightning on the Oklahoma prairie. The matchup seemed too good to be true, as if ripped from the pages of a Hollywood screenplay or an Ernest Hemingway novel.

The beloved, old cowboy versus the rank, unrideable bull.

Tornado entered the National Finals Rodeo as feared as ever. By now, the bull's reputation had drifted into the realm of mythology, a fearsome, hooking bull of Paul Bunyan-type proportions. Hundreds of defeated cowboys had been left in his dusty wake with a number so large, everyone lost count.

Only one thing remained certain: the bull was undefeated.

Crowds loved him. Cowboys loathed him.

Bull rider Ronnie Bowman — a traveling buddy of Freckles from Durant, Oklahoma — ducked into the tiny NFR office on the fairgrounds to inquire about his first-round matchup. He learned he had drawn *Sparring Mate*, one of Harry Knight's nastiest bulls from Colorado. That's where he also discovered Freckles had drawn *Tornado*. As was the case with many bull riders, *Tornado* left a distinctive memory seared into Bowman's brain.

"The first time I ever saw *Tornado* was at a rodeo down in Crockett, Texas," recalled Bowman, as if vividly reliving the moment. "Hank Abbie rode him for about three or four seconds before being bucked off. *Tornado* was so rank, and one of the fastest bulls I had ever seen. It was unreal."[1]

Oklahoma columnist Frank Boggs once wrote of *Tornado*: "His reputation had not been gained smelling flowers. He was rodeo's orneriest critter, a massive assembly of muscle and guts and powerful old bones."[2]

Few cowboys wanted any part of *Tornado*. Clem McSpadden, then an Oklahoma congressman and the NFR's new general manager, once said, "*Tornado* had such a reputation that most cowboys were thrown before they even got on him."[3]

McSpadden knew Freckles wouldn't be one of those cowboys. Freckles possessed a mental toughness forged into his psyche during three decades of riding the nastiest broncs and bulls rodeo had to offer.

Outside of family, McSpadden might have known Freckles as well as anyone. He often called Freckles "a brother," and

Clem McSpadden was one of the most prominent figures in professional rodeo and the state of Oklahoma. In rodeo he was a noted announcer, broadcaster and served as general manager of the National Finals Rodeo. He also served in the Oklahoma Senate and represented Oklahoma in the U.S. House of Representatives. McSpadden was also a grandnephew of Will Rogers and one of Freckles Brown's closest friends. (*Photo courtesy of Ferrell Butler.*)

spent countless evenings at his kitchen table in Soper swapping stories of days past.[4]

McSpadden understood Freckles on the deepest of levels, having shared a similar hardscrabble upbringing on a family farm and ranch. He was born in the rural settlement of Bushyhead, Oklahoma, and raised on a Rogers County ranch owned by his great-uncle Will Rogers, the famed humorist. He could recall the days when Rogers stopped by the ranch unannounced to ride horses in the pasture or eat one of his mother's homemade blueberry pies whole in one sitting.[5]

McSpadden grew up with a strong sense of humility, love of family, and an understanding that life was a fleeting gift. He sometimes harkened back to a tearful day when he was nine, tossing bales of hay from a barn loft. His father walked into the barn, removed his hat, and said somberly, "I have some bad news. Uncle Will has died in a plane crash with Wiley Post."[6]

The moment forever framed his life with perspective.

Years later, inspired by decades of work with rodeos, he penned *The Cowboy's Prayer*. The prayer concludes:

> *Help us, Lord, to live our lives in such a manner that when we make that last inevitable ride to the country up there, where the grass grows lush, green and stirrup high, and the water runs cool, clear, and deep, that you, as our last Judge, will tell us that our entry fees are paid.*[7]

McSpadden wasn't afraid to touch the bone marrow of life. And neither was Freckles. The forty-six-year-old cowboy earnestly desired the rankest bulls on the circuit, thriving on the challenge. His enthusiasm was always evident in his lively descriptions of riding bulls for a paycheck.

"You put your gloved hand in the loop of the rope, clench it with all your strength, and get ready for the explosion," Freckles once told a reporter enthusiastically. "Then they crack the gate, and you are out for an eight-second ride on a 1,500-pound stick of dynamite. That is, if you last that long.

"There is a lot of action when you ride a Brahma. They are unpredictable critters — a lot faster and quicker than a horse."[8]

Six months earlier, in June, Freckles rode just such a "stick of dynamite." He entered a rodeo in Miami, Oklahoma, and drew the 1,725-pound *Big Bad John* — another of Jim Shoulders' nasty bulls. Freckles welcomed the challenge. He successfully rode *Big Bad John* that day to win the top money in bull riding, but upon the dismount, suffered a broken bone when the bull stepped on his leg. The injury sidelined him for weeks.[9]

As a result, Freckles competed in only forty-five rodeos

all season and entered the 1967 Finals seventh in the money standings with $11,753 — far behind the leader Larry Mahan, who had won a total of $20,568 in that event.[10]

Mahan, who represented rodeo's new breed at twenty-four, had already clinched his second straight all-around cowboy world championship before his arrival. He also remained poised to become the sport's first cowboy to surpass $50,000 in total earnings. Mahan came to Oklahoma City with $48,112 in the bank, a total that had already broken an eleven-year-old record held by Shoulders.[11]

Yet now even Mahan stood in the shadows of the Freckles-*Tornado* showdown.

McSpadden reveled in the storyline. And if there was one thing the native Oklahoman understood, it was a captivating story. Perhaps his bloodline had something to do with this knack for sniffing out a good story. Regardless, the aged Freckles riding out of the chute on the back of a raging and unbeaten *Tornado* made for high drama, and the kind of moment that could transcend a sport.

Rodeo needed such a moment.

For all its prestige, the NFR simply had no money. In 1965 — the NFR's first appearance in Oklahoma City — the event made a modest profit of $89,000. Prior to 1965, the NFR continually reported losses.[12]

McSpadden, who replaced Pat Scudder as NFR general manager, saw the balance sheets. They weren't pleasant, and he noted decades later, "There just simply wasn't any money." In those early days, he even solicited money from Oklahoma City merchants so each NFR champion could be presented with a blue blazer, copying the famed green jacket bestowed upon the annual winner at the Masters.[13]

Frankly, the sport needed the publicity of a Freckles-*Tornado* showdown. Even more so, and against all odds, it needed the unimaginable — a successful ride by the old rodeo sage.

In private, Freckles showed no change in his demeanor on the day he was to mount *Tornado*. As usual, he stayed in motion, restlessly busying himself at every turn. Freckles rarely sat still for more than a minute. Still, he appeared relaxed and jovial as he settled into his room with Edith at the swank, thirteen-story Skirvin Tower in downtown Oklahoma City — the city's oldest and grandest hotel.[14]

Finally, the clock signaled the time to depart for the arena. Freckles and Edith met Donna and her husband, Wiley Harrison, in the hallway and entered a hotel elevator. Harrison clutched an 8 mm movie camera so he could capture the ride on film.

The family shared the elevator with Texan Jim Bob Altizer, who won the World Calf Roping Championship in 1959. Typical of rodeo cowboys, Altizer was truly oblivious to the happenings beyond the narrow focus of his event.

Altizer and Freckles exchanged pleasantries on the ride down. Altizer then looked at Freckles and asked who had drawn in the first round.

"I got *Tornado*," Freckles answered.[15]

Altizer replied, "Is he a goodin'?"[16]

"Yep," Freckles said with a nod and polite smile. "He's a goodin.'"[17]

Chapter Twelve
The Ride
"If you believe he can do it, he will."
— Rodeo announcer Pete Logan

Rodeo immortality dangled in front of Freckles like a sack of gold on that frigid December night in 1967. He had been granted one opportunity to forever — and against all odds — be remembered as the first cowboy to ride the "unrideable" *Tornado*, or forever wonder what might have been.

Either way, Freckles now stood moments away from forever.

Across the State Fair Arena, and facing the chutes, sat his family in box seats. June Ivory, the wife of noted stock contractor Buster Ivory, invited the family to sit in her choice section given the potential historic occasion — one Wiley Harrison hoped to capture on film for his father-in-law with his movie camera. Typical of Edith and Donna, they sat calmly and stoically despite the growing buzz in the crowd.[1]

Word of Freckles' showdown with *Tornado* had already filtered throughout the half-filled arena. Despite the announced sellout of 8,000, only 4,112 souls braved the sleet and icy roads outside to be present. Those fans now enjoyed a front-row seat to the drama about to unfold.

Spectators were unsettled by the unknown. Behind chute number two would soon be two of rodeo's living legends

— a 1,725-pound, wildly bucking beast, and a battle-scarred, ageless former world champion well past his prime. Few, if any, gave the forty-six-year-old cowpuncher a chance.

Many feared a dangerous mismatch. The fear appeared contagious.

"Everyone thought Freckles was gonna get bucked off, and *Tornado* wouldn't just buck you off," recalled Ferrell Butler, who stood on the arena's dirt floor that night prepared to photograph the ride. "If you didn't get out of there, he'd camp on you something fierce. Then he'd go to wipe out a barrel. We were all scared."[2]

The anticipation plucked at everyone's nerves.

Butler walked to within thirty feet of chute number two so his 100-watt strobe could cast enough light on Freckles and *Tornado* in the poorly lit arena. Rolls of film bulged from the pockets of his ratty green vest. In addition, the 140-pound photographer shouldered a twenty-pound pack that held two batteries to power his strobe — one that couldn't toss light beyond fifty feet.

He boldly nudged closer as the moment approached.

Pick-up man C.R. Boucher, a grizzled bulldogger from Montana, sat on his horse nearby to await the final ride of opening night. Privately, he worried too about Freckles. Butler noticed Boucher uncharacteristically move in closer. Butler declared, "He was gonna ride in and rope *Tornado* by the horns if he had to . . . yeah, the fear was real."[3]

Three of the best rodeo clowns in the business also took their positions in the arena — Buck LaGrand, Chuck Henson, and barrelman Jim Schumacher. The bullfighters stood with faces painted and in full costume, ready to spring between the raging *Tornado* and the aging Freckles if needed.

The tension mounted as fans began to stand.

Throughout the day, Freckles replayed a highlight reel of *Tornado's* rides and tendencies in his mind. Freckles first saw *Tornado* at a rodeo in Memphis, and afterward never missed a chance to watch him in action. Each time *Tornado's* name was announced, Freckles could be found sitting in front of the chute, scouting the bull he might someday mount.[4]

"Sometimes he was just impossible, and on those days, there wasn't a bull rider alive who could have ridden him," Freckles recalled. "I had never seen *Tornado* have a bad day."[5]

The words were never spoken prior to the ride, but Freckles later admitted he was "tickled" by the draw. He thrived on such challenges. And the thought of not attempting to ride the feared bull never entered his mind. Even at forty-six, he still packed 140 pounds of wiry muscle into his five-foot-seven frame. He also cast a giant shadow among his peers, who considered him as respected and beloved as any man on the circuit.[6]

None of his fellow cowboys doubted his grit and determination.

The recently retired bull rider Ken Roberts — a Kansan who won the Rodeo Association of America bull riding championship from 1943-1945 — witnessed that toughness on numerous occasions. Roberts was overheard that day saying, "*Tornado's* scared a lot of guys off but he's gonna have to buck Freckles off."[7]

The cowboys knew Freckles wouldn't go down without a fight.

Finally, that forever moment had arrived. Fans saw

Freckles come into view as he climbed the chute, pulling his leather riding glove taut on his left hand. He stared down at the bull's massive body covered in red hair and distinctive white face. Gouge marks peppered his horns from seven years of combat in the arena.

Spectators were already standing en masse.

"Ladies and gentlemen — Freckles Brown will come out of chute number two . . ." Pete Logan announced as the crowd fell eerily silent. The twenty-one-year veteran rodeo announcer then uncharacteristically choked-up and paused. He composed himself and began again: "Ladies and gentlemen, Freckles Brown will come out of chute number two — on a bull that has never been ridden — Jim Shoulders' great bull, *Tornado!*"[8]

Freckles lowered down onto *Tornado's* muscular back. He felt a nervous energy surge through his body, although he felt that before every ride. He then shoved his left hand deep into the braided handhold, his pinky finger firmly against the knot. His hand laid parallel to a plait of leather laced into the handhold — an addition reportedly "made by ropemaker Booger Bryant to keep the handhold flat and straight, stable against the rider's grip."[9]

Canadian Marty Wood, a former World Saddle Bronc Riding Champion, suddenly leapt to the side of the chute. He wanted to support his old friend, and aggressively barked, "I wanna pull your damn rope!"[10]

Gateman Harold Leftwich, who stood prepared to open the chute's heavy gate, reached in through the gate's wooden slats to help cinch Freckles' rope from beneath *Tornado*. He noticed Jim Shoulders leaning in above him, assisting

Freckles as well.¹¹

Freckles knew then he was on a bull far different from any of the thousands he had mounted during his thirty-year career. At first, the signs weren't evident. Freckles pushed against the beast to adjust himself and felt plenty of give. *Tornado's* muscles were relaxed.

A tug of the rope changed everything.

"The bull understood what was happening," Freckles said, adding his hide went as hard as a "table."¹²

"His muscles were tensed, like a runner in the blocks," he continued. "It was then that I knew what made *Tornado* different. He was an athlete. He loved the contest; he was tense with anticipation — ready for the gate to crack open."¹³

Latchman Bob Thedford slowly unlatched the gate, allowing the bull to exit cleanly whenever Leftwich pulled the gate open. Both men locked eyes on Freckles to await his command.¹⁴

Silence overpowered the moment. Logan recalled how the tension in the arena "could be felt like a heavy fog." He let the moment breath before leaning into the microphone.

"If you believe he can do it," Logan whispered, "he will."¹⁵

Suddenly, Freckles nodded quickly, and the chute's stout gate burst open.

The mighty *Tornado* violently jerked to the left to clear the chute, and immediately whipped to the right, away from Freckles' riding hand. Freckles remained centered as he pitched forward and then backward, rolling with each jump and twist. He held his right hand high above his head and eyes fixed on the center of the bull's massive hump.

Butler immediately snapped a picture. He feared he might

not get a chance to shoot another.[16]

Tornado fiercely continued to spin to the right, again violently whipping his hind legs before launching into another jump. Freckles overcorrected to the right, and in that moment, appeared vulnerable. The wily veteran instantly straightened up as *Tornado* sprang into a frantic series of bucks, each time angling to the right in a whiplash motion.

The famed bull plunged earthward with his front quarters behind the momentum of his rising hind legs — each thrust and kick intended to dislodge his equally famous rider. Streams of bull snot shot into the air.

Freckles Brown aboard the infamous and supposedly unrideable, *Tornado*, until Freckles conquered him at the National Finals Rodeo for 73 points and the win. The ride would go as one of the most famous rides in rodeo. (*Photo courtesy of Ferrell Butler.*)

"He came out spinning to the right," Freckles said. "He was not only big and powerful, but fast. He kept hooking his head back at me. Somehow, I kept my balance as he spun and pitched. Each second seemed like an hour. I didn't know if I could make the whistle or not."[17]

Fans remained eerily silent.

Then, unbeknownst to the spectators, Freckles felt another moment of vulnerability.

"I just got behind him a little bit," he said. "I threw my foot out there, got my head back in there and did all right. You can feel it. It may not look like you were in a storm, but you can tell it when you're riding."[18]

Freckles survived by digging in his spurs and clenching

Ferrell Butler captured two photographs the night Freckles Brown rode *Tornado*. This is the first shot – an image that went missing for more than fifty years. *(Author's Collection)*

his knees, with a bent left knee he used as a shock absorber. All while his upper body mirrored *Tornado's* wild gyrations.[19]

Butler quickly snapped a second shot.

The crowd erupted in cheers. Fans were now standing in the aisles and on seats, screaming and hollering. The cowboys jumped up and down, and punched the air as they sensed history in the making.

"There weren't enough fans in that place to start a cussin' match," Butler recalled. "But there could've been 100,000 people in there with all that hollering and hooping. I had never heard it that loud in that arena before."[20]

Five seconds . . . six seconds . . . seven seconds . . .

Freckles held on with the might of a death grip.

"I just felt real good," Freckles said. "I got where I wanted to be and that's the first time I got exactly where I wanted to be. Sometimes you don't feel that way. Sometimes out there, about the third or fourth round if they're bucking, you feel like you can ride him regardless of what he does, but not very often. It was just before the whistle when I felt like I had him rode."[21]

Only Freckles never heard the whistle. The deafening cheers in the half-empty arena drowned out the sound of timekeeper Una Beutler's whistle at eight seconds.[22]

Freckles caught a glimpse of one of the clowns moving toward *Tornado*. He knew then he had made the whistle. As the bull launched into his fourteenth buck, Freckles leapt into the air and landed on his feet. The momentum fittingly caused him to scramble into the arms of a grinning Jim Shoulders, who embraced his old friend with an enthusiastic handshake.

"Boy," Shoulders shouted into Freckles' right ear, "I'm proud you rode him."[23]

Thunderous cheers beckoned Freckles to the center of the arena, where he stood hesitantly and doffed his cowboy hat with his right hand. Edith, Donna, and Wiley celebrated the joyous moment, framed by their perspective of his darkest hours of setbacks and sacrifices. Caught up in the moment, Wiley realized he never used the movie camera in his hand to film the ride. He laughed at himself and continued to clap.[24]

The cheers grew louder, as if bouncing off the rafters. Spectator W.K. Stratton, then twelve-years-old, vividly remembered the bedlam at that moment.

"I looked around at the turmoil surrounding me," recalled Stratton, now an award-winning author who grew up north of Oklahoma City in Guthrie. "A middle-aged man with a blond flattop danced a jig in an aisle. Some people had tears streaming down their cheeks."[25]

Freckles stood amidst the shower of applause in the center of the arena for what seemed like an eternity. The applause never died. Even the cowboys were clapping and yelling, including fellow bull riders George Paul and Ronnie Bowman. Both Paul and Bowman turned in marvelous performances that night to finish second and third, respectively. Yet neither friend would think to begrudge Freckles for his winning score of 73 that night aboard *Tornado*.[26]

Finally, Freckles walked off. Only the cheers failed to cease. He looked up at his dear friend, Clem McSpadden, in the stands. McSpadden motioned him back into the arena. He obliged.

"And it started up louder than ever," Freckles recalled. "Never heard anything like it."[27]

Most would never hear it again. One Oklahoma City reporter wrote, "Brown received a standing ovation, a tribute rarely seen in rodeo performance."[28] Years later, Freckles reflected on the moment in his handwritten remembrances, defining his ride on *Tornado* as the "greatest and biggest thrill" of his illustrious rodeo career.[29]

The weight of the moment even overwhelmed the veteran bull rider. Someone saw Freckles exit the arena with his cowboy hat in hand and tears in his eyes. As he walked, he said to no one in particular, "He was overdue."[30]

Humility had long been his calling card.

New Jersey sportswriter Jerry Izenberg witnessed the famed ride. Afterward, as the cowboys packed up for the night, he asked Freckles if was afraid in the chute.

"Hell, mister, only two kinds of people don't have sense to be afraid," Freckles said in his quick cadence. "The first are crazy and the second are dead, and I ain't neither. It's the way you handle that fear that says who you are."[31]

Freckles' newly minted status as living legend would be handled with that same courage and humility. Later that night, as he and his family returned to the Skirvin Tower, Edith noticed her husband wasn't walking with them in the lobby. She turned to McSpadden and asked if he knew where her "Brownie" had gone.

Beyond the hotel doors, sleet continued to pelt the frozen ground. McSpadden replied with a smile, "He's outside talkin' to some old whino."[32]

Chapter Thirteen
Living Legend

"He is one, however, whom I wanted to see again as I had wanted to see [former all-around cowboy champion] Jim Tescher, to reaffirm, while I watch society go soft all around me, that a man, not with just undefinable courage but with determination, can survive poverty and deprivation and still ride adversity out to the whistle."

— **Sportswriter W.C. Heinz**

The Holiday Inn West's cocktail lounge in Oklahoma City brimmed with rodeo cowboys on a December afternoon when a familiar face walked into the crowded room. Retired bull rider Freckles Brown stood as tall as anyone present that day, even at five-foot-seven. He was shadowed by W.C. Heinz, a celebrated American sportswriter who was revisiting former literary subjects for his upcoming book, *Once They Heard the Cheers*.

Freckles' presence immediately caused a commotion.

"Hey, there's Brownie!" one cowboy hollered. "Hey, Freck, come over here!" another shouted. "Hey, Brown you old dog, have a drink!" a third cowboy crowed.[1]

"Come sit down, Freck!" yet another pleaded. "Somebody find a chair for Brown!"[2]

Freckles introduced Heinz to the five cowboys huddled around a table, drinking alcohol and life with equal enthusiasm. This was a festive time of year, another National

Finals Rodeo. The two men plopped down on a couple of chairs when one cowboy leaned into Heinz and said, "You want me to tell you something? You want to listen to me?"[3]

"Why, certainly," Heinz politely replied.[4]

"This man," continued the cowboy, theatrically sweeping one arm toward Freckles, "is an immortal. Did you know that?"[5]

"Yes," Heinz replied. "I did."[6]

"You did?" the cowboy said. "How well do you know this man?"[7]

"Aw, old Bill knows me," Freckles chimed in, embarrassed. "He's been out here before."[8]

"That's right," Heinz said. "During the Finals in '68 I followed Freckles around for nine days and . . ."[9]

"And I was fallin' off everything," Freckles interrupted. "I sure was ridin' sorry."[10]

"That don't matter," said another cowboy, before turning to Heinz. "And I want to tell you something else, too. This man has a million friends, and not an enemy in the world. Did you know that?"[11]

"Aw, not that many," Freckles said, "and I'm sure there's some don't like me."[12]

"Listen," the second cowboy continued, "What I said is right. You haven't got an enemy in the world."[13]

"Well, I just try to live with people," Freckles said humbly and still embarrassed.[14]

"You want to know something else?" yet another cowboy said to Heinz. "You are in the presence of a legend. Did you know that?"[15]

"Yes," Heinz said. "That's why I'm here."[16]

Unrelenting adulation such as this trailed Freckles since the night he rode *Tornado* to the whistle. In that moment, he experienced what few do in this world. He passed into the realm of a living legend — someone whose feats border on mythology and folklore.

Freckles wore this cloak of celebrity uncomfortably at times, given his instinctive nature to walk with humility. Yet he shouldered this fame, nonetheless. He had no choice. The aftershocks of his ride on the invincible *Tornado* reverberated far beyond the rodeo world.

National radio personality Paul Harvey — a Tulsa, Oklahoma, native — used the airwaves in the immediate aftermath to tell America about Freckles' unimaginable ride on *Tornado*. Harvey's glowing words were also later published in a syndicated column, which further brought that improbable moment into the living rooms, offices, and social halls across the country. Harvey spoke of Freckles as if he were speaking of Pecos Bill, an American folk hero who incidentally once lassoed a tornado with a rattlesnake. Harvey's words certainly echoed the spirit of that famous folk hero:

> *Sun and wind and frosty mornings have long since obscured the freckles, but the sky-blue eyes still are. This work-brittle old-timer with a mild manner and mile-wide grin wouldn't weigh 160 pounds with rocks in his pants, but he'd fight a circle saw and give it a three-revolution head start.*[17]

Of *Tornado*, Harvey described the bull as the "most feared animal, weighing more than a ton" and one that "has thrown 200 of the youngest, smartest, toughest who've tried."[18]

Harvey's column dramatically continued:

> *Hospitals from Cheyenne to Tucson remember his victims. The crowd shushed and held its breath when they opened the chute on Tornado . . . The bull snorted and bull-frogged and kicked and shrugged and stumbled and spit like water on a hot stove lid, but Freckles' skinny legs, hard from years of flanking and holding husky calves by a branding fire, clung to the gigantic one-ton bulge for an eight-second lifetime – and a little more. The horn sounded. And the crowd came to its feet whooping and hollering and stomping and throwing hats.*[19]

Old Freckles Brown had bested the best of man and beast. Every boy in that grandstand had his heart in his throat. Every middle-aged man in that mass of humanity was young again. Rugged, pro cowboys on the chutes and in the ring and in the pit and cowboys down by the gate – the ones who'd bet he could and the ones who'd bet nobody could – all stood and cheered.

And the legend of Freckles Brown grew.

Word of Freckles' ride traveled the dark, icy streets of Oklahoma City long before the morning newspapers were tossed onto porches and driveways and lawns. News of his seemingly miraculous ride December 1, 1967, spread quickly into the honky tonks, domino parlors, barber shops, and hotel lobbies, as well as into the historic stockyards on the city's southside.

"What I remember is the next day," Ferrell Butler said. "Paul Harvey — I ain't lyin' — he spent ten minutes of a fifteen-minute radio program describing and telling about Freckles riding him. And that's when people started coming out. Everybody in Oklahoma listened to that Paul Harvey show at noon. And the next day, the crowd got bigger every night."[20]

In truth, a sold-out crowd filled the State Fair Arena the night after Freckles' historic ride — an audience that doubled in size from opening night.[21] Oklahomans awoke the morning of December 2, 1967, to newspaper headlines that read: "Tornado Tamed!"[22] and "Freckles Finally Rides the Tornado."[23]

Wire services also delivered the story into newsrooms nationwide, in places such as Billings, Montana, where one headline shouted: "Brown Bests Unridden Bull."[24] A headline that in all probability was read by Don Snyder, fifty miles away in Wyoming's Sunlight Basin.

In Garwood, Texas, news of *Tornado's* broken unbeaten streak didn't sit well with the bull's previous owner, "Big" John Williams. For years later, whenever someone mentioned the famous ride, Williams would say, "*Tornado* wasn't right that night. He must have ate some hardware."[25]

Williams literally thought the bull had eaten a piece of metal. To Williams, the idea that anyone could ride *Tornado* seemed unfathomable.

Freckles, meanwhile, rode the momentum of his career-defining moment for the remainder of the 1967 Finals. He conquered Jim Shoulders' newest star, *Big Bad John*, one night. The 1,725-pound bull of "red savagery" had been unbeaten in nineteen previous trips that season until meeting his match with Freckles. The next night Freckles rode *Tex M* of Inman's that had only been ridden twice in thirty-eight tries, earning the day's top score with a sterling 74. The ride prompted yet another standing ovation — his third of the Finals.[26]

In the end, Freckles won the NFR overall bull riding competition with a total of 480 points, edging Texas rookie George Paul (465 points) and Larry Mahan (449).[27]

Freckles' string of spectacular performances captured the hearts of rodeo fans to the extent that he even overshadowed Mahan, then the sport's greatest star. Mahan finished the 1967 season as the first cowboy in rodeo history to break the $50,000 barrier with $51,996.37 in total earnings. The amount smashed an eleven-year-old record held by Jim Shoulders.[28]

Mahan would eventually win four more all-around cowboy world championships before he retired, including a five-year run as all-around champ between 1966 and 1970. He finished his illustrious career with six all-around titles (1966-1970 and 1973) and two bull riding championships (1965 and 1967). Freckles also went on to manage his own rodeo immortality, perhaps predictably with grace, humor, and humility.

"Whenever I'd see ol' Freck, I'd always want to go up and shake his hand," said Larry Dawson, a professional bulldogger who witnessed the

Retired bulldogger Larry Dawson of Packsaddle, Oklahoma, witnessed Freckles' ride aboard *Tornado* from the stands of the Oklahoma State Fair Arena December 1, 1967. (Author's Collection)

iconic ride from the stands that night. "He was a legend. But you wouldn't know it. I never heard him so much as mention riding *Tornado*. He just wasn't that kind of guy."[29]

Even on the night of the ride, Freckles chose grace and humility over glory.

"I couldn't have asked for a better place to do it than here in the Finals," he told *The Oklahoman's* reporter Bob Colvin. "*Tornado* is a tough one to handle for sure but to tell the truth, I think he's reaching that point where he just can't buck like he used to. He's getting up in age I guess."[30]

Years later Freckles described *Tornado* as an "honest bull," meaning the animal wouldn't intentionally harm a cowboy. The charismatic Mahan laughed at those gracious words. Mahan unabashedly offered a different perspective when he countered, "Yeah, that's about like that Freckles, make that son of a bitch *Tornado* sound like some kinda white mouse. That bull made the rest of us look like idiots."[31]

The ride unquestionably catapulted rodeo into the mainstream of American sports. Coupled with Mahan's dominant emergence as a bona fide super star athlete and Hollywood good looks, rodeo began to shed its image as a band of rough-and-tumble, barroom brawling cowpokes. Rodeo was becoming downright respectable, and with respectability, trailed an unprecedented period of growth and popularity.

Freckles, viewed now as an unofficial rodeo ambassador more than ever, found the sport's newfound popularity both delightful and amusing.

"I'll tell you what, it's a weird thing, but when tickets go to gettin' scarce, people want to go (to the rodeo) who didn't care about it before," he said. "If you can't get one, then you want it."³²

Tornado's legend also fittingly grew. Ironically, the ride with Freckles ushered the bull's greatness into a larger spotlight.

Shoulders retired *Tornado* after the 1969 NFR in Oklahoma City. Oregonian John Quintana, the youngest bull rider in the Rodeo Cowboys Association, spoiled the retirement party by riding the famous bull to the whistle on December 11, 1969. Quintana, who won the World Bull Riding Championship in 1972, became only the third cowboy to successfully ride *Tornado* over a decade of competition.³³

Jim Charles of Oakdale, California, also rode *Tornado* in the ninth round of the 1967 NFR, while Freckles rode *Tornado* a second time during the summer of 1968 in a matched event in Miami, Oklahoma.³⁴

"I rode him easier the second time," Freckles said of *Tornado*. "I felt that maybe he bucked a little better than he did at the Finals, but there was no pressure the second time. There were better bulls to ride than *Tornado*, but there weren't any as memorable."³⁵

Few were bigger stars on the rodeo circuit than *Tornado*. Oklahoma columnist Frank Boggs — a writer with more than a satchel full of witty, one-liners — once even spent an afternoon at Shoulders' ranch in Henryetta, Oklahoma, during *Tornado's* prime. Boggs told Shoulders he wanted to "interview" *Tornado*. Upon arrival, Shoulders unlatched the gate and stepped into Tornado's spacious patch of ranch real estate. Shoulders motioned Boggs to follow.

Shoulders then walked up to *Tornado*, looked the bull in

the eyes, and began to talk to him.

"It was my own fault," Boggs playfully wrote later. "I was the one who'd mentioned an interview with the world's most famous bull, but I had in mind using the telephone . . . I followed Shoulders so closely we made only one shadow. It was perfect teamwork on my part."[36]

Silence prevailed on that windless, sunny day as Boggs gingerly approached.

"The only sound was that of my own heart, which was dangerously close to busting through my shirt," Boggs wrote. "*Tornado* was watching. He did not blink. I did not blink. I did not even do myself the favor of looking down to see what I might be stepping in, or upon."[37]

Boggs witnessed something shocking to his senses that afternoon — something only Shoulders and his family knew about an animal sometimes referred to as "the meanest bull alive."[38] In the pasture, *Tornado* — a four-time NFR "Bull of the Year" winner — was downright gentle. So gentle, in fact, Shoulders would often pet the bull while talking to him.

For Shoulders, *Tornado* represented far more than just a noteworthy bull that made him some money. *Tornado* symbolized a legacy of greatness he loved and respected as a champion. The decision to retire the bull therefore came from a place of love and respect, stating simply, "He's just got to where he can't do real good."[39]

Shoulders also declared he would not auction the prized bull, adding, "He'll just keep his head in the feed trough."[40]

Tornado spent his final years peacefully grazing the pastures of Shoulders' ranch in eastern Oklahoma. Ever the performer, whenever strangers appeared, the bull would often bellow and kick dirt — or, as Shoulders strongly believed, "almost as tho he wanted all to know he was still a champion."⁴¹

Dean Krakel, the National Cowboy Hall of Fame and Western Heritage Center's managing director, told Shoulders he hoped to bury *Tornado* on the museum's Oklahoma City property. If permitted, *Tornado* would be laid to rest with other famous rodeo livestock such as the great bucking horse, *Midnight*.

"When *Tornado* goes," Krakel recalled Shoulders saying, "I'll let you know and pick the spot."

Tornado died May 4, 1972, at age fifteen. "He simply laid down and never got up," Shoulders told Boggs. "We did everything we could for him, but he was just too old."⁴²

Jim Shoulders mounted *Tornado's* battered horns after the bull's death in 1972. Today, they are on display at the Henryetta (Oklahoma) Chamber of Commerce. *(Author's Collection)*

A sentimental Shoulders had *Tornado's* battered horns removed and mounted. The horns were later placed in the Henryetta Chamber of Commerce, and hung on the equally battered chute number two that once opened for the historic ride of 1967. The old, discarded chute had been salvaged from a dusty storage area deep within the State Fair Arena.[43]

Shoulders additionally typed a brief history of *Tornado* for posterity while the details were fresh in his mind. His

Officials at the National Cowboy & Western Heritage Museum buried *Tornado* in a quiet memorial service on a grassy knoll selected by Jim Shoulders in 1972. *(Institutional Photographic Collection, Dickinson Research Center, National Cowboy & Western Heritage Museum. 0236.005)*

notes show his deep admiration for the bull as an athlete and competitor:

> *Went for years without being ridden . . . Seemed to buck only as hard as he had to . . . When he had a not-so-tough hand he bucked only as hard as was needed to knock him off . . . Harder with tough hand. Greatest rodeo bull there ever was because he not only bucked and rolled the barrels, but he also never hurt anybody — he bucked [and] fought the clowns good ... Never did cripple anybody or jerk 'em down and knock their teeth out ... greatest combination bull [there] ever was . .*

Shoulders selected a grassy knoll on the museum grounds for *Tornado's* final resting place. A backhoe dug a sizeable hole, and the animal was lowered down during a funeral service. Seven months later *Tornado* received a tribute at the National Finals Rodeo in Oklahoma City.[44]

By then, word of *Tornado's* death had already spread throughout the rodeo community. Freckles first heard of the bull's passing in the newspaper. Later, at a Rodeo Historical Society luncheon at the National Cowboy Hall of Fame, Freckles reflected on his iconic ride aboard his old adversary. In typical fashion, he shed his ego and simply said, "I was real fortunate."[45]

Shoulders also walked to the podium that day to pay homage to *Tornado*. His voice grew husky as he reminisced about his famous bull, also reflecting on that historic ride with more than a touch of nostalgia. Turning to his old friend in the crowded room, he said, "I believe I would have rather seen him ride him than do it myself."[46]

Shoulders intimately understood the weight of history. Shoulders knew he, *Tornado*, and Freckles would be forever bonded by that one moment in time — a moment Clem McSpadden aptly described as "the greatest legend-making incident in rodeo."[47]

That moment shadowed Freckles like an old friend wherever he traveled. Once, most likely in 1969, a young bull rider named Doug Brown asked Freckles if he could tell people he was his uncle. Freckles grinned and replied, "Tell 'em anything you want."[48]

Later, the youngster delivered a stellar performance at a rodeo in Salinas, California. Freckles approached the youngster afterward and deadpanned, "Doug, would you mind if I told people you were my nephew."[49]

Freckles spent his final years in rodeo mesmerizing fans with his durability and longevity. In July of 1969, the Cheyenne Frontier Days announcer told the crowd, "Freckles Brown — old unsinkable Mr. Brown — has been riding bulls since *Gone with the Wind* was a new movie, and he'll probably still be riding when it is shown on television."[50]

At another event that year in Dallas, the flank man for *Funeral Wagon* saw Freckles riding the lively bucking horse and marveled at his agility. The man turned to his fellow cowboy Wilkie Braten and asked, "How old is that guy now?"[51]

Braten replied, "Forty-eight."[52]

"Forty-eight!" the man shouted. "Why I'm fifty-three and he was riding when I was a kid!"[53]

Rodeo fans flocked to Freckles. During the 1969 Finals, Boggs wrote, "The crowd loves him. He is a sentimental choice at any rodeo and he's off to a rousing fine start at the finals." On the second day of competition, Freckles rode his final bull — a second-place ride for a score of 81 — and then spent an hour afterward signing autographs in the State Fair Arena lobby.[54]

Boggs watched the fans eagerly mingle with the amiable Freckles, and concluded, "He's easily the most popular cowboy since John Wayne."[55]

One woman asked Freckles to kindly sign her program. The woman asked, "How in the world did you ever work up the nerve to ride the first time?"[56]

Freckles looked at the woman, removed his curled hat, and placed it over his chest as if, as Boggs put it, "the *National Anthem* is about to be played."[57]

"It didn't take no nerve, lady," Freckles answered. "I was just wantin' to cowboy."[58]

Retirement finally cornered Freckles in 1974. Freckles rode his last bull in Tulsa and was bucked off, landing on the back of his head. A specialist who worked with him in the aftermath of his neck surgery delivered his sobering assessment to Edith. Given his widespread arthritis and a neck that would no longer bend, the doctor explained how another bad fall could likely be fatal.[59]

"Did you tell him?" Edith asked the doctor.[60]

He replied, "You tell him."[61]

"I'm not going to," insisted Edith, who then informed Donna of the doctor's grave warning. Donna told her mother to "Tell him."

Edith never did. She refused to be the messenger or play any role in his decision to retire. Freckles eventually learned of the doctor's assessment, and formally retired after an astonishing thirty-seven years in professional rodeo. "I didn't want to rodeo much anymore," he said. "I needed to be home."[63]

In the following months and years, Freckles would jokingly say, "I quit because I was embarrassing the judges."[64]

The truth is his body could finally no longer withstand the rigors of bull riding.

"I couldn't get away from the bulls because of breaks, aches, and pains that came with old falls," Freckles told Willard H. Porter of *Western Horseman*. "Getting off and away from a bull is just as important as riding them. I just couldn't do it anymore."[65]

And no one would dare begrudge Freckles that admission. He was fifty-three — a biblical age for bull riders. His legendary career spanned parts of five decades from 1937 to 1974 and would be forever defined by an eight-second ride aboard an "unrideable" bull on rodeo's grandest stage at age forty-six.

Freckles walked away a living legend, an immortal. Although his legacy represented far more than his legendary feats in the arena. For those who knew Freckles best, his equally extraordinary kindness would echo long after the memory of his last ride.

Fellow bull rider Myrtis Dightman — often called "the Jackie Robinson of rodeo" — never missed a chance to praise his old traveling partner, calling him, "a wonderful man."[66] His words are especially poignant given the period in which Dightman competed. He began his rodeo career in 1961 as a bullfighter, and a few years later began competing as a

Myrtis Dightman – the "Jackie Robinson of Rodeo" – always found a friend in Freckles in an era when prejudice festered throughout the South. *(DeVere Helfrich Rodeo Photographs, Dickinson Research Center, National Cowboy & Western Heritage Museum.81.023.29097-08.)*

bull rider. And not just any bull rider. He was the first African American to qualify for the National Finals Rodeo.

"They ain't gonna treat you right," friends warned him as he ventured into a sport exclusively run and enjoyed by white men.[67]

"I ain't gonna ride white people," Dightman always replied, "I'm gonna ride the bulls."[68]

Dightman's philosophical approach meant little in a sport where white judges and officials held all the power, especially in the Jim Crow South where he primarily competed. Signs posted outside rodeo arenas throughout the South often greeted Dightman with the blunt words of prejudice: "No dogs, no Negroes, no Mexicans."[69]

Few rodeo officials even tried to hide the hate.

Officials sometimes didn't even permit Dightman to ride. Dightman would hear his name announced, and then watch helplessly as his bull was turned out. At other times, if permitted to ride, he had to do some so after the rodeo in front of empty stands.[70]

"He was a cowboy and he wanted to compete," Myrtis Dightman, Jr. said of his father. "So, when you go to a rodeo, and they turn your bull out cause you're black . . . I think that was probably the toughest thing he faced."[71]

Amid this dark atmosphere of prejudice strode the humanity of Freckles Brown.

"If you want to ride bulls, I'll help you," Freckles told Dightman at the start of his career. "Let me know when you get ready."[72]

Dightman credited Freckles as the cowboy who really got him started in bull riding. Freckles taught the Crockett, Texas, native the basics, such as how to pull his rope and how to set his hand.[73]

On the road, Freckles, and other cowboys such as Bobby Berger and Mahan also tried to look out for Dightman the best they could in that era. Motel owners regularly banned Dightman from their property because of his skin color. Back then, the cowboys traveled from rodeo to rodeo like a band of gypsies. They often piled into a motel room to save money. On those occasions, someone would slip Dightman a key to the room, so he had a place to sleep.[74]

Or someone would simply raise the window so he could crawl in under the cover of darkness.[75]

"That was the thing about us cowboys," Dightman said proudly. "It was like going to work. You ride with me. I ride with you.

"Freckles was my friend. I used to go up to Oklahoma where he lived. He used to take me by his house, and I used to stay the night there. Let me tell you, he was just a good guy . . . He would help me in any way he could."[76]

Freckles did so without patronizing Dightman or ignoring the reality of his challenges as a black man in a white man's sport. Once Dightman asked Freckles what he had to do to win a world championship. Freckles delivered his own brand of honesty: "Keep ridin' like you've been ridin' and turn white."[77]

Dightman — and countless other cowboys — experienced Freckles core belief firsthand.

"Down the road," Freckles once said, "if you'll just treat everybody good it'll come back to you."[78]

* * *

Country musician Red Steagall wanted to return to his western roots. He figured he had spent too many years in Hollywood chasing other ventures and drifted away from those who passionately embraced his Texas Swing music.

Friend Ernie Taylor of Hugo, Oklahoma, — the reigning World Calf Roping Champion — presented Steagall with a plan. Taylor invited him to the 1974 National Finals Rodeo in Oklahoma City.

Steagall loved the idea.

"I was living in Nashville at the time, and I wanted to get back into the world of rodeo because I had left it for eight or nine years," Steagall recalled. "I wanted to touch base with that group of people. So, I thought the best way to do that was to go to the Finals and meet some folks."[79]

Steagall met both cowboys and fate.

On a December night, the popular musician walked down the hallway of his Oklahoma City hotel to retrieve his guitar from his room. En route he passed an open door to a room crowded with people and noise. He paused. By then, he had sipped just enough wine to cast his inhibitions aside. He walked into the room uninvited, shaking hands and introducing himself. Warm smiles greeted him in return.

Steagall instantly noticed everyone was watching a

continual eight-second loop of a bull ride on black-and-white film. He then spotted a "little guy" sitting on the arm of a chair — "the man they were paying tribute to."[80]

"I was overwhelmed by the reverence that they paid him," recalled Steagall, whose curiosity drove him to the diminutive man like a magnet. The musician instantly sat down to visit, and the man kindly told him all about the ride in the film.[81]

This is how Steagall first met Freckles Brown.[82]

Afterward, Steagall couldn't get the story of Freckles improbable ride on *Tornado* out of his head. So, on the plane back to Nashville the next morning, he started to write a song about that famous showdown. By the time the plane touched down in Tennessee, Steagall had finished writing the ballad, *Freckles Brown*.

Ever the perfectionist, Steagall wanted to read the lyrics to Clem McSpadden to ensure the words were as accurate as possible. Since he was watching a black-and-white film, one line read: "He lowered himself on dark grey hide and pulled his bull rope tight . . ."[83]

"He was a Braford," McSpadden noted. "So, he was red."[84]

Steagall changed only one word. He believed he had a catchy tune and lyrics — spirited words that read in part:

Two thousand pounds of boiling hell was turnin' wrong side out
And showing four feet to the Lord and giving Freckles hell
Eight thousand fans were on their feet and he couldn't hear a lick
Cause the only sound he listened for was the buzzer then he quit

And tonight bull ridin' history's made and a cowboy gained his crown
His bull was called Tornado and the cowboy Freckles Brown . . .

Eager to play his song for McSpadden, Steagall flew to Denver the next month to attend the Professional

Red Steagall captured one of the most iconic moments in rodeo when he wrote his classic hit, *Freckles Brown*. *(Photo Courtesy of Red Steagall)*

Rodeo Cowboys Association Convention. He stayed at the historic Brown Palace Hotel, where he invited McSpadden to his room to listen to his new tune.

McSpadden loved the song, and immediately said, "Jim (Shoulders) would love to hear it."[85] So McSpadden left to retrieve him. Shoulders loved the song instantly, so much so he teared up.

"Let's go find Freck," Shoulders said. "He needs to hear this."[86]

Finally, Freckles joined McSpadden and Shoulders in Steagall's room. Steagall once again played the ballad; this time for three of rodeo's greatest legends.

Tears fell from the eyes of all three men.[87]

Chapter Fourteen
End of Days

"While the feats of man at times become immortal, man is not."

— The Oklahoman, March 21, 1987

Darkness filled the State Fair Arena on opening night of the 1975 National Finals Rodeo in Oklahoma City. A buzz of unexpected anticipation filtered through the crowd. A spotlight suddenly beamed down upon a lone cowboy, standing in an ocean of black on the arena floor in his chaps and holding a braided, bull rope.[1]

Fans roared at the sight of Freckles Brown doffing his hat.

Another spotlight then shot to a bucking chute, where Red Steagall sat with his trusty guitar in hand. The country star launched into his new ballad, *Freckles Brown*, as a chute gate banged open, releasing a magnificent, high-horned bull into the arena. The bull — representing the great *Tornado* — ran free under a third spotlight, lowered his head, and theatrically kicked dirt up over his back.[2]

Cheers erupted, evoking memories of the famous ride of 1967. At no point during the performance did the two spotlights below touch, presenting an illusion of a vast, deep canyon between Freckles and the bull. Imaginations were stirred.[3]

NFR general manager Clem McSpadden reveled in the nostalgia of the performance. He made sure the act opened each night of the Finals.[4]

"Pretty dramatic," Steagall recalled. "And I always considered that the number one performance of my entire career in over fifty years."[5]

The tribute performance for Freckles and *Tornado* became a tradition at the National Finals. Then, in 1982, the act became something far more profound.

McSpadden introduced his dear friend to the crowd as he had on many other nights at the Finals, but this time he also delivered some sobering news. McSpadden informed fans that five weeks earlier, Freckles had been diagnosed with prostate cancer.

A hush washed over the crowd. Fans looked at one another in disbelief.

Doctors think it's treatable, McSpadden said optimistically, noting Freckles will soon be checking into a cancer clinic in Houston to battle his greatest adversary. He then added, "Freckles told the doctors, 'I got to go up to the Finals before we do all this.' "[6]

Stunned fans whistled and cheered in support.

Later that night rodeo officials held a benefit dance to raise money for Freckles' medical expenses. Country singing sensation and Oklahoma native Reba McEntire performed along with Steagall, who discovered her when she sang the National Anthem at the 1975 NFR. Country western singer Moe Bandy also performed in honor of Freckles. Together, the threesome helped raise enough money to hit "five figures."[7]

Later, Freckles addressed reporters.

"I don't think it's gonna be no sweat," Freckles said that night. "It's just gonna take some time and a lot of money. I gotta take six weeks of them radiation treatments down

Clem McSpadden & Freckles Brown
(Bern Gregory, 1983, safety film negative. Bern Gregory Rodeo Photographs, Dickinson Research Center, National Cowboy & Western Heritage Museum. 1999.025.2218.10.)

there. But they think they'll get it and I do, too."[8]

What else could anyone expect a 5-foot-7, 150-pound man who rode wild, 1,700-pound bucking bulls for a living to say?

A reporter asked Jim Shoulders what he thought of the news. Shoulders bluntly replied, "What does anyone think? . . . You hear about more people having cancer anymore than tonsillitis. It don't sound good; I don't care what they say. But I'll tell you about Freckles Brown, he's had a pretty good life and lots of friends. You don't need to worry much for Freckles. He can handle it, whatever it is."[9]

Shoulders wasn't being overly optimistic. Freckles had always risen to the challenge. Now he planned to tackle cancer with the same mentality he did when he mounted broncs and bulls — boldly and unflinchingly. The sixty-two-year-old began chemotherapy treatments at the MD Anderson Cancer Center in Houston, stubbornly choosing to drive himself in the beginning. The round-trip drives totaled ten hours.[10]

Texas Rodeo Cowboy Hall of Fame inductee Bill George and his wife, Billie, heard of his journeys to Houston for treatment. The Georges owned the American Hat Company in nearby Conroe, Texas, and insisted on him staying at their home whenever needed.[11]

Freckles gratefully accepted the invitation, perhaps learning that the gift is sometimes allowing others to help. Edith eventually joined him in Houston as the treatments continued. During this period, Freckles experienced a dramatic loss of weight and strength.[12]

Despite the physical toll, Freckles told his family, "I think I got this cancer licked."[13]

Everyone prayed it would be so, although Wiley Harrison couldn't help being shocked and saddened by his father-in-law's diminished strength. Eight years earlier, in the immediate aftermath of his retirement, Harrison saw Freckles' strength on full display.

One day he and Freckles stepped into the barn, where Freckles noticed a 100-pound anvil. He walked over, reached down with his left hand, and grabbed the anvil by its narrowing, protruding nose. He then lifted the anvil off the dirt, and in one fluid motion, curled it like a dumbbell.

Harrison watched in astonishment.

"If I hadn't seen it with my own eyes, I wouldn't have believed it," Harrison said. "But I did see it. He was that strong."[14]

Harrison remembered those days as joyous ones on the ranch. Colorful stories and laughter crowded their hours as they baled hay, mended fences, and tended to the horses and cattle. Freckles routinely remained in motion back then, often running from spot to spot in his cowboy boots rather than drive his old pickup. *Pete*, his faithful Australian Shepherd, usually trailed behind. Occasionally, Freckles grabbed the modest, metal entryway to his ranch house and started doing pullups.[15]

Some habits were hard to break, even in retirement.

Lively times were always a sunrise away. By then, Shorty Gordon — Freckles' brother-in-law — had joined the Browns in Oklahoma, having purchased a small patch of acreage near Soper where he grew prize-winning flowers. Gordon moved from Arizona after the tragic loss of his wife, Ella, who died December 20, 1970, when a fire ravaged the Pioneer Hotel in Tucson's downtown district. Ella, a nurse, had been caring for a patient who lived in the hotel when the fire started. The flames trapped them on the tenth floor of the eleven-story building. Ella died from carbon-monoxide poisoning — one of twenty-nine people who perished that dark day.[16]

The old anvil that weighed close to a hundred pounds that Freckles would curl with one hand.
(Courtesy of the Harrison-Brown Family)

Gordon found refuge with Freckles. Or perhaps they found refuge in one another. In his presence, the jovial Gordon rekindled the comic camaraderie they had always shared. He spent nearly every day on the ranch, working and laughing alongside Freckles and Harrison. The three men became inseparable.

"Shorty and Freckles were always cuttin' up," Harrison recalled with a chuckle. "They were quite a pair."[17]

One year — and Harrison couldn't recall which one — Muddy Boggy Creek flooded out of banks. The waters rose quickly, leaving the neighbor's cattle submerged and in danger of drowning. Several of the cows were seen swimming to the safety of higher ground; some with their calves latched onto their backs with tilted heads.

"I think we ought to try to see if we can save some of those cows," Freckles told Harrison.[18]

James "Shorty" Gordon and Wiley Harrison enjoying a laugh, circa 1980. *(Courtesy of the Harrison-Brown Family)*

Freckles borrowed a neighbor's small boat, and along with Harrison and Gordon, quickly began rowing to where they could see bull horns poking from the murky water. They lassoed the bull which had become tangled in some submerged branches. Slowly, they struggled to pull the bull out of the entanglement by rowing against the swift current. They rowed toward a small island with a lone tree. As the boat neared the island, Freckles instructed Harrison to tie the

A retired Freckles enjoying company at his Soper ranch in July 1980. *(Courtesy of the Harrison-Brown Family)*

rope to the tree.

Harrison stepped from the boat and onto the parcel of high ground to look for a sturdy branch. To his great alarm and dismay, the branches were draped with snakes.

"Freck," he said wearily, "there are snakes all over this tree."[19]

"Aw, just shake'em off," Freckles replied without hesitation. "They're not gonna bother ya."[20]

As usual, the old cowpuncher never blinked. An unnerved Harrison gingerly did as Freckles requested, and miraculously avoided being bitten. They saved the bull in the process, but Gordon's mind quickly shifted to a playful endeavor. He spotted a giant rattlesnake skimming across the water.

"Hey Freck," Gordon said with a grin. "Let's go catch that

giant rattlesnake."[21]

Harrison shook his head in amusement. Freckles immediately rigged a piece of hay string to some baling wire, and within minutes, they were chasing that snake with a makeshift lasso. Moments later, they were dragging the massive snake across the rushing water and back to shore.

"That snake was as angry as could be, hissing and striking out at anything that moved," Harrison recalled. "But ol' Freck walked up to that snake, grabbed it behind the head, and tossed it into an old feed sack. He said he would take it into Hugo the next day and sell it to the circus people."[22]

To Harrison, Freckles always cast a larger-than-life shadow whether riding a raging bull or snatching an angry rattlesnake with his bare hand.

Retirement allowed Freckles time to enjoy rodeos at his leisure, as well. He frequently traveled to larger rodeos across the country, often judging or making appearances for his sponsors — Wrangler and Laramie Boots. Wherever he went, Freckles always armed himself with a warm smile and a lively story. He loved being around the cowboys and they loved being around him. They were his people.[23]

Unsurprisingly, Freckles also made time for fans. He always engaged with them earnestly as he shook hands and signed autographs. Many referred to him as "my hero." Fans inevitably referenced his legendary ride aboard *Tornado* — countless claiming to have witnessed the famous ride. The claims became so frequent in fact, they became humorous to Freckles and others who were present that night. For if every claim were true, there would have been enough fans to fill the 47,879-seat Houston Astrodome multiple times in 1967, let alone the 8,000-seat State Fair Arena in Oklahoma City.[24]

Freckles felt honored by the attention, just as he always felt a natural inclination to give back in this world. In many respects, he never forgot that teenager who once leapt from a steam-engine train in Cody, Wyoming, covered in black soot and tattered clothes.

Long before retirement, Freckles volunteered his time to tutor aspiring rodeo cowboys. For several years, he even made an annual pilgrimage to South Dakota, where he helped American Indian youngsters with their annual rodeo seminar.[25]

One of his greatest sources of pride was Lane Frost, the son of one of his old traveling buddies, Clyde Frost, from Atoka, Oklahoma. Clyde once rode saddle and bareback broncs on the professional circuit, while his son gravitated to bull riding due to his admiration of Freckles. As a child, Lane studied old photographs and later videos of Freckles riding bulls.[26]

In time, Freckles and Lane developed a close relationship, akin to a grandfather and grandson. Freckles watched Lane ride bulls at various arenas, discussing techniques and providing pointers. In 1981, when Lane competed in the National High School Rodeo Finals in Douglas, Wyoming. Freckles traveled to cheer him on.

Lane won the championship.

A year later Lane won the first annual Youth National Finals in Fort Worth, Texas. Lane, who turned professional in 1983, grew to proudly call Freckles "my idol, teacher, and friend."[27]

Freckles, meanwhile, continued to spread goodwill

wherever he traveled in the rodeo world. In December 1982, he made his annual appearance at the National Finals Rodeo in Oklahoma City, where he encountered longtime rodeo announcer Bob Chambers of Oregon. Chambers had announced the Pendleton Round-Up each year since 1967 and had become a fan favorite at that legendary rodeo.

But, for Chambers, the 1982 National Finals Rodeo marked the first time he had been invited to work the most prestigious rodeo in the sport. Freckles noticed Chambers looked visibly nervous.

"You're kind of sweating this," Freckles said to Chambers. "Just calm down. It's just another rodeo, Bob. You know why you're here. It's because what you've done in other places. Just do it. Just do anything you want to. What the hell."[28]

A calmness settled over Chambers thanks to Freckles' pep talk. Chambers later reflected on that moment, saying, "That helped me so much. Just knowing that little bull rider was behind me and wishing me the best. I calmed right down."[29]

Little did Chambers — or nearly anyone else — know at the time, Freckles had already been diagnosed with cancer. As usual, he still took time to think of someone else. Everyone would learn the news several days later when McSpadden made the diagnosis public on the NFR's final night.

Two months earlier, Freckles first felt some pain and discomfort — enough to prompt the rugged cowboy to drive two hours to see his family physician, Dr. Eugene Foster, in Gilmer, Texas. Freckles trusted Foster, who often drove an old, dented pickup loaded with hay bales and farm equipment.[30]

Foster told Freckles he feared he had cancer. Foster urged Freckles to see oncologists at the MD Anderson Cancer

Center in Houston, where the doctor's suspicions would be confirmed. Freckles then completed the six weeks of radiation treatment. An oncologist informed Freckles he was clear of cancer by June 1983, but cautioned him that it could always return.[31]

A month later Freckles spoke like a man who never met a challenge he couldn't handle. As far as Freckles was concerned, he had a lifetime of experiences that inspired such confidence.

"They say it could come back, but it looks real good right now," Freckles told a reporter. "You just got to believe you're going to win."[32]

Reporter Jo Berry of *ProRodeo Sports News* asked Freckles about his cancer a month later. Freckles smiled and said assuredly, "I'll be okay real soon, don't worry." Berry knew Freckles, and added, "somehow you couldn't help but wonder if it wasn't what he wanted everyone to believe, so nobody would worry."[33]

Months trickled into years. By the fall of 1986, the public conversation regarding his cancer had essentially subsided. The cancer remained in remission. Freckles even celebrated his induction into the Rodeo Hall of Fame that year at the National Cowboy & Western Heritage Museum in Oklahoma City. Yet his strength remained greatly diminished.

"It was heartbreaking to see him in that condition," said Harrison, who stepped up without complaint to do most of the work on the ranch.[34] Freckles always felt guilty he couldn't do more to help.

Freckles' guilt drove him into the field one day while Harrison was baling hay. A ball bearing went out on the flywheel of a square baler. Harrison removed the flywheel but couldn't dislodge the ball bearing. He crawled under the baler with a crowbar, struggling to pry it loose.³⁵

Suddenly, he heard Freckles rumble up in his pickup and climb out. Within moments, Freckles stood atop the baler with a long crowbar, trying to help jerk the bearing loose. Harrison then watched, while on his back, Freckles tumbled backward off the baler.³⁶

Freckles landed so hard on the ground he broke a collar bone and knocked himself out cold. Harrison scrambled from underneath the baler to be by his side. He feared the worst. Freckles appeared lifeless.³⁷

Yet his chest moved up and down, much to Harrison's relief. Freckles was unconscious but breathing. Harrison desperately struggled to lift his father-in-law into the pickup. All dead weight. Eventually, perhaps only because of the adrenaline, he succeeded. The truck barreled down the country roads as Harrison sped toward a hospital in Paris, Texas, forty-five miles away on the Red River.³⁸

En route, Freckles awoke and asked, "Where are we goin'?"³⁹

As a son-in-law, Wiley Harrison grew as close to Freckles as anyone other than Edith and Donna. He considered Freckles a "father figure." *(Author's Collection)*

The accident signaled a dramatic change in health for Freckles and coincided with the return of his cancer — perhaps discovered in the aftermath of the incident as the doctors ran a series of tests. Over the next several months MD Anderson's oncologists hospitalized Freckles in Houston multiple times.[40]

During one return home, Freckles called Wiley and Donna into his bedroom where he was resting. Edith sat by his side.

"Wiley," Freckles said, "I want ya'all to get a deed fixed up and I want to deed the place to ya'all."[41]

The words were jarring.

"You're doin' all the work around here anyway," Freckles continued. "If I don't make it, it will just save a bunch of expense in probate and all that stuff. Get that done."[42]

The weight of Freckles' words pressed on Harrison's heart for more than a few moments. He stood speechless. The ranch represented the fruition of a lifelong dream for Freckles. He transformed the property into a working ranch — a showplace where friends and family were free to congregate and enjoy life. He literally built it with his own blood, sweat, and broken bones.[43]

Freckles loved his ranch.

"Freck," Harrison finally replied, "we'll do what you want to do, but this will always be your place regardless of who has the deed."[44]

Now, for the first time, Harrison realized that Freckles knew his days were numbered.[45]

If Edith had any doubts, those vanished when doctors in Houston again hospitalized her sixty-six-year-old "Brownie" in early 1987. Word spread quickly about Freckles decline. Myrtis Dightman lived nearby in Crockett and made a few trips to the hospital to visit his old friend and pay his respects. Red Steagall flew into the Houston airport, where Donna and Wiley waited to whisk him away so he could be at the bedside of a man he greatly admired.[46]

Steagall wasn't alone.

Lane Frost flew in from Fort Worth so he could spend the night with his beloved friend and mentor. Frost vowed he would win a world championship for Freckles that year. At one point during Frost's stay, he glanced at Freckles who was doing pullups from the overhead trapeze bar above his hospital bed.

"Ya know," Freckles said, "I should get one of these for home."[47]

Frost marveled at how Freckles harnessed a flash of his old spunk. But the cancer was ravaging his body.

Donna, who inherited her father's understated toughness, could no longer deny the inevitable. She broke down several times in Houston, probably when no one was looking. The tears left her pained and exhausted.[48]

Edith never cried. She lived — and survived — by wearing the armor of a stoic. She instead reached for the telephone and called her husband's closest friend, Clem McSpadden.[49]

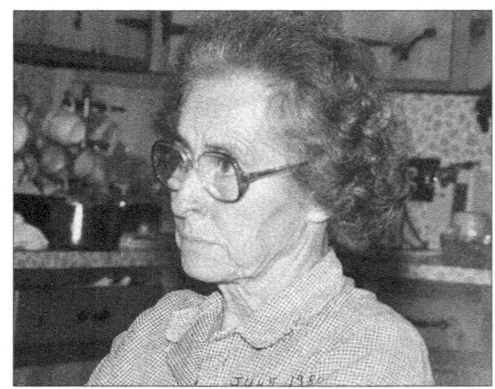

Edith Brown as she appeared at her ranch home in July 1980 – seven years before her husband's death. *(Courtesy of the Harrison-Brown Family)*

"Clem," Edith said bluntly, "if you want to see Brownie, you better come now."

McSpadden caught the first flight to Houston, and was soon sitting by Freckles' side, trying to chat like old times. But those times were long gone, memories now as frail as life itself. And they both knew it, too. Once alone, McSpadden said, "Freck, I'm gonna pray for you."[50]

The gesture moved Freckles to a moment of deep reflection. Freckles told his dear friend how he and Edith had been attending a pleasant church in Soper, and how he often prayed for others who had experienced hardships or the loss of some kind.[51]

McSpadden nodded and smiled in gratitude. Listening silently, McSpadden never forgot what Freckles said next.

"The Lord has been good to me," Freckles quietly added. "I just don't know if I have ever thought to pray for myself."[52]

For McSpadden, those two sentences defined the man he grew to love as a brother.[53]

March brought spring showers to the family's Kelly Bend Ranch and a renewal of plush, green pastures. The ranch teamed with life, from whitetail deer and flocks of wild turkey to the croaking of giant bull frogs emanating from the dense tree line along the banks of Muddy Boggy Creek.

Freckles also returned home at this time, whether by cruel irony or the fitting glory of a life lived in every breath.

Healthcare workers moved a hospital bed into his bedroom, a modest space of roughly 289-square-feet. The room didn't feature any of his rodeo memorabilia or trophies, but rather a family photo that sat atop a humble dresser. Here, Freckles was made as comfortable as possible.[54]

Billie Trent, a neighbor who lived on a ranch north of Soper, stayed with the family to help care for Freckles. Occasionally, Wiley and Donna ran to town to retrieve medicine from the local pharmacy, although Donna mostly remained close to her father. They had always been inseparable throughout her life, now more than ever before as the hours turned precious.[55]

McSpadden, meanwhile, refused to sit still. He ramrodded a fund-raising auction for Freckles for Sunday, March 22, at the Holiday Inn in McAlester, Oklahoma, — seventy-three miles from Soper in the heart of the state's southeastern region. This is where Freckles wasn't just a living legend, but rather a flesh-and-blood neighbor and friend to all who crossed his path.[56]

Oklahoma City journalist Frank Boggs announced the fundraiser in a personally moving column that ran March 13.

"So much pleasant time now has passed since the day I met Freckles Brown I don't remember the exact circumstances," Boggs wrote. "But I know he smiled and tipped his cowboy hat and made me feel like the most important person he'd ever visited . . .

"Now the man loved by everybody is in trouble."[57]

Western sculptor Harry Jackson donated a bronze statue titled, *Pony Express II*, to the auction. Charles Banks Wilson, another artist, generously chipped in a print of a portrait he did of Freckles. The auction would also include dinner with Oklahoma Governor Henry Bellmon, tickets to the National Finals Rodeo in Las Vegas, tickets to University of Oklahoma football games, and numerous antiques. For those unable to attend, organizers reminded people they could always send checks to the Freckles Brown Fund in nearby Chelsea.[58]

Boggs' column also featured a few words from

McSpadden, who said he often heard people use the term "beautiful human being" over the years. In reference to Freckles, McSpadden said, "But I never knew what the term 'beautiful human being' really meant until I met this man."[59]

Inspired by McSpadden's comment, Boggs ditched his trademark wit for something personal, words that sprang from his heart:

> *I have sat around hotel rooms and visited with Freckles and his wife, Edith. I have stood around in rodeo arenas and marveled at the courage that made Freckles one of history's great bull riders.*
>
> *Mostly, I just marveled at how any person can be that thorough a gentleman. Always smiling. Always speaking in a low, calm voice. Always wondering what he might do to help someone else. Always finding time for someone else.*
>
> *Always a beautiful human being.*[60]

Sunshine splashed across the Kelly Bend Ranch on Friday, March 20, 1987, — two days before the auction. Inside the Brown's two-bedroom home, Edith and Donna sat in the living room, while Wiley filtered in and out of the house, intentionally staying busy. By then, healthcare workers had Freckles on an IV drip of morphine to primarily dull the pain. Each tried to talk to him at various times, although they were uncertain whether he heard what they were saying. For nearly two days he laid motionless in bed with his eyes closed and his breathing faint. They talked anyway.[61]

Freckles took his last breath sometime in the afternoon, slipping quietly into eternity.[62]

The man who became a rodeo legend riding raging, 1,700-pound bulls before roaring crowds now laid lifeless in a hospital bed. Gone was his leprechaun grin, disarming wink, joyous laughter, and endless repertoire of humorous stories.

Cancer stole it all.

Edith never cried. She reached instead for a camera. Whether overwhelmed by the reality of her loss or motivated by another reason, she intended to photograph her beloved "Brownie" on his deathbed. Appalled by the thought, Donna vehemently protested. No one would take a picture of her father in a state of death. She took the camera from her mother's hands, and demanded the subject be discussed no further.[63]

A tearful Wiley approached his wife and asked, "How are you doing?"[64]

Donna replied, "I done my crying in Houston."[65]

The inevitability of death had shadowed the family. Not for days, but weeks. The finality still struck like a bolt of lightning on a hot-wire fence. Wiley and Freckles spent countless hours together, working on the ranch as they laughed, reminisced, and talked about life. Wiley drew as close to Freckles as nearly anyone on the planet, and he loved him like a father.[66]

Wiley walked to the barn alone. There, he wept out loud.[67]

* * *

News of Freckles' death traveled with the swiftness of a prairie fire. Tributes poured in from all corners of the country, especially in Oklahoma where he made his home and became a living legend on a magical night in 1967. *The*

The back numbers worn on each of Freckles' eight National Finals Rodeo appearances are proudly on display at John Harrison's ranch in Soper, Oklahoma. Harrison is Freckles' grandson and a noted rodeo clown and entertainer who has won numerous awards in professional rodeo. *(Author's Collection)*

Oklahoman dedicated the entire top of its front page to the news: "Legendary Rodeo Cowboy 'Freckles' Brown Dies."[68] The story summed up the historic passing with one eloquent, profound sentence that read, "While the feats of man at times become immortal, man is not."[69]

The death of Freckles Brown — "The Unsinkable Mr. Brown" — inspired moving prose, such as those used by rodeo journalist Willard H. Porter in *Western Horseman*. Porter, who had interviewed Freckles on countless occasions, personally knew the man's story and heart. He opened his story by writing, "It was just another obituary. But it wasn't just another cowboy."[70]

And no one would argue Porter's point.

"He is the most wonderful, unselfish human being I've ever known," McSpadden told *The Oklahoman*. "He is a credit to his family and the sport of rodeo."[71]

The auction took place as planned in McAlester, and supporters raised more than $41,000 toward the pile of medical bills left in the wake of Freckles' last battle.

Thousands of mourners later attended his funeral in neighboring Hugo, many of whom were rodeo royalty. Lane Frost and his family were also present when Freckles' casket was lowered into the grave at the Mount Olivet Cemetery in Hugo.

Nine months later Frost kept his promise to Freckles. He won the World Bull Riding Championship.

Frost tragically died two years later, on July 30, 1989, at age twenty-five. He died in Cheyenne, Wyoming, after riding a bull named, *Takin' Care of Business*. Frost fell face-first in the mud of the arena when the bull turned and plowed into his back, breaking ribs, and puncturing his lungs. His parents buried him at the Mount Olivet Cemetery in a grave next to Freckles, his mentor and hero.[72]

Time only seasoned the legend of Freckles Brown. And wherever people uttered his name, they spoke of his famous ride aboard the "unrideable" *Tornado*. Steagall's ballad *Freckles Brown*, further immortalized that iconic moment as the song became a staple at every rodeo in the nation. The ballad seemingly carried the ride into a realm somewhere between history and mythology.

Ever since, writers have groped for the perfect words to describe the drama and grandeur of those legendary eight seconds — arguably the most important eight seconds in

Even in death Freckles and *Tornado* ride on with an etching of the famous ride engraved on Freckles' footstone.

rodeo history.

Prior to his death in 2008, McSpadden frequently spoke of his dearly departed friend and that historic moment during interviews. He talked about Freckles' advanced age of forty-six, and the greatest of his accomplishment against contestants with an average age of twenty-four. He spoke of *Tornado's* unbeaten streak. He also noted the bull's feared reputation, and Freckles equally legendary grit and determination.[73]

All were true and worthy of remembrance.

Only McSpadden saw a grander picture of what truly made that moment so magical, beyond the legend. He saw the character of the man.

"Everyone was pulling for Freckles," McSpadden explained to author W.K. Stratton. "You see, he was the most genuine, most humble, nicest man I've ever known. If the world was full of Freckles Browns, you wouldn't need locks on any of your doors. All he ever knew his whole life was hard work, so you had to hope something good would happen for him."[74]

Against all odds, it did. The beloved man became a beloved legend.

McSpadden loved the man. Hell, everyone did.

Freckles and Edith Brown were laid to rest in Mount Olivet Cemetery in Soper, Oklahoma.

Lane Frost became a world champion bull rider and died from injuries he suffered competing at the Cheyenne Frontier Days Rodeo in 1989. His grave is adjacent to his friend and mentor, Freckles Brown in Mount Olivet Cemetery.

Freckles Brown Honors

1962 - World Champion Bull Rider
1979 – ProRodeo Hall of Fame
1986 – National Rodeo Hall of Fame
1993 - Oklahoma Sports Hall of Fame
2006 – Cheyenne Frontier Days Hall of Fame
2015 – Bull Riding Hall of Fame
2017 – Molalla Rodeo Walk of Fame
2025 – PBR Hall of Fame

Qualified For the National Finals Rodeo

Year	Final Season Ranking
1959	14
1960	6
1961	3
1962	1*
1966	3
1967	5
1968	3
1969	7

Unable to compete due to injuries, but still won the World Championship.

Freckles Brown

By Red Steagall

Well, the year was sixty-seven National Finals Rodeo
December one's the Friday night that all bull riders know
There's cowboy heroes made and born at rodeos like this
'Cause the cowboys are the toughest, the stock's the best there is

Then Chuck announced that in chute two is the cowboy we all know
He's a young man now of forty-six and he's made him a mighty draw
His bull is from Jim Shoulder's string, Tornado's how he's known
Yes, Freckles Brown has drawed a bull no one has ever rode

Chorus:
And tonight bull ridin' history's made, a cowboy gained a crown
His bull was called Tornado and the cowboy, Freckles Brown

He lowered himself on dark red hide, he pulled his bull rope tight
He wrapped her twice and jerked her hard made sure he pulled her right
then two big old shiny horns looked Freckles in the eye
With a snort and a nod the chute gate swung as Freckles yelled, "let's ride"

Two thousand pounds of boilin' hell was turnin' wrong side out
And showin' four feet to the Lord and givin' Freckles hell
Eight thousand fans were on their feet and he couldn't hear a lick
'Cause the only sound he listened for was the buzzer and then he quit

It seemed the world exploded as Freckles hit the ground
And he swung his hat around his head and he shouted with the crowd
A cowboy hero born that day and Freckles totes the load
Two hundred times that bull had bucked the first time he'd been rode

Chorus:
And tonight bull ridin' history's made, a cowboy gained a crown
His bull was called Tornado and the cowboy, Freckles Brown

Now while we're giving credit where we know the credit's due
Yes, Freckles is a hero but Tornado gets some, too
'Cause without the bull to show him off a cowboy's got no call
And the only time he'll ever win's get lucky when he draws

So if bulls have got a Heaven and somehow we're sure they do
Let's hope Tornado's up there and the Lord has let him through
Hope his pasture is the greenest and his stock tanks never dry
And I hope there ain't a single spur to gouge his ugly hide
And I hope them cowboys up there keep him fat and treat him kind
And I hope he lives forever on bunch grass belly high

Acknowledgments

Authors often live a lonely existence.

Yes, I love people. And as a professional writer of 40 years, I have been privileged to meet people from all walks of life, from astronauts and governors to legendary athletes and working-class heroes. I fundamentally even subscribe to the belief that all stories ultimately trail back to people, and the human drama that unfolds daily before our eyes.

So where is the loneliness? For an author, everywhere.

Countless hours are spent in libraries and archival collections, meticulously combing over books, transcripts, letters, official documents, scribbled notes, old newspapers, and photographs for those handful of sources that will bring a story to life. I've long called it "panning for gold," which requires hours of tedious, back-breaking work for those who dare to dream. Sometimes, those sources – my gold nuggets – might contribute nothing more than a sentence in a book. But when those sources are stitched together, they can create a beautiful mosaic.

Therefore, no source is too small.

Endless hours are naturally also dedicated to reading in solitude. I routinely begin and end my days reading chapters from a book or papers from my stacks of files. On the road, where I retrace the footsteps of my subjects, I've spent lonely nights in hotels, restaurants, and driving in rental cars to my next destination. I welcome solitude because it gives me time to think about my research and to contemplate the lives I'm writing about in bold, black type.

Writing, might I add, alone. Hour after hour. Day after day. A writer essentially writes in an empty arena. Make no mistake, I absolutely love what I do. And I learned long ago to enjoy my own company.

Yet here's the irony: No book is produced solely by the efforts of one person. I also learned this long ago. With each new literary journey I've taken, I've met dozens of people along the way who have contributed in some way to the final manuscript and ensuing publication. Those contributions have been both big and small, and all were important and necessary to create the mosaic. *The Ride* is no exception.

So, here's a heartfelt thanks to those I will never forget.

Librarian Karen Spilman of the National Cowboy and Western Heritage Museum in Oklahoma City assisted me from day one without fail. Spilman helped me maneuver through the archives of the Dickinson Research Center, which houses the single largest collection of historical rodeo files in the country.

Other librarians and archivists also helped me on my journey. Laura Martin, deputy director of the research division for the Oklahoma Historical Society, has long been a great help to me in my many forays into American Western history. Martin secured a CD for me of an interview with Freckles Brown from April 24, 1971. The interview was the first time I heard Freckles' voice.

In Tucson, Arizona, Perri Pyle – a research archivist for the Arizona Historical Society – took extra steps to help me track the whereabouts of Hulon McMinn, who taught Freckles how to wrangle horses as a teenager. Later, while walking amid the giant saguaro of the Sabino Canyon Recreational Area, I had a chance encounter with volunteer rangers Chuck Houy and Connie Whippo. Both Houy and Whippo give talks to visitors about the geology of the canyon and showed me the rock foundations of a rock house once occupied by McMinn. Freckles undoubtedly rode horses through this magnificent canyon while working for McMinn.

In Willcox, Arizona, Kathy Klump – a volunteer archivist and librarian for the Chiricahua Regional Museum and Research Center – came in on her day off to give me access to the center's rich holdings. Thanks to Klump, I was able to establish the exact dates of Freckles' first bull ride in 1937.

My research also carried me to Cody, Wyoming, where I met Brian Beauvais. He is the curator of the Park County Archives, and frankly, they're fortunate to have him. I informed Beauvais I wanted to travel fifty miles north of Cody into the remote Sunlight Basin, where Freckles secured work as a teenager during the Great Depression on Simon Snyder's pioneering dude ranch. Beauvais not only offered to accompany me on the trip, but also invited Sue (Snyder) LaFever, Simon's granddaughter.

LaFever graciously agreed to join us. Together, they gave me an unforgettable tour of the majestic basin and the history of the people who lived there when Freckles did. LaFever took me back in time with her family stories of the Sunlight Ranch where she was raised, while Beauvais provided great insight into the basin's unique geology and the pioneers who boldly made it their home.

Later, Sally (Snyder) Holberg – LaFever's sister – invited us to her home in Cody so I could make copies of images from old family photo albums. Holberg and LeFever also provided me with an unpublished excerpt on Freckles written by their father, Don Snyder, as well as an article written by Chuck King, who also worked on the Synder's ranch. King's article, "Those Snyder Horses," appeared in the October 1991 issue of *Western Horseman*, and provided rich, firsthand details of the ranch's operations.

My gratitude also extends to a number of other folks: My Mother and Father; Bryan Painter, a former colleague of mine at *The Oklahoman* who unknowingly planted the seed for this book; the late Sharon Shoulders – beloved wife of Jim Shoulders – who once wrote me an inspiring letter of thanks for a 2011 newspaper feature entitled, "The Ride"; Jacquelyn Reese, librarian at the world-class Western History Collections at the University of Oklahoma in Norman; Wendy Schall who provided written notes from her mother, Eva Lively – the last surviving child of Hulon McMinn; my dear and long-time friend, Lee White, a research guru; Dollie Riddle and Vickie Shireman, whose mother Una Beutler served as the official timekeeper the night Freckles rode *Tornado*; and my gang of friends and supporters from my hometown of Vacaville, California, especially Jeep and Larriann Grima, Andy Grima, and Kim Reeves. I always found refuge in their supportive words.

A special thanks must also go out to my "Special Counsel," veteran editor and writer Nicole Nortier whom I entrusted with my deepest thoughts on research, writing, and storytelling. Your fingerprints are on these pages. Thank you and much gratitude.

Nor can my appreciation for my publisher Billy Huckaby be understated. Frankly, I couldn't have hand-picked a better publisher for *The Ride*. Huckaby is a cowboy who has dedicated much of his life to rodeo through his announcing and publishing. He knows the sport, its history, and its people. And he loves them all. Thank you, Billy.

Beyond my extensive research, I had the grand privilege of interviewing several of his contemporaries – friends and competitors who traveled the country together like a unique band of brothers from one rodeo to the next. They often piled into the same vehicle or motel room as they traveled, keeping each other company with colorful stories and sometimes afloat with a helping hand. I believe it was a special brotherhood from a bygone era, and one that shouldn't be forgotten. If this story comes to life for readers, these men deserve much of the credit: Bobby Berger; the late C.R. Boucher; Ronnie Bowman; Larry Dawson; Myrtis Dightman; Bill Kornell; Harold Leftwich; Marvin Paul Shoulders; and Bob Thedford. All are legends in their own right.

Country western singer/songwriter Red Steagall should also be counted among those cowboys. Steagall kindly told me the story of how he met Freckles and the origin of his timeless hit song, "Freckles Brown" – a ballad that catapulted the legend of Freckles and Tornado into another stratosphere.

Two men deserve special recognition: Wiley Harrison, Freckles' son-in-law; and Ferrell Butler, who photographed Freckles' historic ride aboard Tornado that night long ago in Oklahoma City. Harrison graciously gave me access to Freckles' private letters, rodeo paraphernalia, and photographs, as well as a tour of his ranch in Soper, Oklahoma. Butler's remembrances not only transported me back to a golden era of rodeo, but also placed me within thirty feet of the bucking chute when Freckles burst into the arena aboard Tornado December 1, 1967. In recent years, both fielded my calls and questions without fail, in honor of Freckles and the cowboys who gave their lives to the sport. I love and respect both gentlemen.

Lastly, I'd like to thank my family. They always sacrifice the most when I embark on a new literary project, and it's important they know how much I recognize those sacrifices. Frankly, this book would not have been possible without their love and support. So, from the bottom of my heart, thank you Jeannia, Ashley, Tristan, Missouri, Emma, Shelby, and Sage. I hope this book does some justice to all that you each have given.

Author Bio

Ron J. Jackson, Jr. is a bestselling author and award-winning journalist who has been writing professionally for 40 years. He is the author of six books, including the ground-breaking *Joe the Slave Who Became an Alamo Legend* (2015) – winner of

The Philosophical Society of Texas Award of Merit for nonfiction – *Fight to the Finish: "Gentleman" Jim Corbett, Joe Choynski, and the Fight that Launched Boxing's Modern Era* (2019); and *Bebes and the Bear: Gene Stallings, Coach Bryant, and Their 1968 Cotton Bowl Showdown* (2019).

Jackson is also a regular contributor for several magazines, including *Colorado Life, Utah Life, Nebraska Life,* and *Maui No Ka Oi,* and was among the reputed stable of contributors who wrote for the prestigious *Wild West* magazine. In addition, he is a proud member of the Western Writers of America, is a frequent guest on national podcasts, and has worked as a consultant for History Channel. Further information about his books and career can be found at https://www.ronjjacksonjr.com.

End Notes

Chapter One

1. W.K. Stratton. *Chasing The Rodeo*. (New York: Harcourt, Inc., 2005), 1-3. Stratton's opening chapter provides the best account of that night by a spectator.

2. Ibid, 2; *The Daily Oklahoman, December 2, 1967*.

3. The 1967 *National Finals Rodeo Program* (Author's collection); Stratton, *Chasing The Rodeo*, 15; Wiley Harrison interview with author, Soper, Oklahoma, January 21, 2023.

4. The 1967 *National Finals Rodeo Program*, 88; *The Ada* (Oklahoma) *Evening News*, December 5, 1967; *The Oklahoman*, September 5, 1982; Michael Wallis, "Freckles," *Oklahoma Today* (March-April 1985), 17; W.C. Heinz. *Once They Heard the Cheers* (Garden City, New York: Doubleday & Company, Inc., 1979), 193; Jim Shoulders' Inductee File (Box 30, Folder 2), The Dickinson Research Center, National Cowboy and Western Heritage Museum, Oklahoma City, Oklahoma.

5. *Associated Press*, July 3, 1983.

6. Ferrell Butler telephone interview with author, April 2, 2023.

7. Ibid.

8. Heinz, *Once They Heard the Cheers*, 182.

9. Ronnie Bowman telephone interview with author, March 30, 2023.

10. Freckles Brown Inductee File (Box 39, Folder 19), The Dickinson Research Center, National Cowboy and Western Heritage Museum, Oklahoma City, Oklahoma. The source is a four-page synopsis of his career in Freckles' own handwriting. Hereafter known as "Freckles' Own Words."

11. Heinz, *Once They Heard the Cheers*, 183; Wallis, "Freckles," 15; *Associated Press*, July 3, 1983; *Rodeo Sports News*, June 1, 1974.

12. Brown's Inductee File.

13. Wiley Harrison interview with author, Soper, Oklahoma, July 6, 2021; Harrison interview, January 21, 2023; Heinz, *Once They Heard the Cheers*, 188-190; "Freckles' Own Words."

14. "You Don't Forget A Guy Like Freckles," *The Ketch Pen*, August 1989; Wallis, "Freckles," 17; "Freckles' Own Words."

15. "Building A Better Bull," *Rodeo Sports News*, July 10, 1996.

16. "You Don't Forget A Guy Like Freckles," *The Ketch Pen*, August 1989.

17. Ibid.

18. Ibid.

Chapter Two

1. Fremont, John Charles. *Report of an Expedition of the Country Lying between the Missouri River and the Rocky Mountains on the Line of the Kansas and Great Platte Rivers*, (Washington, D.C.: 1843), 46-47. The source of the name Goshen has long been debated. Some suggest the name originated with an Indian warrior or French trapper. Others suggest it derives from the fertile Land of Goshen in Egypt as cited in the *Book of Genesis*. (Vickie Zimmer, "Goshen County, Wyoming," *WyoHistory.org*, November 2014, 2.)

2. Zimmer, "Goshen County, Wyoming," 1.

3. *The Guernsey Gazette*, February 4, 1921.

4. Pettis County, Missouri Marriage Records (1800-1901); 1930 United States Census, Goshen County, Wyoming; *Wind Pudding and Rabbit Tracks: A History of Goshen County*, (Torrington, Wyoming: Goshen County History Book Committee, 1989), 364-365.

5. Heinz, *Once They Heard the Cheers*, 186; *Wind Pudding and Rabbit Tracks*, 364; Zimmer, "Goshen County," 3.

6. Gregory Nickerson, "The Burlington Railroad: Wyoming's Second Transcontinental Railroad," *WyoHistory.org*, 4.

7. Zimmer, "Goshen County," 3.

8. *Wind Pudding and Rabbit Tracks*, 364.

9. Ibid, 212-213; Zimmer, "Goshen County," 3-4.

10. "Freckles' Own Words."

11. Ibid, 364.

12. Wallis, "Freckles," 15; Heinz, *Once They Heard the Cheers*, 186.

13. Heinz, *Once They Heard the Cheers*, 187.

14. Ibid.

15. 1930 United States Census, Goshen County, Lingle Precinct.

16. Ibid.

17. *Wind Pudding and Rabbit Tracks*, 364.

18. Ibid.

19. *The Torrington Telegram*, August 31, 1922.

20. Wallis, "Freckles," 15.

21. Warren "Freckles" Brown interview with Pen Woods, April 24, 1971, Oklahoma Historical Society Living Legends Collection.

22. "Freckles Own Words"; Willard H. Porter, "Freckles: A tribute of the best-liked rodeo cowboys of all-time, the famous Freckles Brown, who died on March 20 at age 66," *The Western Horseman* (June 1987), 92.

23. Brown interview with Woods, April 24, 1971.

24. *Wind Pudding and Rabbit Tracks*, 364.
25. Ibid, 364-365.
26. Ibid, 365.
27. Ibid, 364.
28. Ibid.
29. *The Oklahoman*, March 22, 1987.
30. Heinz, *Once They Heard the Cheers*, 187.
31. Ibid.
32. Ibid.
33. Ibid.
34. Ibid.
35. *The Oklahoman*, December 9, 1976.
36. Heinz, *Once They Heard the Cheers*, 188.
37. Ibid.
38. Ibid.
39. Ibid.

Chapter Three

1. Heinz, *Once They Heard the Cheers*, 188; Wallis, "Freckles," 15; Porter, "Freckles," 92; "Freckles' Own Words."
2. Don Snyder, "Freckles," from an unpublished memoir. Courtesy of Snyder's daughters, Sue LaFever, and Sally Holberg, both of Cody, Wyoming.
3. Tucson's population in 1930 was 32,506, an increase of 12,214 residents recorded in 1920. (1930 and 1920 United States Census); "Freckles' Own Words."
4. Errol Lincoln Uys. *Riding the Rails: Teenagers on the Move During the Great Depression* (New York: TV Books, L.L.C., 1999), 35.
5. John Bret Harte. *Portrait of a Desert Pueblo* (Woodland Hills, California: Windsor Publication, Inc., 1980), 131.
6. Uys, *Riding the Rails*, 35.
7. *Tucson City Directory 1937* (Tucson, Arizona: Keddington-Mission Printing Co., 1937), 133.
8. *Tucson 1935 Classified Directory* (Tucson, Arizona: *The Arizona Daily Star*, 1935).
9. Sabino Canyon vertical file, Arizona History Museum Library and Archives, Tucson, Arizona; David Wentworth Lazaroff. *Sabino Canyon: The Life of a Southwestern Oasis* (Tucson, Arizona: The University of Arizona Press, 1993), 97-99.
10. Heinz, *Once They Heard the Cheers*, 189.
11. Harte, *Portrait of a Desert Pueblo*, 97.
12. Snyder, "Freckles."

13. Harrison interviews, January 21, 2023, and July 6, 2021.

14. Ibid.

15. Ibid.

16. Ibid.

17. "Freckles' Own Word."

18. Porter, "Freckles," 92; Wallis, "Freckles," 15. Wallis quotes Freckles as saying the man who delivered the famed line as a rancher near Wilcox, Arizona. In yet another interview, Freckles claims the dairyman said, "Well, I'll call you Freckles." ("He Said It," *The Oklahoman*, March 22, 1987). A slight variation in the quote is understandable given the hundreds of interviews Freckles gave over his illustrious, 37-year-career.

Wiley Harrison maintains Tucson rancher Stanley "Buck" Fletcher gave his father-in-law his famous nickname. Freckles, however, most often said the man who gave him the nickname owned a dairy. Fletcher was a prominent Pima County cattleman who provided rough stock for rodeos and later movie companies.

19. Ibid.

20. Heinz, *Once They Heard the Cheers*, 188.

21. Ibid.

22. Ibid.

23. Ibid.

24. Ibid.

25. Ibid.

26. Ibid.

27. Ibid.

28. Bert Haskett, "Early History of The Cattle Industry in Arizona," *Arizona Historical Review* (v. 6, no. 4, 1935), 23.

29. Ibid, 22; Ron J. Jackson, Jr., "The Parting: In 1913 the freed Apache prisoners of 'Geronimo's band' had to choose whether to remain in Oklahoma or move to a reservation in New Mexico," *Wild West* (August 2021), 42-49; Bill Cavaliere, "Geronimo's Final Surrender," *Wild West* (August 2021), 36-41; Angie Debo. *Geronimo*. (Norman, Oklahoma: University of Oklahoma Press, 1976), 292-293.

30. C.L. Sonnichsen. *Tucson: The Life and Times of an American City*. (Norman, Oklahoma: University of Oklahoma Press, 1987), 221; Harte, *Portrait of a Desert Pueblo*, 129.

31. Harte, *Tucson: Portrait of a Desert Pueblo*, 126, 129.

32. National Register of Historic Places, El Montevideo Historic District, July 21, 1994.

33. 1940 United States Census for Pima County, Arizona; Arizona World War II Draft Registrations; Harrison interview, July 6, 2021; *Hoofs and Horns*, August 1941; *The Tucson Daily Star*, May 3, 1940; *The Tucson Daily Star*,

November 3, 1955. In August 1941, Fletcher also staged Tucson's first night rodeo (*Hoofs and Horns*, August 1941).

34. Harrison interview, July 6, 2021.

35. 1920 United States Census, Coryell County, Texas; Eva Lively, the last surviving child of John Hulon and Harriet McMinn's four children, provided an oral history of her father to her daughter, Wendy Schall, in February 2023. In her remembrances, Lively noted that her father and uncle, Weston McMinn, also provided Columbia Pictures with horses for its filming of *Arizona* in 1940.

36. Heinz, *Once They Heard the Cheers*, 189.

37. Lively oral history.

38. *Tucson City Directory 1936* (Tucson, Arizona: Arizona Directory, Co., 1936), 352; 1930 United States Census, Pima County; *The Coolidge Examiner*, August 12, 1932.

39. Heinz, *Once They Heard the Cheers*, 189.

40. Ibid.

41. Uys, *Riding the Rails*, 11-12.

42. Heinz, *Once They Heard the Cheers*, 189.

43. Ibid.

44. Uys, *Riding the Rails*, 32.

45. Ibid, 37.

46. Heinz, *Once They Heard the Cheers*, 189.

47. Ibid; *Tucson City Directory 1937* (Tucson, Arizona: Arizona Directory Co., 1937); *The Arizona Daily Star*, February 20, 1957.

48. Heinz, *Once They Heard the Cheers*, 189. McMinn eventually moved his family into a rock house above Rattlesnake Creek in Sabino Canyon, where he worked for the government. The McMinns appeared to have moved into Sabino Canyon in 1938 since Hulon doesn't appear on the *Tucson City Directory* that year. In the 1940 Census for Pima County, Hulon and Harriet are listed as living in Supervisorial District 1 – Sabino Canyon. The foundations of that historic rock house – the only one ever built in Sabino Canyon – remain today. The author is indebted to Sabino Canyon Recreational Area volunteer park rangers Chuck Houy and Connie Whippo for generously providing some history of the canyon and the rock house. Houy and Whippo freely give of their time to provided tours of the canyon.

49. Brown interview with Wood, April 24, 1971; *The Oklahoma Journal*, December 12, 1969; *Arizona Range News*, December 18, 1936.

50. Vernon B. Schultz. *Southwestern Town: The Story of Willcox, Arizona* (Tucson, Arizona: The Board of Regents of the Universities and State College of Arizona, 1964), 17-18.

51. Morris E. Opler, *An Apache Life-Way* (Chicago: University of Chicago Press, 1941), 216; Debo, *Geronimo*, 145.

52. *Arizona Range News*, July 9, 1937.

End Notes

53. O.E. Meinzer and F.C. Kelton. *Geology and Water Resources of Sulphur Springs Valley* (Washington, D.C.: Government Printing Office, 1913), 214.

54. Schultz, *Southwestern Town*, 66.

55. *Arizona Range News*, December 18, 1936. Wooten served as Livestock Sanitary Commission Inspector for Willcox District No. 6.

56. Brown interview with Wood, April 24, 1971; *The Oklahoma Journal*, December 12, 1969; *Arizona Range News*, July 9, 1937.

57. *Arizona Range News*, July 9, 1937.

58. The Seventy-Six Ranch Vertical File, Willcox Historical Society, Willcox, Arizona.

59. G.W. "Boozer" Page Vertical File, Willcox Historical Society, Willcox, Arizona.

60. Ibid; *Arizona Range News*, June 18, 1937.

61. Ibid.

62. Ibid.

63. *Arizona Range News*, June 18, 1937.

64. Brown interview with Woods, April 24, 1971; *The Oklahoma Journal*, December 12, 1969; *Arizona Range News*, June 18, 1937. Page's rodeo on June 26 and 27 was the only rodeo held in Willcox in 1937, and while the rodeo grounds were located three-quarters of a mile outside of town, it was considered a Willcox rodeo. The *Arizona Range News* – Willcox's weekly newspaper – also reported the rodeo as being "held in Willcox."

65. Wilcox Rodeos Vertical File. Willcox Historical Society, Willcox, Arizona.

66. Kathy Klump and Peta-Anne Tenney. *Images of America, Willcox* (Charleston, South Carolina: Arcadia Publishing, 2009), 38.

67. *Arizona Range News*, June 18, 1937.

68. *Arizona Range News*, June 25, 1937.

69. *Arizona Range News*, June 18, 1937.

70. Brown interview with Woods, April 24, 1971.

71. Ibid. The *Arizona Range News* never reported the winners of the bull riding competition in its July 2, 1937, issue. In a 1969 interview with columnist Tom Wright of *The Oklahoma Journal*, Freckles said he "split a third of the day money." Wright's column also stated that the 1937 Willcox rodeo was a Rodeo Cowboy Association (RCA) event. This is a mistake. The only RCA rodeos in Arizona during 1937 were held in Casa Grande (January 30-31), Florence (5-7), Phoenix (February 12-15), Tucson (February 20-22), Wickenburg (February 26-28), and Prescott (July 2-5), according to *Hoofs and Horns* (May 1937 issue). Page's Willcox rodeo was a non-association rodeo.

72. "Freckles' Own Words."

73. Snyder, "Freckles."

74. Heinz, *Once They Heard the Cheers*, 189; Harrison interviews, January 21, 2023, and July 6, 2021.

75. Heinz, *Once They Heard the Cheers*, 189.

76. Ibid.

77. Ibid.

78. Ibid; Harrison interview, July 6, 2021.

79. Heinz, *Once They Heard the Cheers*, 190; Harrison interview, July 6, 2021.

80. Harrison interviews, July 6, 2021, and January 21, 2023.

Chapter Four

1. Heinz, *Once They Heard the Cheers*, 190; Harrison interviews, July 6, 2021, and January 21, 2023. Don Snyder, "Freckles."

2. Harrison interviews, July 6, 2021, and January 21, 2023.

3. Snyder Family Vertical File, Simon Snyder interview with Lucille Patrick, 1968. Park County Archives, Cody, Wyoming.

4. Chamblin, Thomas S, ed. *The Historical Encyclopedia of Wyoming* (Wyoming: Wyoming Historical Institute, 1970), v. 2, 1289; Harrison interviews, July 6, 2021, and January 21, 2023; Don Snyder, "Freckles."

5. Red Steagall telephone interview with author, July 1, 2020.

6. Harrison interviews, July 6, 2021, and January 21, 2023; Snyder interview with Patrick, 1968. Heinz, *Once They Heard the Cheers*, 190.

7. Heinz, *Once They Heard the Cheers*, 190.

8. Chuck King, "Those Snyder Horses," *Western Horseman* (October 1991), 91. Thomas Molesworth built his iconic, western furniture between 1931 and 1961 at his shop in Cody.

9. King, "Those Snyder Horses," 90.

10. King, "Those Snyder Horses," 90-91; Sue LaFever telephone interview with author, September 18, 2022.

11. Ibid.

12. King, "Those Snyder Horses," 91.

13. Harrison interview, January 21, 2023. The author would like to thank Park County Archives curator Brian Beauvais and Sue LaFever – Don Snyder's daughter – for their memorable tour of the Sunlight Basin and Sunlight Ranch on September 13, 2022. Beauvais possesses an extensive knowledge of the basin, from the history of its earliest settlers to its ancient geology. He is truly a credit to his profession. As for LaFever, she dared to step back in time for what was clearly an emotional experience, all to honor her family and its pioneer legacy in Wyoming.

14. Heinz, *Once They Heard the Cheers*, 190.

15. Ibid.

16. Don Snyder, "Freckles."; King, "Those Snyder Horses," 98; Simon Snyder interview with Patrick, 1968; Snyder Family Vertical File, Park County Archives, Cody, Wyoming. Don Snyder was born March 10, 1911, in Cody to Simon and Ora Snyder. He was the eldest of three children, including Catharine Pickard (born in 1912) and Jack Snyder (born April 10, 1918). Jack

died May 22, 1936, of pneumonia. Don married Faye Davies of Iowa October 20, 1935, in Cody. Together, they had two daughters, Sue LaFever, and Sally Holberg.

17. Don Snyder, "Freckles."

18. Ibid.

19. Ibid.

20. Ibid.

21. Ibid.

22. Ibid.

23. Ibid.

24. Ibid.

25. Ibid.

26. Ibid.

27. Ibid.

28. Ibid.

29. Ibid.

30. Ibid.

31. Heinz, *Once They Heard the Cheers*, 190; Darla Worden, "Hemmingway's Wyoming: A Cockeyed Wonderful Country," *Big Sky Journal* (Spring 2016); Sue LaFever interview, September 18, 2022.

32. LaFever interview, September 18, 2022.

33. Heinz, *Once They Heard the Cheers*, 190-191.

34. Ibid, 190.

35. Don Snyder, "Freckles."

36. Snyder Family Vertical File, Don Snyder, "Cyrus P. 'Pap' Snyder," Park County Archives, Cody, Wyoming. Prior to 1893, businessmen George Beck and Horace Alger of Sheridan, Wyoming purchased water rights to irrigate a large swath of land along the south side of the Shoshone River. William F. "Buffalo Bill" Cody met that year with the two businessmen, who were more than eager to bring aboard the famed soldier and showman as an investor and promoter. They created the Shoshone Land and Irrigation Company – later the Shoshone Irrigation Company – and began digging the Cody Canal in 1895 – three years before Cyrus R. Snyder's arrival to Wyoming.

37. Don Snyder, "Cyrus R. 'Pap' Snyder."

38. Ibid.

39. Ibid.

40. Snyder Family Vertical File, Simon Snyder's "My Early Days in the Buffalo Bill Country," Park County Archives, Cody, Wyoming.

41. Ibid.

42. Ibid.

238 THE RIDE

43. Robert E. Bonner, "Town Founder and Irrigation Tycoon: The Buffalo Bill Nobody Knows," *Wyohistory.org* (October 25, 2015); Don Snyder, "Cyrus R. 'Pap' Snyder." Cyrus and Mary Catherine Snyder later had two more children, Harold and Gladys.

44. Ibid; Snyder Family Vertical File, Catherine Pinckard interviews with Ester Johansson Murray, January 4, 2000, and January 26, 2000, Park County Archives, Cody, Wyoming.

45. Snyder Family Vertical File, Park County Archives, Cody, Wyoming; *The Cody Enterprise*, February 14, 1923.

46. Catherine Pinckard interviews, January 4, 2000, and January 26, 2000.

47. William T. Painter deed of sale to Simon Snyder, dated August 28, 1923, Park County Clerk's Office, Warranty Deed Record Book 58, p. 300; Snyder Vertical File, Park County Archives, undated newspaper clipping; *The Cody Enterprise*, February 14, 1923.

48. Sunlight Basin Vertical File, Ted Ladd's "A History of the Sunlight Valley: A Tributary of Clark's Fork Creek, Park County, Wyoming," p. 15, Park County Archives, Cody Wyoming; Snyder Family Vertical File, Don Snyder interview, undated, Park County Archives, Cody, Wyoming; King, "Those Snyder Horses," 100; Snyder Family Vertical File, Simon Snyder interview with [?] Siggins, undated, Park County Archives, Cody, Wyoming.

49. Dewitt Dominick and Mary Dominick Chivers. *Doctor Dewey: Stories from the Life and Career of Dr. Dewitt Dominick of Cody, Wyoming* (Cody, Wyoming: WordsWorth, 1996), 44.

50. Catherine Pickard interviews, January 4 and January 26, 2000.

51. Ibid.

52. Ibid.

53. Ibid.

54. Sue LaFever interview, September 18, 2022.

55. Catherine Pickard interviews, January 4, and January 26, 2000; Sue LaFever interview, September 18, 2022.

56. Heinz, *Once They Heard the Cheers*, 190.

Chapter Five

1. King, "Those Snyder Horses," 91.

2. Sunlight Ranch Vertical File, Park County Archives, Cody, Wyoming.

3. Sue LaFever interview, September 18, 2022.

4. King, "Those Snyder Horses," 98.

5. Ibid.

6. Ibid.

7. Ibid.

8. *The Cody Enterprise*, March 26, 1941.

9. *The Cody Enterprise*, April 23, 1941.

10. *The Cody Enterprise*, April 30, 1941.

11. Ibid.

12. *The Cody Enterprise*, August 7, 1929; Heinz, *Once They Heard the Cheers*, 191.

13. *Hoofs and Horns*, July 1941.

14. John Clayton, "The Old West's Female Champion: Caroline Lockhart and Wyoming's Cowboy Heritage," *WyoHistory.org*, November 8, 2014.

15. *The Cody Enterprise*, Special Souvenir Edition, July 4, 1968.

16. Ibid.

17. *The Cody Enterprise*, June 28, 1939; *The Cody Enterprise*, June 26, 1940; *The Cody Enterprise*, July 3, 1940.

18. *The Cody Enterprise*, July 9, 1941; *The Cody Enterprise*, June 14, 1939.

19. *The Cody Enterprise*, June 25, 1941; Cody's Nite Rodeo Vertical File, Park County Archives, Cody, Wyoming.

20. *The Cody Enterprise*, June 25, 1941.

21. King, "Those Snyder Horses," 98.

22. Dominick and Chivers, *Doctor Dewey*, 45.

23. Walter's Inn Vertical File, Park County Archives, Cody, Wyoming; Simon Snyder interview with Patrick, date unknown.

24. Ibid.

25. Heinz, *Once They Heard the Cheers*, 191.

26. *The Cody Enterprise*, July 2, 1941.

27. *The Cody Enterprise*, June 11, 1941.

28. *The Cody Enterprise*, July 2, 1941.

29. *The Cody Enterprise*, July 2, 1941.

30. Ibid.

31. Ibid; *The Cody Stampede*, July 9, 1941.

32. *The Cody Stampede*, July 9, 1941.

33. Ibid.

34. Ibid.

35. Ibid.

36. Heinz, *Once They Heard the Cheers*, 191.

37. Ibid; Wallis, "Freckles," 15.

38. Wallis, "Freckles," 15.

39. *The Cody Enterprise*, July 9, 1941.

40. *The Western Horseman* (June 1987), 92.

41. Heinz, *Once They Heard the Cheers*, 191.

42. Ibid.

43. Ibid; Warren Granger Brown, Wyoming, World War II Registration Cards, 1940-1945.

Chapter Six

1. Wallis, "Freckles," 16.

2. Warren Brown letter to Edith Gregory, August 9, 1943. The letters are part of the family's private collection and were graciously shared with this author.

3. Ibid.

4. Ibid.

5. Warren Brown letter to Edith Gregory, August 10, 1943.

6. Ibid.

7. Joe Berry, "Freckles is still Winning," *ProRodeo Sports News*, August 10, 1983.

8. Ibid.

9. *Hoofs and Horns*, v. 12, no. 8 (February 1943).

10. Warren Brown letter to Edith Gregory, March 10, 1943.

11. Ibid; *Hoof and Horns*, v. 7, no. 4 (April 1943).

12. Digital Collections at Dickinson Research Center, National Cowboy and Western Heritage Museum, Oklahoma City, Oklahoma.

13. Warren Brown letter to Edith Gregory, August 18, 1943.

14. Warren Granger Brown's Office of Strategic Services World War II File, Serial 17054334, Box 86, Location 230/86/28/01, National Archives, Washington, D.C.; Wallis, "Freckles," 16; Warren Brown letter to Edith Gregory, August 21, 1943.

15. Ibid.

16. Warren Brown letter to Edith Gregory, August 22, 1943.

17. Warren Brown letter to Edith Gregory, September 4, 1943.

18. Warren Brown letter to Edith Brown, November 17, 1943.

19. Ibid.

20. Warren Brown letter to Edith Brown, November 19, 1943.

21. Warren Brown letter to Edith Brown, November 22, 1943.

22. Lucretia Brown letter to Warren and Edith Brown, March 15, 1944; Lucretia Brown's certificate of death, May 17, 1944, Tucson, Pima County, Arizona.

23. Lucretia Brown's certificate of death.

24. Stanley H. Kosinski letter to the "National Cowboy Hall of Fame," October 5, 2002, in Brown's Inductee File; Heinz, *Once They Heard the Cheers*, 191.

25. Heinz, *Once They Heard the Cheers*, 191.

26. Brown's Inductee File.

27. Stanley H. Kosinski letter to the "National Cowboy Hall of Fame," July 2002, in Brown's Inductee File.

28. Maochun Yu. *OSS In China: Prelude to Cold War* (New Haven: Yale University Press, 1996), 1.

29. Evan Thomas, "Spymaster General," *Vanity Fair* (March 2011).

30. Ibid.

31. Ibid.

32. Ibid.

33. Heinz, *Once They Heard the Cheers*, 192.

34. *The Oklahoma Journal*, December 12, 1969.

35. Heinz, *Once They Heard the Cheers*, 192.

36. Brown's OSS File.

37. Warren Brown postcard to Edith Brown, March 30, 1945.

38. Warren Brown letter to Edith Brown, March 30, 1945.

39. Ibid.

40. Warren Brown letter to Edith Brown, April 5, 1945.

41. Warren Brown to Edith Brown, April 18, 1945.

42. *The Stars and Stripes*, May 2, 1945.

43. Warren Brown letter to Edith Brown, May 18, 1945; Warren Brown letter to Edith Brown, May 23, 1945; Warren Brown letter to Edith Brown, May 25, 1945. In a letter written June 4, 1945, Freckles tells Edith, "I have seen Jerusalem and Bethlehem," presumably when his unit was in Egypt. Unfortunately, he makes no other reference to having visited the Holy Land. In the same letter, he also tells his wife he "rode on an elephant the other night," and pictures were taken. By then, he's clearly in India.

44. Warren Brown letter to Edith Brown, May 18, 1945.

45. Ibid.

46. Warren Brown letter to Edith Brown, May 21, 1945.

47. Warren Brown letter to Edith Brown, May 23, 1945.

48. Warren Brown letter to Edith Brown, June 1, 1945.

49. United States War Department letter to Warren Brown, November 23, 1945.

50. *The Oklahoma Journal*, December 12, 1969.

51. Yu, *OSS In China*, 226.

52. Brown's OSS File.

53. Yu, *OSS In China*, 214.

54. Heinz, *Once They Heard the Cheers*, 192.

55. Warren Brown letter to Edith Brown, June 25, 1945.

56. Warren Brown letter to Edith Brown, June 21, 1945.

57. Warren Brown letter to Edith Brown, August 15, 1945.

58. Wallis, "Freckles," 16; Heinz, *Once They Heard the Cheers*, 192; Chuck King, "Riding The Rimrock," *The Western Horseman* (January 1966), 8.

59. Warren Brown letter to Edith Brown, July 22, 1945.

60. Ibid.

61. Ibid.

62. Heinz, *Once They Heard the Cheers*, 192.

63. King, "Riding the Rimrock," 8; Warren Brown letter to Edith Brown, August 15, 1945.

64. King, "Riding the Rimrock," 8.

65. Wallis, "Freckles," 16.

66. Warren Brown letter to Edith Brown, September 10, 1945.

67. Warren Brown letter to Edith Brown, September 4, 1945.

Chapter Seven

1. *The Oklahoman*, March 22, 1987.

2. Ibid.

3. *The Oklahoman*, December 13, 1982.

4. Warren Brown telegram to Edith Brown, October 24, 1945.

5. Brown interview, April 24, 1971; *The Oklahoman*, October 13, 1907; *Lawton Semi-Weekly Star*, October 19, 1907.

6. Brown interview, April 24, 1971.

7. Heinz, *Once They Heard the Cheers*, 199.

8. Ibid, 197.

9. Ibid, 199.

10. Don Snyder letter to Warren Brown, December 20, 1945.

11. Simon and Ora Snyder deed of sale to Donald and Faye Snyder, dated November 26, 1945, Park County Clerk's Office, Warranty Deed Record Book 116, p. 624-625.

12. Don Snyder to Warren Brown, December 20, 1945.

13. Ibid.

14. Berry, "Freckles is Still Winning," 3.

15. *ProRodeo Sports News*, July 15, 1947; "Freckles' Own Words." During this period, Freckles also dealt with the death of his father, Richard. The elder Brown passed away March 14, 1947, in Tucson at the age of 73 (Arizona State Department of Health, Certificate of Death, Pima County, Arizona).

16. James Cathey (1917-1978) snapped photographs over a thirty-year career, capturing images that ranged from rodeos to working cowboys to the western way of life. Today, more than 68,000 photographic negatives are preserved as part of The James Cathey Heritage Collection at The Dickinson Research Center of the National Cowboy and Western Heritage Museum in

Oklahoma City.

17. Wallis, "Freckles," 16.

18. Berry, "Freckles is Still Winning," 3.

19. Ibid.

20. *The Arkansas Gazette*, October 11, 1960.

21. Porter, "Freckles," 92.

22. Heinz, *Once They Heard the Cheers*, 197.

23. Ibid, 185.

24. Ibid.

25. Heinz, *Once They Heard the Cheers*, 199.

26. Ibid.

27. Ibid.

28. Ibid.

29. Ibid.

30. *Stillwater News Press*, July 3, 1963; Wallis, "Freckles," 16-17. Wallis never stated the exact time when Freckles accomplished through extraordinary feats; "Freckles' Own Words."

31. *The Arkansas Gazette*, October 11, 1960.

32. Heinz, *Once They Heard the Cheers*, 194.

33. John M. Duffy, "Casey Tibbs: 'America's Most Beloved Cowboy,' " *South Dakota History*, v. 32, no. 4, (Winter 2002), 310-330.

34. Kendra Santos, "Friends relived days with Casey Tibbs," *ProRodeo Sports News*, February 21, 1990, 6.

35. Duffy, "Casey Tibbs," 320.

36. Shoulders Inductee File, (Box 30, File 1).

37. Loudon Kelly, "Champion Of The Suicide Circuit," *Hoof and Horns* (June 1959), 4.

38. Shoulders Inductee File, (Box 30, File 1).

39. Ibid.

40. Barbara J. Brown, "The Bull Riding Stylist," *The Western Horseman* (July 1981), 30-33; Harry Tompkins Inductee File, Rode Historical Society Records, The Dickinson Research Center, National Cowboy and Western History Museum, Oklahoma City, Oklahoma.

41. Brown, "The Bull Riding Stylist," 33.

42. Ibid.

43. Kristen M. White, "Riding into history," *ProRodeo Sports News*, March 15, 2006; Harry Tompkins Inductee File; Casey Tibbs Inductee File (Box 30, Files 8 and 10), The Dickinson Research Center, National Cowboy and Western Heritage Museum, Oklahoma City, Oklahoma.

44. *The Oklahoman*, March 22, 1987.

45. John G. Sawyer, "Born Daredevils: The Bull Riders," *Ketch Pen* (Summer 1994), 16.
46. Ibid.
47. Ibid, 17.
48. Ibid.
49. Ibid.
50. Ibid.
51. Ibid.
52. Ibid.
53. The 1962 Rodeo Annual, *Rodeo Sports News*, 39.
54. Ibid.
55. Ibid, 39-40.
56. Ibid, 11-12.
57. Ibid, 40.
58. Ibid.
59. "Freckles' Own Words."
60. The 1962 Rodeo Annual, 40.

Chapter Eight

1. The 1962 Rodeo Annual, 40.
2. Ibid.
3. RCA Standings, March 15; April 1; April 15; May 1; May 15; June 15; July 1; July 15; August 1, 1962, published in *Rodeo Sports News*.
4. "Freckles Brown Is Back In The Lead," *Rodeo Sports News*, August 15, 1962.
5. "Durable Freckles Brown Wins On Deadwood's Tough Bulls," *Hoofs and Horns* (October 1962), 30.
6. "Standings Show Close Title Races," *Rodeo Sports News*, August 15, 1962.
7. "Freckles' Own Words"; Jerry Armstrong, "Picked Up In The Rodeo Arena," *The Western Horseman*, 40.
8. [Willard H. Porter], "In an Exclusive Hoofs and Horns Interview, Freckles Brown, World's Champion Bull Rider from Lawton, Oklahoma, Discusses the Wreck That Injured Him Last October, His Convalescent Months, and His Decision to Ride Again ...," *Hoofs and Horns* (October 1963), 12; Heinz, *Once They Heard the Cheers*, 184.
9. "Freckles Brown Badly Hurt In Bull Riding," *Rodeo Sports News*, November 1, 1962.
10. [Porter], "In an Exclusive Hoofs and Horns Interview...," 12.
11. Ibid.
12. Ibid.
13. Ibid.

14. Ibid.
15. Ibid.
16. Ibid; Heinz, *Once They Heard the Cheers*, 184.
17. Heinz, *Once They Heard the Cheers*, 184.
18. Ibid.
19. Ibid.
20. Heinz, *Once They Heard the Cheers*, 184.
21. "Freckles Brown Badly Hurt in Bull Riding," *Rodeo Sports News*, November 1, 1962.
22. Ibid.
23. *The Oklahoma Journal*, December 12, 1969.
24. *The Oklahoman*, November 22, 1987.
25. 1963 Rodeo Annual, *Rodeo Sports News*.
26. According to the May 23, 1972, issue of *The Greeley* (Colorado) *Daily Tribune*, the front fusion operation had been "perfected in Japan."
27. Heinz, *Once They Heard the Cheers*, 184.
28. Ibid.
29. 1963 Rodeo Annual, *Rodeo Sports News*, 39.
30. [Porter], "In an Exclusive Hoofs and Horns Interview …," 12.
31. 1963 Rodeo Annual, *Rodeo Sports News*, 39; 1962 Rodeo Annual, *Rodeo Sports News*, 39; "Freckles Own Words."
32. 1963 Rodeo Annual, *Rodeo Sports News*, 39.
33. [Porter], "In an Exclusive Hoofs and Horns Interview …," 12.
34. Harrison interview, July 6, 2021.

Chapter Nine

1. Heinz, *Once They Heard the Cheers*, 194.
2. [Porter], "In an Exclusive Hoofs and Horns Interview …," 12.
3. Ibid.
4. Ibid.
5. "From the Top of This Hill: An Interview With Freckles Brown," *Hoofs and Horns* (September 1969), 20.
6. Heinz, *Once They Heard the Cheers*, 193.
7. *The Oklahoman*, March 22, 1987; Harrison interview, July 6, 2021.
8. [Porter], "In an Exclusive Hoofs and Horns Interview," 12.
9. Harrison interview, July 6, 2021; Todd Whatley Vertical File, The Dickinson Research Center, National Cowboy and Western Heritage Museum, Oklahoma City, Oklahoma.
10. Whatley Vertical File.

11. Ibid.

12. Harrison interview, July 6, 2021; "Southeastern Oklahoma – Soper," *Strum's Oklahoma Magazine* (June 1912), v. 5, no. 2, 16; Wallis, "Freckles," 12.

13. Heinz, *Once They Heard the Cheers*, 199; Harrison interview, July 6, 2021.

14. Harrison interview, July 6, 2021.

15. [Porter], "In an Exclusive Hoofs and Horns Interview," 12.

16. Ibid.

17. Ibid.

18. Ibid, Heinz, *Once They Heard the Cheers*, 185.

19. [Porter], "In an Exclusive Hoofs and Horns Interview," 36; Heinz, *Once They Heard the Cheers*, 185.

20. Heinz, *Once They Heard the Cheers*, 185.

21. [Porter], "In an Exclusive Hoofs and Horns Interview," 36.

22. Ibid.

23. Ibid.

24. Ibid.

25. Ibid.

26. Heinz, *Once They Heard the Cheers*, 183.

27. Martin, who qualified for five National Finals Rodeos, retired from rodeo in 1971 and was inducted into the Texas Rodeo Cowboy Hall of Fame in 2000. He died July 13, 2014, of a heart attack at the age of 83.

28. Heinz, *Once They Heard the Cheers*, 183-184.

29. Porter, "Freckles," 91.

30. The celebrated sportswriter W.C. Heinz even dedicated a chapter in his 1979 book *Once They Heard the Cheers* to Freckles titled, "The Unsinkable Mister Brown."

31. Harrison interview, July 6, 2021; "Freckles' Own Words"; Heinz, *Once They Heard the Cheers*, 199.

32. Harrison interview, July 6, 2021.

33. Ibid; "Freckles' Own Words"; Wallis, "Freckles," 12.

34. Ibid.

35. King, "Riding The Rimrock," 8.

36. "Freckles' Own Words."

37. Heinz, *Once They Heard the Cheers*, 185. Whatley's life would be snuffed out two years later. A drunken Edward R. Kizer shot Whatley to death on June 17, 1966, outside a rodeo dance at the Hugo, Oklahoma fairgrounds when he found the rodeo champion in a car with his wife, Opal. Kizer fired several shots through the car window, killing Whatley and wounding his wife. Opal was shot three times but survived. On November 15, 1967, a jury of nine men and three women found Kizer guilty of first-degree manslaughter. He received a sentence of five years in prison. The trial was Kizer's second.

The first resulted in a hung jury (*The Oklahoman*, November 30, 1967).
38. Ibid.
39. Ibid, 185-186.
40. Ibid, 186.
41. Ferrell Butler interview with Tristan Jackson and author, Ringold, Oklahoma, June 29, 2021.
42. Ibid.
43. Ibid; Ferrell Butler telephone interview with author, June 19, 2020.
44. Ibid.
45. Butler interview, June 29, 2021.
46. Ibid.
47. Ibid.
48. Bill Kornell Vertical File, The Dickinson Research Center, National Cowboy and Western Heritage Museum, Oklahoma City, Oklahoma.
49. Jerry Izenberg, "Look What's Happened to Rodeo!" *True The Man's Magazine* (August 1968), 49-51, 70-71.
50. Larry Mahan Inductee File, The Dickinson Research Center, National Cowboy and Western Heritage Museum, Oklahoma City, Oklahoma; Kornell Vertical File; Cheryl Leverton Larsen, "Bobby Berger, Descent and the Black Hills Roundup," *Tri-State Livestock News*, July 16, 2015.
51. Bobby Berger telephone interview with author, May 30, 2020.
52. Ibid.
53. Ibid.
54. Bill Kornell telephone interview with author, July 23, 2021.
55. *The Oklahoman*, December 7, 2008.
56. Ibid.
57. Ibid.
58. Ibid.
59. Ibid.
60. "Freckles' Own Words."
61. *The Oklahoman*, March 22, 1987; *The Oklahoman*, September 5, 1982.
62. *The Oklahoman*, December 6, 1968.
63. Ibid.
64. *The Oklahoman*, March 22, 1987.
65. John G. Sawyer, "Born Daredevils: The Bull Riders," *Ketch Pen* (Summer 1994), 16.

Chapter Ten

1. Gail Hughbanks Woerner. *Cowboy Up: The History of Bull Riding* (Austin, Texas: Eakin Press, 2001), 135. Woerner inaccurately stated that Tornado sold

at auction in the "spring of 1961," but Jim Shoulders – Tornado's long-time owner – always said Tornado first began to appear in rodeos in 1960 (Jim Shoulders Inductee File).

2. Bill L. Olsen telephone interview with author, October 27, 2021.

3. Woerner, *Cowboy Up*, 135.

4. Ibid.

5. Olson interview; Marvin Paul Shoulders interview with author, Henryetta, Oklahoma, January 16, 2020.

6. Marvin Paul Shoulders interview, January 16, 2020.

7. Jim Shoulders Inductee File; "Clive Runnells, Jr.," *The Cattleman Magazine* (July 2019), online. Runnells died April 26, 2019, at the age of 93.

8. Jim Blackburn. *The Book of Texas Bays* (College Station, Texas: Texas A&M University Press, 2004), 133.

9. Chris Emmett, "Pierce, Abel Head [Shanghai]," *Handbook of Texas Online*, accessed July 19, 2023, https://www.tshaonline.org/handbook/entries/pierce-abel-head-shanghai; Blackburn, *The Book of Texas Bays*, 133.

10. Olson interview; Woerner, *Cowboy Up*, 133.

11. Neal Gay, Ben Johnson Award File, Rodeo Historical Society Records, The Dickinson Research Center, National Cowboys and Western Heritage Museum, Oklahoma City, Oklahoma; Woerner, *Cowboy Up*, 133; Marvin Paul Shoulders interview, January 16, 2020.

12. Marvin Paul Shoulders interview, January 16, 2020.

13. Ibid.

14. Butler interview, June 19, 2020.

15. Ferrell Butler telephone interview, Ringold, Oklahoma, July 16, 2023; Butler interview, June 29, 2021.

16. Butler interview, June 19, 2020. Scudder went on to find a more peaceful occupation as National Finals Rodeo general manager. He became instrumental in bringing the Finals to Oklahoma City in 1964.

17. Marvin Paul Shoulders interview, January 16, 2020.

18. *Associated Press*, July 3, 1983.

19. Myrtis Dightman, Sr interview with author, Houston, Texas, December 20, 2018.

20. Ibid.

21. Harold Leftwich telephone interview with author, Elk City, Oklahoma, June 25, 2020.

22. The 1967 *National Finals Rodeo Program*.

23. Ibid.

24. *The Oklahoman*, January 5, 1964.

25. Berger interview, May 30, 2020.

26. Ibid.

27. Butler interview, July 16, 2023.

28. Marin Paul Shoulders, January 16, 2020.

Chapter Eleven

1. Ronnie Bowman interview with author, Calera, Oklahoma, February 8, 2020.

2. *The Oklahoman*, May 18, 1972.

3. W.K. Stratton, "Sitting Atop A Tornado," *Sports Illustrated*, May 25, 1987.

4. Clem McSpadden interview with Gail Woerner, the Dickinson Research Center, National Cowboy and Western Heritage Museum, Oklahoma City, Oklahoma, October 20, 2006; Berger interview, May 30, 2020.

5. *The New York Times*, July 14, 2008; McSpadden interview, October 20, 2006.

6. Ibid.

7. *The New York Times*, July 14, 2008.

8. Richard McCall, "Brownie, You're Quite A Guy ..." *Rodeo Sports News* August 1, 1969.

9. "Freckles' Own Words"; *The Oklahoman*, November 28, 1967.

10. The 1967 *National Finals Rodeo Program*; The *Oklahoman*, November 28, 1967.

11. *The Oklahoman*, December 1, 1967.

12. J.D. Ackerman letter to Freckles Brown, July 8, 1983, in the Freckles Brown Inductee File.

13. McSpadden interview, October 20, 2006.

14. *The Oklahoman*, March 22, 1987; Wiley Harrison telephone interview with author, July 22, 2023.

15. Harrison interview, July 6, 2021.

16. Ibid.

17. Ibid.

Chapter Twelve

1. Harrison interview, July 23, 2023.

2. Ferrell Butler telephone interview with author, September 10, 2009.

3. Butler interview, April 2, 2023.

4. Wallis, "Freckles," 17.

5. Ibid.

6. *The Oklahoman*, December 15, 1972.

7. *The Oklahoman*, December 13, 1982.

8. "You Don't Forget A Guy Like Freckles," *The Ketch Pen*, August 1989

9. *The Oklahoman*, March 22, 1987; Larry Pointer, "Freckles vs. Tornado: one ride the NFR will never forget," *World of Rodeo and Western Heritage* (December 1979), 11.

10. *The Oklahoman*, December 13, 1982.
11. Leftwich interview, June 25, 2020.
12. Pointer, "Freckles vs. Tornado," 11.
13. Ibid.
14. Bob Thedford telephone interview with author, Elk City, Oklahoma, June 24, 2020; Leftwich interview, June 25, 2020.
15. "You Don't Forget A Guy Like Freckles," *The Ketch Pen*, August 1989.
16. Butler interview, June 19, 2020.
17. "You Don't Forget A Guy Like Freckles," *The Ketch Pen*, August 1989.
18. *The Oklahoman*, December 15, 1972.
19. Pointer, "Freckles vs. Tornado: one ride the NFR will never forget," *World of Rodeo and Western Heritage* (December 1979), 11.
20. Butler interview, June 19, 2020.
21. *The Oklahoman*, March 22, 1987.
22. *The Oklahoman*, March 22, 1987; *The Oklahoman*, September 5, 1982; Wallis, "Freckles," 17. Dollie Riddle, Una's daughter, inherited the whistle her mother used on that fateful night. To this day, the cherished whistle been tied to her stopwatch for more than two decades of timing rodeos (*The Hutchinson News*, July 17, 2015).
23. *The Oklahoman*, December 15, 1972.
24. Harrison interview, July 23, 2023.
25. Stratton, *Chasing The Rodeo*, 17.
26. The 1967 *National Finals Rodeo Program*.
27. Wallis, "Freckles," 17
28. *The Oklahoma City Times*, December 2, 1967.
29. "Freckles' Own Words."
30. Wallis, "Freckles," 17.
31. *The Newark Star-Ledger*, October 1, 2006.
32. Harrison interview, July 6, 2021.

Chapter Thirteen

1. Heinz, *Once They Heard the Cheers*, 181.
2. Ibid.
3. Ibid.
4, Ibid.
5. Ibid, 182.
6. Ibid.
7. Ibid.
8. Ibid.

9. Ibid.
10. Ibid.
11. Ibid.
12. Ibid.
13. Ibid.
14. Ibid.
15. Ibid.
16. Ibid.
17. *Daily Herald* (Provo, Utah), February 17, 1968.
18. Ibid.
19. Ibid. Harvey's column originally stated "ten-second," clearly meant to be "eight-second." Hence, the change.
20. Butler interview, June 19, 2020.
21. The 1967 *National Finals Rodeo Program*.
22. *The Oklahoman*, December 2, 1967.
23. *Oklahoma City Times*, December 2, 1967.
24. *Billings Gazette*, December 2, 1967.
25. Olson interview, October 27, 2021.
26. *The Oklahoman*, December 6, 1967; *The Oklahoman*, December 8, 1967.
27. *The Oklahoman*, December 9, 1967; *The Oklahoman*, December 10, 1967; *The Oklahoman*, December 11, 1967.
28. *The Oklahoman*, December 10, 1967.
29. Dawson interview, March 22, 2023.
30. *The Oklahoman*, December 2, 1967.
31. Wallis, "Freckles," 17; Stratton, *Chasing The Rodeo*, 15.
32. *The Oklahoman*, March 22, 1987.
33. "Champ Turned Out To Pasture," undated and unidentified newspaper, Freckles Brown Vertical File, The Dickinson Research Center, National Cowboy and Western Heritage Museum, Oklahoma City, Oklahoma; *The Ada Evening News*, December 12, 1969.
34. Ibid; Woerner, *Cowboy Up*, 135; "Freckles Triumphs against Tornado," *ProRodeo Sports News*, July 1, 1998.
35. "Freckles Triumphs against Tornado," *ProRodeo Sports News*, July 1, 1998.
36. *The Oklahoman*, May 18, 1972.
37. Ibid.
38. *The Enid Morning News*, December 12, 1972.
39. "Champ Turned Out To Pasture," undated and unidentified newspaper, Freckles Brown Vertical File.
40. Ibid.

41. Shoulders Inductee File, Box 30, Folder 2.

42. *The Oklahoman*, May 18, 1972. *Tornado's* age was reported as sixteen, but the bull was born in 1957, meaning he was in the fifteenth year of his life when he died.

43. *The Daily Free-Lance* (Henryetta, Oklahoma), May 7, 1972.

44. *The Daily Free-Lance* (Henryetta, Oklahoma), December 8, 1972.

45. *The Morning News*, December 12, 1972.

46. Ibid.

47. Wallis, "Freckles," 17.

48. *The Oklahoman*, March 22, 1987.

49. Ibid. Doug Brown went on the win the World Bull Riding Championship in 1969 (Doug Brown Vertical File, The Dickinson Research Center, National Cowboy and Western Heritage Museum, Oklahoma City, Oklahoma).

50. *Rodeo Sports News*, August 1, 1969.

51. *The Oklahoma City Journal*, December 2, 1969.

52. Ibid.

53. Ibid.

54. *The Oklahoma City Times*, December 8, 1969.

55. Ibid.

56. Ibid.

57. Ibid.

58. Ibid.

59. Heinz, *Once They Heard the Cheers*, 195-196.

60. Ibid, 196.

61. Ibid.

62. Ibid.

63. Ibid.

64. Porter, "Freckles," 91.

65. Ibid.

66. Christian Wallace, "The Jackie Robinson of Rodeo," *Texas Monthly* (July, 2018); Kendra Santos, "Dightman still smiling, still riding," *ProRodeo Sports News*, March 20, 1991.

67. Dightman, Sr. interview, December 20, 2018.

68. Ibid.

69. Wallace, "The Jackie Robinson of Rodeo."

70. Dightman, Sr. interview, December 20, 2018; Wallace, "The Jackie Robinson of Rodeo."

71. Myrtis Dightman, Jr.. interview in Houston, Texas, December 20, 2018.

72. Dightman, Sr. interview, December 20, 2018.
73. Ibid.
74. Ibid.
75. Ibid.
76. Ibid.
77. Myrtis Dightman Inductee File, The Dickinson Research Center, National Cowboys and Western Heritage Museum, Oklahoma City, Oklahoma.
78. *The Oklahoma City Times*, December 8, 1969.
79. Steagall interview, July 1, 2020.
80. Ibid.
81. Ibid.
82. Ibid.
83. Ibid.
84. Ibid.
86. Ibid.
87. Ibid.

Chapter Fourteen

1. Steagall interview, July 1, 2020.
2. Ibid. The *Tornado* stand-in was a Florida bull named *Osceola*.
3. Ibid.
4. Ibid.
5. Ibid.
6. *The Oklahoman*, December 13, 1982.7. Ibid.
8. Ibid.
9. Ibid.
10. Harrison interview with author, Soper, Oklahoma, January 21, 2023.
11. Ibid.
12. Ibid.
13. Ibid.
14. Harrison interview, July 6, 2021.
15. Harrison interview, January 21, 2023.
16. Berry, "Freckles is still winning," 5; Harrison interview, January 21, 2023; *The New York Times*, December 21, 1970.
17. Harrison interview, January 21, 2023.
18. Ibid.
19. Ibid.
20. Ibid.

21. Ibid.
22. Ibid.
23. Berry, "Freckles is still winning," 5.
24. Ibid.
25. Randy Witte, "Ol' Freck just goes on and on …," *Rodeo Sports News*, v. 22, no. 13, Jun 1, 1974.
26. Berry, "Freckles is still winning," 3; www.lanefrost.com.
27. www.lanefrost.com.
28. Michael Bales and Ann Terry Hill, *Pendleton Round-Up At 100: Oregon's Legendary Rodeo* (Portland, Oregon: Graphic Arts Books, 2009), 217.
29. Ibid.
30. Harrison interview, January 21, 2023.
31. Ibid; *The Associated Press*, July 3, 1983.
32. *The Associated Press*, July 3, 1983.
33. Berry, "Freckles is still winning," 3.
34. Harrison interview, January 21, 2023.
35. *The Oklahoman*, March 21, 1987; Harrison interview, January 21, 2023.
36. Harrison interview, January 21, 2023.
37. Ibid.
38. Ibid.
39. Ibid.
40. Ibid.
41. Ibid.
42. Ibid.
43. Ibid.
44. Ibid.
45. Ibid.
46. Ibid.
47. Ibid; McSpadden interview, October 20, 2006.
48. Harrison interview, January 21, 2023.
49. Ibid.
50. McSapdden interview, October 20, 2006.
51. Ibid.
52. Ibid.
53. Ibid.
54. Harrison interview, January 21, 2023; Wiley Harrison telephone interview with author, Soper, Oklahoma, August 13, 2023.
55. Harrison interview, January 21, 2023.

56. *The Oklahoman*, March 13, 1987.
57. Ibid.
58. Ibid; Brown Induction File, Box 39, Folder 20.
59. *The Oklahoman*, March 13, 1987.
60. Ibid.
61. Ibid.
62. Ibid.
63. Ibid.
64. Ibid.
65. Ibid.
66. Ibid.
67. Ibid.
68. *The Oklahoman*, March 21, 1987.
69. Ibid.
70. Porter, "Freckles," 89.
71. *The Oklahoman*, March 21, 1987.
72. *Tulsa World,* July 31, 1989; www.lanefrost.com.
73. Stratton, "Sitting Atop A Tornado," *Sports Illustrated,* May 25, 1987.
74. Stratton, *Chasing the Rodeo*, 18.

Bibliography

Primary Sources
Archival & Private Collections

Arizona Historical Society, Tucson, Arizona
   Sabino Canyon. Vertical File.
   Tanque Verde Ranch. Vertical File.
Chiricahua Regional Museum & Research Center, Willcox, Arizona
   G.W. "Boozer" Page. Vertical File.
   Willcox Rodeos. Vertical File.
   Seventy-Six Ranch. Vertical File.
Donald C. & Elizabeth Dickinson Research Center, National Cowboy & Western Heritage Museum, Oklahoma City
   Hoofs and Horns Collection
   Rodeo Sports News Collection
   Rodeo Historical Society Records

Vertical Files:
- Bobby Berger
- Jake Beutler
- John "Jiggs" Beutler
- Warren G. "Freckles" Brown
- Jim Charles
- Descent
- Ben Johnson
- Doug Jones
- Chuck King
- Bill Kornell
- Clem McSpadden
- Marvin Shoulders
- Ernie Taylor
- Tornado
- Todd Whatley

Rodeo Oral History Project:
- Jim Charles
- Neal Gay
- Larry Mahan
- Clem McSpadden
- Jim Shoulders
- Marty Wood

Inductee Files:
- Elra Beutler
- John "Jiggs" Beutler
- Lynn Beutler
- Warren G. "Freckles" Brown
- Myrtis Dightman, Sr.
- Ben Johnson
- Pete Logan
- Larry Mahan
- George Paul
- Jim Shoulders
- Casey Tibbs
- Harry Tompkins
- Harry Vold
- Todd Whatley
- Marty Wood

Correspondence Files:
Warren G. "Freckles" and Edith Brown

Nominee Files:
Bobby Berger

Ben Johnson Award:
Neal Gay
Clem McSpadden
Jim Shoulders

Harrison-Brown Family Papers
Warren G. "Freckles" Brown. Letters.
Lucretia Brown. Letters.

Lively Family Papers
Eva Lively. Family History Notes.

National Archives, Washington, D.C., Office of Strategic Services
Warren Granger Brown. OSS Personnel Files.

Oklahoma Historical Society, Oklahoma City
Warren G. "Freckles" Brown taped interview with Pen Woods, April 24, 1971, Living Legends Collection.
Clem McSpadden taped interview with Gail Hughbanks Woerner, October 20, 2006, Living Legends Collection.

Park County Archives, Cody, Wyoming
Carlie Downing. Vertical File.
Catharine Snyder. Oral History Interview.
Chief Joseph Highway. Vertical File.
Cody Nite Rodeo. Vertical File.
Cody, Wyoming Telephone Directories, 1925, 1941.
Don Snyder. Oral History Interview.
Darling Family. Vertical File.
Simon Snyder. Oral History Interviews.
Simon Snyder. Vertical File.
Snyder Family. Vertical File.
Snyder, Don. "Cyrus R. 'Pap' Snyder," undated.
Snyder, Simon. "My Early Days in the Buffalo Bill Country," undated.
Sunlight Ranch. Vertical File.
Sunlight Basin. Vertical File.
Walters' Inn. Vertical File.

Snyder Family Papers
Don Snyder's historical sketch "Freckles," from an unpublished memoir.

Court Records

Park County, Wyoming, County Clerk's Office
William T. Painter sale to Simon Snyder, Warranty Deeds Book 58.
Simon and Ora Snyder sale to Donald and Faye Snyder, Warranty Deeds Book 116.

Government Records

Arizona Department of Health
  Lucretia Brown death certificate, May 17, 1944.
  Richard Brown death certificate, March 14, 1947.
Oklahoma Vital Records Division
  Warren G. "Freckles" Brown death certificate, March 20, 1987.
  Edith Brown death certificate, January 7, 2000.

Books and Pamphlets

Arizona Road Map. Chicago: The H.M. Gousha Company, 1935.

Arizona State Business Directory, 1937. Denver: The Gazetteer Publishing & Printing Co., 1937.

Bard, Floyd C. *Horse Wrangler: Sixty Years in the Horse Saddle in Wyoming and Montana.* Norman, Oklahoma: University of Oklahoma Press, 1960.

Chambers III, John Whiteclay. *OSS Training in the National Parks and Service Abroad in World War II.* Washington, D.C.: U.S. National Parks Service, 2008.

Dominick, Dewitt and Mary Dominick Chives. *Doctor Dewey: Stories from the Life and Career of Dr. Dewitt Dewey, Cody, Wyoming.* Cody, Wyoming: WordWorth, 1996.

Fremont, John Charles. *Report of an Expedition of the Country Lying between the Missouri River and the Rocky Mountains on the Line of the Kansas and Great Platte Rivers.* Washington, D.C., 1843.

Heinz, W.C. *Once They Heard the Cheers.* Garden City, New York: Doubleday & Company, Inc., 1979.

Horses and Mules and National Defense. Washington, D.C.: United States Army, Quartermaster Corps, 1958.

Jameson, W.C., ed. *Notes From Texas: On Writing in the Lone Star State.* Fort Worth: Texas Christian University Press, 2008.

Meinzer, O.E. and F.C. Kelton. *Geology and Water Resources of Sulphur Springs Valley.* Washington, D.C.: Government Printing Office, 1913.

National Finals Rodeo Program & Scorecard, Oklahoma City, 1967.

National Register of Historic Places: El Montevideo Historic District.

Snyder, Don. "Freckles" from an unpublished memoir. Courtesy of his daughters, Sally (Snyder) Holberg and Sue (Snyder) LaFever.

The Cody Stampede Program, July 4, 1941.

The Tucson Daily Star 1935 Classified Directory. Tucson: The Tucson Daily Star, 1935.

Tucson City Directory, 1936. Tucson: Arizona Directory Co., 1936.

Tucson City Directory, 1937. Tucson: Keddington-Mission Printing Co., 1937.

Tucson City Directory, 1938. Tucson: Keddington-Mission Printing Co., 1938.

Tulk, Rusty. *Ride 'Em As They Come: The Life of John "Rusty" Tulk, 1886-1977.* Deming, New Mexico: NWJ Publishing, 2005.

United States Census. Goshen County, Wyoming, 1930.

United States Census. Park County, Wyoming, 1920, 1930, 1940.

United States Census. Pima County, Arizona, 1930, 1940.

United States Census. Cochise County, Arizona, 1930, 1940.

United States Census. Coryell County, Texas, 1920

Uys, Errol Lincoln. *Riding The Rails: Teenagers on the Move During the Great Depression.* New York, New York: TV Books, L.L.C., 1999.

Wind Pudding and Rabbit Tracks: A History of Goshen County. Torrington, Wyoming: Goshen County History Book Committee, 1989.

Wright, Gordon. *The Cavalry Manual of Horsemanship and Horsemastership.* Fort Riley, Kansas: The Cavalry School, 1942.

Stratton, W.K. *Chasing the Rodeo: On Wild Rides and Big Dreams, Broken Hearts and Broken Bones, and One Man's Search for the West.* San Diego: Harcourt, 2004.

Newspapers

Arizona Range News (Willcox, Arizona), December 18, 1936.
Arizona Range News (Willcox, Arizona), January 15, 1937.
Arizona Range News (Willcox, Arizona), January 29, 1937.
Arizona Range News (Willcox, Arizona), February 5, 1937.
Arizona Range News (Willcox, Arizona), March 5, 1937.
Arizona Range News (Willcox, Arizona), March 19, 1937.
Arizona Range News (Willcox, Arizona), May 21, 1937.
Arizona Range News (Willcox, Arizona), June 18, 1937.
Arizona Range News (Willcox, Arizona), June 25, 1937.
Arizona Range News (Willcox, Arizona), July 2, 1937.
Arizona Range News (Willcox, Arizona), July 9, 1937.
Arizona Range News (Willcox, Arizona), September 17, 1937.
Arizona Range News (Willcox, Arizona), October 29, 1937.
Arizona Range News (Willcox, Arizona), November 5, 1937.
Arizona Range News (Willcox, Arizona), December 23, 1938.
Associated Press, July 3, 1983.
Billings Gazette, December 2, 1967.
Daily Herald (Provo, Utah), February 16, 1967.
Eagle Lake (Texas) *Headlight,* September 7, 2006.
Hoofs and Horns, May 1937.
Hoofs and Horns, July 1941.
Hoofs and Horns, August 1941.
Hoofs and Horns, February 1943.
Hoofs and Horns, April 1943.
Lawton Semi-Weekly Star, October 19, 1907.
Rodeo Sports News, March 15, 1962.
Rodeo Sports News, April 1, 1962.
Rodeo Sports News, April 15, 1962.
Rodeo Sports News, May 1, 1962.
Rodeo Sports News, May 15, 1962
Rodeo Sports News, June 15, 1962.
Rodeo Sports News, July 1, 1962.
Rodeo Sports News, July 15, 1962.
Rodeo Sports News, August 1, 1962.

Rodeo Sports News, August 1, 1969.
Rodeo Sports News, June 1, 1974.
Rodeo Sports News, July 10, 1996.
ProRodeo Sports News, July 15, 1947.
ProRodeo Sports News, July 1, 1998.
The Ada (Oklahoma) *Evening News*, December 5, 1967.
The Ada (Oklahoma) *Evening News*, December 12, 1969.
The Arizona Daily Star, February 2-, 1957.
The Arkansas Gazette, October 11, 1960.
The Billings Gazette, December 2, 1967.
The Cody Enterprise, February 14, 1923.
The Cody Enterprise, June 29, 1927.
The Cody Enterprise, August 7, 1929.
The Cody Enterprise, June 14, 1939.
The Cody Enterprise, June 28, 1939.
The Cody Enterprise, June 19, 1940.
The Cody Enterprise, June 25, 1940.
The Cody Enterprise, June 26, 1940.
The Cody Enterprise, July 3, 1940.
The Cody Enterprise, October 23, 1940.
The Cody Enterprise, March 26, 1941.
The Cody Enterprise, April 23, 1941.
The Cody Enterprise, April 30, 1941.
The Cody Enterprise, June 4, 1941.
The Cody Enterprise, June 11, 1941.
The Cody Enterprise, June 25, 1941.
The Cody Enterprise, July 2, 1941.
The Cody Enterprise, July 9, 1941.
The Cody Enterprise, July 16, 1941.
The Cody Enterprise, November 12, 1941.
The Cody Enterprise, July 4, 1968.
The Cody Enterprise, September 20, 1999.
The Cody Enterprise, November 17, 2010.
The Coolidge (Arizona) *Examiner*, August 12, 1932.
The (Henryetta, Oklahoma) *Daily Free-Lance*, May 7, 1972.
The (Henryetta, Oklahoma) *Daily Free-Lance*, December 8, 1972.
The Denton Record-Chronicle, December 3, 1967.
The Greeley (Colorado) *Daily Tribune*, May 23, 1972.
The Guernsey (Wyoming) *Gazette*, February 4, 1921.
The Hutchinson (Kansas) *News*, July 17, 2015.
The (Enid, Oklahoma) *Morning News*, December 12, 1972.
The (Santa Fe) *New Mexican*, May 21, 1972.
The New York Times, December 21, 1970.
The New York Times, January 31, 1979.
The New York Times, December 13, 1982.

The New York Times, July 14, 2008.
The Newark Star-Ledger, October 1, 2006.
The (Stillwater, Oklahoma) *News Press*, July 3, 1983.
The Nevada-Reno State Journal, December 23, 1969.
The Northern Wyoming Herald (Cody, Wyoming), June 13, 1923.
The Oklahoma City Times, December 2, 1967.
The Oklahoma City Times, December 8, 1969.
The Oklahoman, October 13, 1907.
The Oklahoman, January 5, 1964.
The Oklahoman, November 28, 1967.
The Oklahoman, November 30, 1967.
The Oklahoman, December 1, 1967.
The Oklahoman, December 2, 1967.
The Oklahoman, December 6, 1967.
The Oklahoman, December 8, 1967.
The Oklahoman, December 9, 1967.
The Oklahoman, December 10, 1967.
The Oklahoman, February 27, 1968.
The Oklahoman, December 6, 1968.
The Oklahoman, December 8, 1969.
The Oklahoman, October 29, 1970.
The Oklahoman, May 18, 1972.
The Oklahoman, December 15, 1972.
The Oklahoman, December 9, 1976.
The Oklahoman, September 5, 1982.
The Oklahoman, December 13, 1982.
The Oklahoman, March 13, 1987.
The Oklahoman, March 21, 1987.
The Oklahoman, March 22, 1987.
The Oklahoman, November 22, 1987.
The Oklahoman, December 7, 2008.
The Oklahoma Journal, December 12, 1969.
The (Syracuse) *Port-Standard*, March 24, 1987.
The Portland Reporter, October 1962.
The Rapid City (South Dakota) *Journal*, June 30, 2015.
The Stars and Stripes, May 2, 1945.
The Torrington (Wyoming) *Telegram*, November 28, 1912.
The Torrington (Wyoming) *Telegram*, December 12, 1912.
The Torrington (Wyoming) *Telegram*, July 3, 1913.
The Torrington (Wyoming) *Telegram*, June 20, 1920.
The Torrington (Wyoming) *Telegram*, October 7, 1920.
The Torrington (Wyoming) *Telegram*, November 3, 1921.
The Torrington (Wyoming) *Telegram*, August 31, 1922.
The Wheatland (Wyoming) *Times*, December 5, 1917.
The Tucson Daily Star, May 3, 1940.

The Tucson Daily Star, November 3, 1955.
The Tulsa World, July 31, 1989.
The (Enid, Oklahoma) *Morning News*, December 12, 1972.
Tri-State Livestock (Belle Fourche, South Dakota) *News*, July 16, 2015.
Park County Enterprise, December 9, 1911.

Articles

Armstrong, Jerry. "Picked Up In The Rodeo Arena," *Western Horseman* (January 1963).

Berry, Jo. "Freckles is still winning," *ProRodeo Sports News*, August 10, 1983.

Brown, Barbara J. "The Bull Riding Stylist," *Western Horseman* (July 1981).

"Building A Better Bull," *Rodeo Sports News*, July 10, 1996.

"Clive Runnells, Jr.," *The Cattleman Magazine* (July 2019).

Dean, Ernie. " 'Suicide Circuit' Pays Off for 'Freckles' Brown," *Arkansas Gazette*, October 11, 1960.

"Durable Freckles Brown Wins On Deadwood's Tough Bulls," *Hoofs and Horns* (October 1962).

"Evans, Thomas. "Spymaster General," *Vanity Fair* (March 2011).

"Freckles Brown Is Back In The Lead," *Rodeo Sports News*, August 15, 1962.

"Freckles Brown Q&A," *Hoofs and Horns* (October 1963).

"Freckles Brown Badly Hurt In Bull Riding," *Rodeo Sports News*, November 1, 1962.

"Freckles Triumphs Against Tornado," *ProRodeo Sports News*, July 1, 1998.

"From the Top of This Hill: An Interview with Freckles Brown," *Hoofs and Horns* (September 1969).

Hein, Rebecca. "Horses of War: A Market for Wyoming Stockmen," *WyoHistory.Org* (March 2016).

Izenberg, Jerry. "Look What's Happened to Rodeo!" *True, The Man's Magazine* (August 1968).

Kelly, Loudon. "Champion Of The Suicide Circuit," *Hoofs and Horns* (June 1959).

King, Chuck. "Those Snyder Horses," *Western Horseman*, (October 1991).

– "Riding the Rimrock," *Western Horseman* (January 1966).

Krakel, Dean. "Requiem To A Bull," *Persimmon Hill*, v. 9, no. 1, 1973.

Ladd, Ted, comp. "A History of Sunlight Valley: A Tributary of Clark's Fork Creek, Park County, Wyoming," Park County Historical Society. Undated.

Larsen, Cheryl Leverton. "Bobby Berger, Descent and the Black Hills Roundup," *Tri-State Livestock News*, July 16, 2015.

Lawson, Jay. "Home on the Range," *Wyoming Wildlife* (December 2006).

McCall, Richard. "Brownie, You're Quite A Guy…," *Rodeo Sports News* (August 1, 1969).

McCormick, David. "Carry on Horse, Mules Kept Army Moving," *Army*, v. 72, no. 8, 2020.

Nickerson, Gregory. "The Burlington Railroad: Wyoming's Second Transcontinental Railroad," *WyoHistory.org* (November 2014).

1961 Rodeo Annual, *Rodeo Sports News*.

1962 Rodeo Annual, *Rodeo Sports News*.
1963 Rodeo Annual, *Rodeo Sports News*.
"One of Rode's Greatest Moments," *Persimmon Hill*, v. 10, no. 1, 1980.
"You Don't Forget A Guy Like Freckles Brown," *The Ketch Pen* (August 1989).
Porter, Willard H. "Freckles Rides 'Em Rough," *Hoofs and Horns* (February 1953).
– "Freckles: A tribute to one of the best-liked rodeo cowboys of all-time, the famous Freckles Brown, who died on March 20 at age 66," *Western Horseman* (June 1987).
– "In an Exclusive Hoofs and Horns Interview, Freckles Brown, World's Champion Bull Rider from Lawton, Oklahoma, Discusses the Wreck That Injured him Last October, His Convalescent Months, and His Decision to Ride Again …" *Hoofs and Horns* (October 1963).
Reid, Neal. "The legend of legends: Shoulders' death leaves lasting legacy, but also void in ProRodeo world," *ProRodeo Sports News*, July 4, 2007.
Santos, Kendra. "Dightman still smiling, still riding," *ProRodeo Sports News*, March 20, 1991.
Sawyer, John G. "Born Daredevils: The Bull Riders," *The Ketch Pen* (Summer 1994).
"Southeastern Oklahoma – Soper," *Strum's Oklahoma Magazine*, v. 5, no. 2 (June 1912).
"Standings Show Close Title Race," *Rodeo Sports News*, August 15, 1962.
Stratton, W.K. "Sitting Atop A Tornado," *Sports Illustrated*, May 25, 1987.
Toohey, John. "Rodeo Hands Facing Rising Costs," *Hoofs and Horns* (March 1967)
Wallace, Christian. "The Jackie Robinson of Rodeo," *Texas Monthly* (July 2018).
Wallis, Michael. "Freckles," *Oklahoma Today* (March-April 1985).
White, Kristen M. "Riding into history," *ProRodeo Sports News*, March 15, 2006.
Witte, Randy. "Ol' Freck just goes on and on …" *Rodeo Sports News*, June 1, 1974.
Zimmer, Vickie. "Goshen County, Wyoming," *WyoHistory.org* (November 2014).

Interviews

Bobby Berger telephone interview with author, Pearsall, Texas, May 30, 2020.
C.R. Boucher telephone interview with author, Pryor, Montana, June 26, 2020.
Judy Bowman interview with author, Calera, Oklahoma, February 8, 2020.
Ronnie Bowman interview with author, Calera, Oklahoma, February 8, 2020.
Ronnie Bowman telephone interview with author, Calera, Oklahoma, March 30, 2023.

Ferrell Butler telephone interview with author, Red Oak, Oklahoma, September 10, 2009.

Ferrell Butler telephone interview with author, Ringold, Oklahoma June 19, 2020.

Ferrell Butler telephone interview with author, Ringold, Oklahoma, June 25, 2020.

Ferrell Butler interview with author and Tristan Jackson, Ringold, Oklahoma, June 29, 2021.

Ferrell Butler telephone interview with author, Ringold, Oklahoma, April 2, 2023.

Ferrell Butler telephone interview with author, Ringold, Oklahoma, July 16, 2023.

Larry Dawson interview with author, Packsaddle, Oklahoma, March 22, 2023.

Myrtis Dightman, Jr. interview with author, Houston, Texas, December 20, 2018.

Myrtis Dightman, Sr. interview with author, Houston, Texas, December 20, 2018.

Wiley Harrison interview with author, Calera, Oklahoma, February 8, 2020.

Wiley Harrison interview with author, Soper, Oklahoma, July 6, 2021.

Wiley Harrison telephone interview with author, Soper, Oklahoma, January 21, 2023.

Wiley Harrison telephone interview with author, Soper, Oklahoma, July 22, 2023.

Wiley Harrison telephone interview with author, Soper, Oklahoma, August 13, 2023.

Chuck Houy and Connie Whippo interview with author, Sabino Canyon Recreational Area, Coronado National Forest, Tucson, Arizona, February 28, 2023.

Bill Kornell telephone interview with author, Rio Rico, Arizona, June 19, 2020.

Sue (Snyder) LaFever interview with author, Sunlight Basin, Park County, Wyoming, September 13, 2022.

Sue (Snyder) LaFever telephone interview with author, September 18, 2022.

Harold Leftwich telephone interview with author, Calera, Oklahoma, June 25, 2020.

Bill L. Olsen telephone interview with author, Houston, Texas, October 27, 2021.

Jim Prather telephone interview with author, Fredericksburg, Texas, May 30, 2020.

Dollie Riddle telephone interview with author, Vernon, Texas, June 18, 2020 & June 23, 2020.

Vickie Shireman telephone interview with author, Elk City, Oklahoma, June 26, 2020.

Marvin Paul Shoulders interview with author, Henryetta, Oklahoma,

January 16, 2020.
Red Steagall telephone interview with author, Fort Worth, Texas, July 1, 2020.
Bob Thedford telephone interview with author, Enid, Oklahoma, June 23, 2020.

Secondary Sources
Books and Pamphlets

Bales, Michael and Ann Terry Hill. *Pendleton Round-Up at 100: Oregon's Legendary Rodeo*. Portland, Oregon: Graphic Arts Books, 2009.

Bay City Story. Bay City, Texas: Bay City Chamber of Commerce, 1957.

Blackburn, Bob and Paul B. Strasbaugh. *A History of the State Fair of Oklahoma*. Oklahoma City: Western Heritage Books, 1994.

Blackburn, Jim. *The Books of Texas Bays*. College Station, Texas: Texas A&M University Press, 2004.

Chamber III, John Whiteclay. *OSS Training in the National Parks and Service Abroad in World War II*.

Chamblin, Thomas S., ed. *The Historical Encyclopedia of Wyoming*, v. 2. Wyoming: Wyoming Historical Institute, 1970.

Debo, Angie. *Geronimo*. Norman, Oklahoma: University of Oklahoma Press, 1976.

Harte, John Bret. *Tucson: Portrait of a Desert Pueblo*. Tucson, Arizona: Tucson Metropolitan Chamber of Commerce, 1980.

Historical Matagorda County, 3 vols. Matagorda County Book Committee, comp. Houston: D. Armstrong Co., Inc., 1986-1989.

Hogan, Jr., David W. *U.S. Army Special Operations in World War II*. Center of Military History, 1992.

Hyde, Robert M. *Range Survey on Sunlight Basin, Park County, Wyoming*, 1937.

Kahn, Margot. *Horses That Buck: The Story of Champion Bronc Rider Bill Smith*. Norman: University of Oklahoma Press, 2011.

Katz, Barry M. *Foreign Intelligence: Research and Analysis in the Office of Strategic Services, 1942-1945*. Cambridge, Mass: Harvard University Press, 1989.

Klump, Kathy and Peta-Anne Tennsey. *Images of America Willcox*. Charleston, South Carolina: Arcadia Publishing, 2009.

Lazaroff, David Wentworth. *Sabino Canyon: The Life of a Southwestern Oasis*. Tucson: University of Arizona, 1993.

Lockwood, Frank C. *Tucson: The Old Pueblo*. Phoenix: The Manufacturing Stationers, Inc., 1930.

Opler, Morris E. *An Apache Life-Way*. Chicago: University of Chicago Press, 1941.

Ruskowsky, Nancy Heyl. *Two Dot Ranch: A Biography of a Place*. Greybull, Wyoming: Pronghorn Press, 2008.

Schultz, Vernon B. *Southwestern Town: The Story of Willcox, Arizona*. Tucson: The Board of Regents of the Universities and State Colleges of Arizona, 1980.

Centennial edition. Originally published in 1964.

Schellie, Don. *The Tucson Citizen: A Century of Arizona Journalism*. Tucson, Arizona: Tucson Daily Citizen, 1970.

Smith, R Harris. *OSS: The Secret History of America's First Central Intelligence Agency*. Berkeley, California: University of California Press, 1972.

Sonnichsen, Charles L. *Tucson, the Life and Times of an American City*. Norman, Oklahoma: University of Oklahoma Press, 1987.

Southern Arizona Bank & Trust. *Fifty Years of Growth, 1903-1953*. Tucson, Arizona: Southern Arizona Bank & Trust, 1953.

Stieghorst, Junann J. *Bay City and Matagorda County: A History*. Austin: Pemberton Press, 1965.

Warren, Christopher Miles. *Ernest Hemingway in the Yellowstone High Country*. Helena, Montana: Riverbend Publishing, 2019.

Wilcoxson, Billy. *The CB Cowboys: The Saga of the Legendary Christensen Family*. Austin, Texas: Sunbelt Eakin, 2003.

Witte, Randy. *A History of Western Horseman: 75 Years of the World's Leading Horse Magazine*.

Woerner, Gail Hughbanks. *Cowboy Up: The History of Bull Riding*. Austin, Texas: Eakin Press, 2001.

Yu, Maochun. *OSS in China: Prelude to the Cold War*. New Haven. Conn.: Yale University Press, 1996.

Articles

Annals of Wyoming, Index, 1925-1942.

Asay, Paul. "Building a Better Bull," *Rodeo Sports News*, July 10, 1996.

Bonner, Robert E. "Town Founder and Irrigation Tycoon: The Buffalo Bill Nobody Knows," *WyoHistory.org* (October 2015).

Cassity, Michael. "Wyoming Will Be Your New Home: Ranching, Farming and Homesteading in Wyoming, 1860-1960." Cheyenne, Wyoming: Wyoming State Preservation Office, 2011.

Cavaliere, Bill. "Geronimo's Final Surrender," *Wild West* (August 2021).

Clayton, John. "The Old West's Female Champion: Caroline Lockhart and Wyoming's Cowboy Heritage," *WyoHistory.org* (November 2014).

Duffy, John M. "Casey Tibbs: 'America's Most Beloved Cowboy,' *South Dakota History*, v. 32, no. 4 (Winter 2002).

Emmett, Chris. "Pierce, Abel Head [Shanghai]," *Handbook of Texas Online*, accessed July 19, 2023, https://www.tshaonline.org/handbook/entries/pierce-abel-head-shanghai.

Haskett, Bert. "Early History of the Cattle Industry in Arizona," *Arizona Historical Review*, v. 6, no. 4 (October 1935).

Hawkins, C.E. "The American Remount Association," *Cavalry Journal*, v. 30, no. 123 (April 1921).

Hein, Rebecca. "Horses of War: A Market for Wyoming Stockmen," WyoHistory.Org (March 2016).

Jackson, Jr., Ron J. "The Parting: In 1913 the freed Apache prisoners of

'Geronimo's band' had to choose whether to remain in Oklahoma or move to a reservation in New Mexico," *Wild West* (August 2021).

Klump, Kathy. "Livestock Auctions," *Currents* (July/August 2022).

Moran, Eugene V. "Ernest Hemingway in the Sunlight Basin of Wyoming," *Annals of Wyoming 77* (Winter 2005).

Pointer, Larry. "Freckles vs. Tornado: one ride the NFR will never forget," *World of Rodeo and Western Heritage* (December 1979).

Santos, Kendra. "Friends relived days with Casey Tibbs," *ProRodeo Sports News*, February 21, 1960.

Thomas, Evans. "Spymaster General," *Vanity Fair* (March 2011).

Worden, Darla. "Hemingway's Wyoming: 'A Cockeyed Wonderful Country," *Big Sky Journal* (February 2016).

Online

Familysearch.org
Missouri Marriage Records (1800-1901)
Warren Granger Brown, World War II Draft Registration Cards, 1940-1945.
www.lanefrost.com.

Theses

Hyde, Robert M. *Vegetation in the Sunlight Basin, Park County, Wyoming*. University of Oklahoma, 1964.

Norris, Frank B. *The Southern Arizona Guest Ranch as a Symbol of the West*, Tucson, Arizona, 1976.

Schultz, Vernon B. *A History of Wilcox, Arizona, and Environs*. University of Arizona, Tucson, 1957.

Index

Symbols
1st Special Forces Group 100
24th Annual World Championship Rodeo 109
100 (bull) 140

A
Abbie, Hank 159, 164
Abilene, Texas 40, 138
Absaroka Mountains 47, 67
Ace in the Hole (horse) 89
Akers, Ira 145
Albuquerque, N.M. 127
Altizer, Jim Bob 163, 168
American Hat Company 202
American Magazine 25
Apache (Native American tribe) 30
Apache, Okla. 138
Arizona Historical Society 224, 256
Arizona 31
Arizona Polo Association 31
Arizona Range News 38, 234, 235, 259
Arizona Star 36
Arizona (state of) 4, 7, 21, 29-31, 34, 36, 38, 40, 42, 46-48, 53, 55, 68, 81, 86, 91, 94, 107, 123, 141, 203, 224-225, 232, 233-235, 240, 242, 256, 258- 260, 264-267
Arizona Territory 30
Arkansas Live Stock Show 89
Arkansas (state of) 89, 114, 127, 143, 147, 243, 260, 262
Arthur, Jean 31
Asia 100
Astor Expedition 10
Atoka, Okla. 207
Autry, Gene 109
Axis powers 98

B
Baker, Ross E. 16
Battiest, Okla. 136
Bay City, Texas 152, 265
Bear Canyon 24
Beauvais, Brian 225, 236
Bebes and the Bear: Gene Stallings, Coach Bryant, and Their 1968 Cotton Bowl Showdown 8, 229
Belle Fourche, S.D. 109, 148, 262
Bellmon, Henry Gov. 214
Benson Highway 31
Berger, Bobby 9, 146-148, 160, 195, 227, 247, 256-257, 262-263
Berlin, Germany 98
Beutler and Brothers Rodeo Co. 159
Beutler, Elra 139
Beutler, Jiggs 139
Beutler, Una 176, 226
Big Bad John (bull) 166, 183
Bighorn Basin 47
Billings, Mont. 59, 183
Bisbee, Ariz. 38
Black Hills Roundup 109, 148, 247, 262
Black Smoke (bull) 123, 125, 127-131, 133, 135, 139
Bobby Berger's Basic Bullriding: A Fundamental Instruction Manual 148
Bockscar (bull) 104
Boggs, Frank 150, 164, 186, 187, 214
Boucher, C.R. 3, 170, 227, 263
Bowman, Ronnie 4, 164, 177, 227, 230, 249, 263
Boy Scouts of America 17
Bozeman Trail 10
Braten, Wilkie 191
Bridger, Jim 10
Broadus, Mont. 120
Bronze Campaign Star 104

Index

Brooks, Oregon 147
Brown, Bryson 14-15, 22, 33-34, 43, 44-45
Brown, Donna 106-107, 132-133, 142, 144
Brown, Donna Lucretia 93, 104
Brown, Doug 191, 252
Brown, Edith 84-87, 89-93, 97-102, 104, 106, 110-112, 130-132, 134, 137, 138, 142, 144, 150, 168-169, 177-178, 192, 202, 210-213, 215-216, 220, 240-242, 257, 258
Brown, Ella 15, 26
Brown, Lillian 15
Brown, Lucretia 10, 13, 21, 93, 240, 257-258
Brown, Lucretia Wilson 12
Brown, Mable 58
Brown, Mildred 15
Brown, Molly 142
Brown, Orpha 15
Brown, Parson 14-15
Brown, Richard 10, 13-16, 19, 20, 21
Brown, Richard Granger 11-12
Brown, Richard Jr. 15
Brown, Warren Granger "Freckles" 2-9, 12, 21, 23, 25, 27-29, 31-58, 64-68, 70-71, 73-94, 96-114, 118-145, 147-151, 163-186, 190-222, 224-228, 230-233, 235-236, 237, 239-247, 249-258, 262-263, 267
Bruce, Col. David K.E. 95
Buffalo Bill's Wild West Show 71, 76
Burlington Railroad 11-12, 231, 262
Burwell, Neb. 147
Bushyhead, Okla. 165
Butler, Ferrell 2-3, 118, 121, 144-147, 152, 156-158, 165, 170, 173-176, 182, 227-228, 230, 247-251, 264

C

Calgary, AB. 149
California Polytechnic State University, San Luis Obispo 147
California (state of) 10, 17, 34, 124, 147, 159, 186, 191, 226, 232, 266
California Trail 10
Camdenton, Mo. 137
Capital Hill Rodeo 103
Carlsbad, N.M. 111
Carrillo, Don Emilio 35
Carroll, Howard 159
Casper, Wyo. 82, 126
Cathey, James 109, 242
CBS Radio 82
Central Intelligence Agency 95, 266
Chambers, Bob 208
Charles, Jim 159, 186, 256
Chelsea, Okla. 214
Cheyenne Frontier Days 124, 125, 147, 191, 221
Cheyenne, Okla. 86, 90
Chickasha, Okla. 92, 112
China-Burma-India Theatre 97-98
China (country of) 94, 97-98, 100-101, 103-104, 123, 241, 266
China Offensive Campaign 104
Chiricahua Apache 30, 36
Chiricahua Mountains 36
Chiricahua Regional Museum and Research Center 225
Choctaw County, Okla. 136
Choctaw Nation 136
Christensen Brothers 127
Cimarron Ranch 117
Clarksville, Texas 147
Clark, S.W. 41
Cochise County, Ariz. 38, 258
Cody Canal 60, 237
Cody Enterprise,The 69, 71, 77, 81, 238-239, 260
Cody Pup Rodeo 73
Cody Stampede 70-74, 78-81, 142, 239, 258
Cody Stampede Association 70, 72-73
Cody Trading Company 76
Cody, William F. "Buffalo Bill" 48-59, 61, 71-73, 76, 237-238, 257, 266
Cody, Wyo. 43, 47-49, 53, 59-62, 69, 71, 74-76, 107, 207, 225, 232, 236-239, 257-258, 261

Coleman, Texas 138
Colorado County, Texas 152
Colorado Life 229
Colorado Springs Gazette-Telegraph 119
Colorado (state of) 9, 119, 152, 164, 229, 245, 260
Columbia Pictures 31, 234
Colvin, Bob 185
Comanche (Native American tribe) 136, 148
Conroe, Texas 202
Copenhaver, Deb. 115
Coryell County, Texas 32, 234, 259
Cowboys' Turtle Association 6
Cow Palace 124, 127
Crockett, Texas 164, 195, 211
Crow Indian Agency 73
Crow Indian Reservation 60
Crow (Native American tribe) 78
Crump, Pete 125, 126
Cummings, Gene 156, 157

D

Dallas County, Texas 155
Dallas Power and Light 147
Dallas State Fair Coliseum 121
Dallas, Texas 113, 114, 120-122, 127, 145, 147, 155, 191
Daly City, Calif. 124
Darnell, Fred 39
Davidson, Okla. 145
Dawson, Larry 184, 227, 264
D-Day 95
Dead Indian Creek 74
Dead Indian Mountain 62-63, 67, 74
Dead Indian Pass 61, 74
Deadwood, S.D. 126, 244, 262
Deane, Ernie 105, 114
Denver Bob 35
Denver, Colo. 31, 34-35, 132, 197, 258
Depression, The Great 1, 6, 7, 19, 21-22, 33-34, 36, 42, 46, 52, 114, 139, 225, 232, 259
Descent (horse) 148, 247, 256, 262
Dewey, Okla. 158
Diamond Jubilee of the Pony Express 17

Dickinson Research Center 4, 90, 116, 124-125, 128, 132, 139, 155, 157, 161, 189, 194, 201, 224, 230, 240, 242-243, 245, 247-249, 251-253, 256
Dightman, Jr., Myrtis 194, 252, 264
Dightman, Myrtis 9, 149, 158, 193, 194-196, 211, 227, 248, 252-253, 256, 263-264
Disney, Walt 4
Dobbins, Carlina 112
Dobbins, Mabel 112
Donovan, Maj. Gen William Joseph "Wild Bill" 95, 104
Dos Cabezas Mountains 36, 39, 42
Doubleday, Ralph R. 89-90
Downing, Carl 73
Dragoon, Ariz. 38
Dragoon Mountains 36, 39
Dude Ranchers Association, The 30
Durant, Okla. 164
Durnen, Bill 70
Dyer, John 23

E

Egypt 24, 98, 99, 231, 241
El Conquistador Hotel 31
Elk City, Okla. 159, 248, 250, 264
Elk Creek 64, 74
El Paso, Texas 34
Emergency Relief Administration 25
Emmanuel Hospital 129
Empire of Japan 82, 104
Englewood, Colo. 35
Enola Gay 104
Entrance Celebration 72
Ephrata, Wash. 11
Esperero Canyon 24
Europe 69, 94, 95, 98

F

Farmers Home Administration 137
Fiesta de los Vaqueros 31
Fight to the Finish: "Gentleman" Jim Corbett, Joe Choynski, and the Fight that Launched Boxing's Modern Era 8, 229
Five Minutes to Midnight (horse) 89-90

Flagstaff, Ariz. 86
Fletcher, Lloyd 31
Fletcher, Stanley "Buck" 31-32, 43, 45-46, 233
Flying High (horse) 87
Fort George G. Meade, Md. 96
Fort Laramie, Wyo. 10-12, 18
Fort Lowell, Ariz. 35
Fort Riley, Kan. 94, 100, 259
Fort Sill, Okla. 84-86, 88, 106, 136
Fort Worth, Texas 31, 109, 207, 212, 258, 265
Foster, Dr. Eugene 208
Freckles Brown (song) 1, 5, 7, 8, 9, 2, 8, 12, 79, 80, 81, 84, 89, 90, 105, 106, 119, 123, 126, 130, 132, 134, 141, 148, 150, 165, 172, 174, 175, 179, 182, 191, 195, 197, 198, 199, 201, 214, 217, 218, 221, 222, 224, 227, 230, 231, 244, 245, 249, 251, 262, 263
Fremont, John C. 10
Frost, Clyde 207
Frost, Lane 207, 212, 218, 220
Funeral Wagon (horse) 191
Furnace Woods, N.Y. 117

G

Galiuro Mountains 30, 36
Gardner, Claude 41
Garstad, Gid 159
Garwood, Texas 152, 183
Gaudin, D.J. 145
Gay, Neal 104, 145-146, 155-156, 158, 248, 256, 257
Gene Lamb Collection 90
George, Bill 202
George, Billie 202
German Third Reich 98, 100
Germany 69
Geronimo 30, 36-37
Getzwiller, Pierre 41
Gilmer, Texas 208
Glover, David 159
Gone with the Wind 123, 191
Gordon, Ella (Brown) 203
Gordon, James "Shorty" 26-27, 203-204
Goshen County, Wyo. 9,-11, 13, 15, 20, 231, 258-259, 263
Grant, Bob 145
Great Britain 69
Great Depression, The 6-7, 21-22, 33-34, 36, 46, 114, 139, 225, 232, 259
Great Falls, Mont. 126
Green Acres, Wash. 125
Green Ridge, Mo. 11
Gregory, Edith (Brown) 84, 90, 92, 240
Grima, Andy 226
Grima, Jeep 226
Grima, Larriann 226
Guernsey Gazette 11, 231
Guernsey, Wyo. 11, 12
Guthrie, Okla. 177

H

Harrison-Brown Family 12, 86, 88, 103, 109, 138, 143, 144, 203-205, 212, 257
Harrison, Donna (Brown) 93, 98, 104, 106-107, 130, 132-133, 138, 142, 144, 168-169, 177, 192, 210-212, 214, 215-216
Harrison, John 217
Harrison, Wiley 133, 137-138, 165, 168-169, 177, 202-204, 206, 209-212, 214-216, 227, 230, 233, 249, 254, 264
Hartville, Wyo. 12
Harvey, Paul 181-183
Hawaiian Islands 82
Heinz, W.C. 28, 179-180, 230-246, 250, 252, 258
Helfrich, DeVere 4, 89, 116, 124, 125, 128, 132, 139, 155, 194
Hemingway, Ernest 56, 163, 266-267
Hemingway, Pauline 57
Henryetta Chamber of Commerce 160, 188, 189
Henryetta, Okla. 156, 160, 186, 188-189, 248, 252, 260, 264
Henson, Chuck 170
Hiroshima, Japan 104
History Channel 229
Hitler, Adolph 69, 98

Holberg, Sally 47-48, 50-51, 54, 56, 58, 232, 237, 226, 232, 237, 258
Holden, William 31
Holds-the-Enemy, Al 73, 78, 80
Holiday Inn West 179
Honey (horse) 40
Hoofs and Horns 89, 233, 234-235, 239-240, 244-246, 256, 259, 262-263
Hooker, Col. Henry C. 30, 37
Houston Astrodome 206
Houston, Texas 154, 200-202, 206, 209, 211-213, 216, 248, 252, 264-265
Houy, Chuck 225, 234, 264
Huckaby, Billy 227
Hudson River 117
Hugo, Okla. 136, 196, 206, 218, 246
Hunt, Wilson Price 10
Hyattville, Wyo. 77

I

India (country of) 96-100, 241
Indianola, Texas 154
Indian Territory 136
Inman, Hoss 183
Irma Hotel 61, 71
Isom, Charles Bernard 69
Ivory, Buster 169
Ivory, June 169
Izenberg, Jerry 178, 247

J

Jackson, Harry 214
Jackson, Jr., Ron J. 1, 229, 233
James, Will 16
Japan 82, 98, 104, 245
J Lazy S Ranch 156
Joe the Slave Who Became an Alamo Legend 229
Johnson, H.A. "Hackberry Slim" 41
Jordan, Andy 107

K

Kelly Bend Ranch 9, 137, 142, 213, 215
Kencke, John Ward 69
Kiamichi Mountains 142
King, Chuck 52, 67, 103, 226, 236, 242, 256

Kiowa (Native American tribe) 136
Klamath Falls, Ore. 89
Klump, Kathy 225, 235
Knight, Harry 120, 121, 164
Kornell, Bill 9, 147, 227, 247, 256, 264
Kosinski, Stanley H. 94, 240-241
Krakel, Dean 7, 188
Kunming, China 100-104

L

LaFever, Sue (Snyder) 47- 48, 50- 51, 54, 56, 58, 232, 236-238, 258, 264
LaFollette-Costigan Committee 23
LaGrand, Buck 170
La Grande, Ore. 43
LaGuardia Airport 98, 104
Landres-et-St. Georges, France 95
Laramie Boots 206
Laramie County, Wyo. 12
Las Vegas, Nev. 214
Lawton, Okla. 85-86, 88, 92-93, 97, 106-107, 109, 112, 123-124, 126, 132, 136, 142, 242, 244, 259, 263
Leftwich, Harold 159, 172, 227, 248, 264
Levi (bull) 116
Life 115
Lingle, Hiram D. 13
Lingle Review 13
Lingle Supply Company 13
Lingle, Wyo. 11, 13, 15, 18-20, 22, 231
Little Blue (horse) 111
Little Brown Jug (horse) 56-57
Little Rock, Ark. 89
Lively, Eva 226, 234, 257
Lockhart, Caroline 71, 239, 266
Lockhart, Catherine 72
Logan, Pete 169, 172, 256
London Flats, Wyo. 9, 11, 13, 15, 17, 19, 68
Lone Cowboy: My Life Story 16
Longview, Texas 35
Los Angeles, Calif. 126, 131, 159
Louisiana (state of) 147, 153
Louks, Wayne 87-88

M

Madison Square Garden 109, 111, 117, 123, 136
Madland, Donna 130
Madland, Ken 130
Mahan, Larry 147-149, 167, 184-185, 195, 247, 256
Maley, Ariz. 36
Marquette Creek 59, 60
Martin, George "Tex" 140
Martin, Laura 224
Matagorda Bay 154
Matagorda County, Texas 154, 265-266
Maui No Ka Oi 229
McAlester, Okla. 214, 218
McEntire, Reba 200
McMinn, John Hulon 32, 43, 55, 94, 225-226
McMinn, Ray 33
McMinn, Weston 33
McSpadden, Clem 164-167, 177-178, 191, 197-201, 208, 212-215, 218-219, 249, 254, 256, 257
MD Anderson Cancer Center 201, 208
Medal of Honor 95
Meeteetse, Wyo. 69
Memphis, Tenn. 171
Mesquite Championship Rodeo 145, 155
Mesquite, Texas 145-146, 155, 156, 158
Mexico 36, 48
Meyers, C.L. 22
Miami, Okla. 166, 186
Midnight (horse) 188
Miller, Harriet Huntington (McMinn) 33
Misenhimer, J.L. "Tab" 39
Mission Ridge, S.D. 114
Missouri River 9, 231, 258
Missouri (state of) 9-11, 17, 137, 228, 231, 258, 267
Mitchell, Margaret 123
Mitchell, Neb. 19, 20
Mixer, Orren 161
Molesworth, Thomas 49, 236
Mongolia (country of) 96
Montana (state of) 3, 59, 73, 120, 126, 170, 183, 258, 263, 266
Moore, Capt. W.R. 96
Mormon Trail 10
Mount Graham 39
Mount Lemmon 33
Mount Olivet Cemetery 218, 220
Mt. Lemmon 24
Muddy Boggy Creek 137, 204, 213

N

Nafzger, Carl 159
Nagasaki, Japan 104
Nashville, Tenn. 196, 197
National Anthem 192, 200
National Cowboy Hall of Fame and Western Heritage Center 4, 90, 116, 124-125, 128, 132, 139, 155, 157, 161, 188-189, 194, 201, 209, 256
National Finals Rodeo 1, 113, 120-121, 126, 131, 146, 149-150, 159, 160, 163, 165, 174, 179, 190, 194, 196, 199, 208, 214, 217, 221-222, 230, 248-251, 258
National Old Timers Rodeo Assn. 121
Nazi Germany 69
Nebraska Life 229
Nebraska (state of) 9, 12, 15, 19-20, 59, 109, 127, 147, 229
Never a Day Goes By 91
New Deal 22
New Mexico (state of) 30, 34, 48, 127, 2   33, 258, 267
New York City, N.Y. 98, 104, 109, 123
New York Times, The 95, 249, 253, 260-261
New York Zoological Park 106
Nile River Valley 24
Nitro (bull) 121
No Doze (bull) 120
Nogales, Ariz. 42
Normandy, France 94
North Dakota (state of) 62
North Platte River 9-13, 15-17
Northport, Neb. 12
Nortier, Nicole 226

O

Oahu, Hawaii. 83
Oakdale, Calif. 186
O'Connell, Helen 91
Odessa, Texas 111
Office of Strategic Services (OSS) 9-101, 240, 241, 257-258, 265-266
Oklahoma City, Oklahoma 1, 7, 103, 127, 163, 167-168, 177-179, 182, 186, 188, 190, 196, 199, 207-209, 214, 224, 227, 230, 240, 243, 245, 247-253, 256-258, 261, 265
Oklahoma Historical Society 224, 231, 257
Oklahoma State Fairgrounds 163

Oklahoma (state of) 1, 4, 7, 85-88, 90, 92, 101, 103-106, 109, 112, 116, 120, 121, 126-127, 136, 138, 142, 145, 147, 150, 156, 158-160, 163-168, 177-184, 186-188, 190, 195-196, 199-200, 203, 207- 209, 214, 216-217, 220-221, 224, 226-228, 230-231, 233-235, 240-267
Old Pueblo (Tucson, Ariz.) 24, 265
Omaha, Neb. 109, 127
Once They Heard the Cheers 28, 179, 230-250, 252, 258
Oregon (state of) 10-11, 17, 43-44, 47, 89, 123, 127, 130, 147, 149, 208, 254, 265
Oregon Trail 10-11, 17
Oregon Trail Memorial Association 17
Osborne, Sam 76

P

Pacific International Rodeo 127
Pacific Northwest 43
Pacific Ocean 22, 38, 43, 83, 85, 127, 158
Pacific Theatre 85, 158
Packsaddle, Okla. 184, 264
Page and Misenhimer Cattle Co. 39
Page, Gordon Winfield "Boozer" 39

Painter, Mary 62
Painter Ranch 62-63
Painter, William 62
Palm Springs, Calif. 147
Paris, Texas 210
Park County Archives 225, 236-239, 257
Park County Enterprise, The 71, 262
Park County, Wyo. 62, 69, 71, 225, 236- 239, 242, 257, 258, 262, 264-265, 267
Pat O'Hara Creek 75
Paul, George 177, 184, 256
Pearl Harbor 82
Pearson, Harold Edward 69
Peekskill, N.Y. 117
Pendleton, Ore. 44, 47-48, 123, 127, 208, 254, 265
Pendleton Round-Up 123, 208, 254, 265
Pete (dog) 203
Peth, Wick 121
Pettis County, Mo. 11, 231
Pettys, Ora (Snyder) 61
Philosophical Society of Texas Award of Merit 229
Phoenix, Ariz. 4, 89-90, 134-135, 137, 139, 141, 143, 145, 147, 149, 151, 235, 265
Phoenix World's Championship Rodeo 89
Pierce, Abel Head "Shanghai" 154
Pierce Estate Ranch 154
Pikes Peak or Bust Rodeo 119
Pima County, Ariz. 33, 233-234, 240, 242, 258
Pinaleno Mountains 30, 36
Pine Bluff, Ark. 127
Pioneer Hotel 203
Pitchfork, Wyo. 69
Platte County, Wyo. 12
Pleasant Mound, Texas 145
Ponca City, Okla. 120
Pond Creek, Okla. 105
Pony Express 10, 17, 214
Pony Express II 214
Porter, Willard H. 21, 111, 140, 193, 217, 231, 244
Portland, Ore. 127, 129-131, 135, 254, 261, 265

Post, Wiley 165
Powell, Wyo. 69, 77
Professional Rodeo Cowboys Association 6, 197
ProRodeo Hall of Fame 146, 221
ProRodeo Sports News 117, 209, 240, 242-243, 251-252, 260, 262-263, 267
Pruett, Gene 146
Public Works Administration 22
Pyle, Perri 224

Q

Quanah, Texas 31
Quintana, John 186

R

Ranger, Texas 32
Rattlesnake Canyon 24, 234
Reclamation Act of 1902 12
Red Cross 102
Red River 31, 136, 210
Reese, Jacquelyn 226
Reeves, Kim 226
Remount Service 31-32, 52, 54
Riddle, Dewey 70
Riddle, Dollie 226, 250, 264
Rincon Mountains 35
Rinestine, Bill 125-127, 130, 131
Rix, Al 41
RMS Titanic 142
Roberts, Ken 171
Roberts Ranch 39
Robinson, Bob 159
Robinson, Jackie 193- 194, 252, 263
Rock Island, Texas 152
Rocky Mountain Fur Company 10
Rocky Mountain Rendezvous 10
Rocky Mountains 149, 231, 258
Rodeo Association of America 71, 171
Rodeo Cowboys Association (RCA) 124, 136, 138, 147, 155, 186, 198, 235, 244
Rodeo Hall of Fame 209, 221
Rodeo Historical Society 190, 248, 256
Rodeo Sports News Annual 141

Rodeo Sports News 123, 126, 129, 132, 141, 146, 230, 244-245, 249, 252, 254, 256, 259-260, 262-263, 266
Rogers County, Okla. 165
Rogers, Will 165
Roosevelt, Pres. Franklin Delano 17, 22, 69, 82, 95
Rossen, Ronnie 120-122, 131
Rufe, Okla. 136
Runnells, Clive 154, 248, 262
Russell Creek 67

S

Sabino Canyon 24-25, 225, 232, 234, 256, 264-265
Sabino Canyon Dam and Recreation Area 25, 225, 234, 264
Sabino Creek 24
Sacramento, Calif. 17
Salinas, Calif. 191
Salt Peter (bull) 79
San Bernardino, Calif. 130
San Luis Obispo, Calif. 147
San Pedro River 38
Santa Catalina Mountains 24, 28, 33, 36
Say, Mary 63, 75
Schmitt, Ernest William 69
Schumacher, Jim 170
Scottsbluff Community College 15
Scudder, Pat 158, 167
Selective Training and Service Act 69
Seven (bull) 139
Seventy-Six Ranch 39, 235, 256
Sheppard, Bob 159
Sheridan, Texas 152
Shireman, Vickie 226, 264
Shoshone Irrigation Company 60, 237
Shoshone Mining District 61
Shoshone Reservoir 60
Shoshone River 59-61, 73, 76, 237
Shoulders, Jim 2, 8, 105-106, 116-118, 121, 137, 141, 145-146, 151, 154-156, 158-162, 166-167, 172, 176-177, 183-184, 186-191, 198, 201, 226-227, 230, 243, 248-249, 252, 256-257, 263-264

Shoulders, Marvin Paul 9, 154, 160, 162, 227, 248, 264
Shoulders, Sharon 226
Sidney, Iowa 140
Sierra Bonita Ranch 30
Skeleton Canyon 30
Skirvin Tower 168, 178
Slim (horse) 18
Smith, Jedediah 10
Smith, Red 3
Smoky the Cowhorse 16
Snow White and the Seven Dwarfs 5
Snyder, Catherine 62-64
Snyder, Cyrus 61
Snyder, Cyrus R. 59-60, 237
Snyder, Don 46, 51-58, 62-64, 68, 107-108, 183, 226, 232, 236-238, 242, 257
Snyder, Faye 51, 107
Snyder, Gladys 61
Snyder, Glen 60
Snyder, Harold 61
Snyder, Jack 62-64
Snyder, Loyd 60
Snyder, Mary Catherine 60, 63-64, 238
Snyder, Merrill 60
Snyder, Ora 48, 51, 236, 242, 257
Snyder, Perry 60
Snyder, Roy 60
Snyder, Sally 51, 58
Snyder, Simon 42-43, 45-47, 50-54, 56-57, 59-60, 62-64, 67, 70, 73, 81-83, 103, 109, 225, 236-239, 257
Sonoran Desert 21
Soper, Okla. 9, 137, 142, 165, 203, 205, 213-214, 217, 220, 228, 230, 246, 253-254, 263-264
Sorrel (horse) 78
South Dakota (state of) 109, 114, 126, 148, 207, 243, 261-262, 266
Southern Pacific Railroad 22, 38
South Fork of the Shoshone River 59-61
Sparring Mate (bull) 164
Spilman, Karen 224
Springdale, Ark. 143
Stafford Nite Hawks 41
Stanton, Ken 159

State Fair Arena 169, 183-184, 189, 192, 199, 207
St. Denis, Mr. 28
Steagall, Red 196, 198-199, 212, 222, 227, 236, 265
Steamboat Mountain 74
Steinbeck, John 1
Stetson Hat Co. 7
St. Joseph, Mo. 17
St. Mary's Hospital 25, 93
St. Paul, Ore. 149
Stratton, W.K. 177, 219, 230, 249
Sublette, Joel 159
Sulphur Springs Valley 30, 36-37, 39, 235, 258
Sunlight Basin, Wyo. 9, 43, 45, 47-48, 50, 61-63, 66, 70, 74-75, 81, 83, 94, 103, 183, 225, 236, 238, 257, 264-265, 267
Sunlight Creek 49, 51, 67, 74
Sunlight Ranch 4, 46, 47, 49, 51, 53, 55, 57, 59, 61, 63, 64-65, 67, 70, 73, 81-82, 103, 107, 225, 236, 238, 257
Sunrise, Wyo. 12
Syracuse, N.Y. 113

T

T4 Ranch 136
Takin' Care of Business (bull) 218
Tanque Verde, Ariz. 33, 35, 55, 256
Tanque Verde Ranch 35, 256
Taylor, Ernie 196, 256
Tennessee (state of) 197
TE Ranch 61, 77
Tescher, Jim 179
Texas Canyon 38
Texas Rodeo Cowboy Hall of Fame 202, 246
Texas Slim 35
Texas (state of) 31-35, 38, 40, 109, 111, 119, 121, 127, 138, 145-147, 152-155, 158, 164, 183-184, 195-196, 202, 207-208, 210, 229, 234, 246-248, 252, 258-259, 263-266
Tex M (bull) 183

Thanksgiving Day 131
The Cowboy's Prayer 166
The Daddy of Them All (Cheyenne
	Frontier Days Rodeo) 125
Thedford, Bob 173, 227, 250, 265
The Grapes of Wrath 1
The Oklahoman 7-8, 185, 199, 216, 218,
	226, 230, 232-233, 242-243,
	245, 247-255, 261
The Ride 7, 8, 9, 169, 171, 173, 175, 177,
	224, 226-227
Thompson, Claude 80
Tibbs, Casey 114-116, 118, 130, 243,
	256, 266-267
Tibbs, John 114
Tibet (country of) 100
Tiger (horse) 67, 68
Todd, Brown 153
Tombstone, Ariz. 40
Tompkins, Harry 116-118, 120, 137,
	145, 243, 256
Tornado 2-3, 7-8, 121, 145, 151-164,
	167-178, 181-191, 197, 199-200,
	206, 218-219, 222, 226-228,
	247-253, 255-256, 262-263, 267
Torrington, Wyo. 12, 231, 259, 261
Trent, Billie 213
Triangle Bar Ranch 61
Tucson, Ariz. 21-28, 30-31, 33-36,
	38, 42-43, 48-89, 92-93, 182,
	203, 224, 232-235, 240, 242,
	256, 258, 261-262, 264-267
Tucson Classified Directory 23, 232,
	258
Tucson Organized Charities 23
Tucumcari, N.M. 34
Tulsa, Okla. 105, 116, 181, 192, 255,
	262
Two Dot Ranch 63, 265

U

United States Army Field Artillery
	School 85
United States Forest Service 61-62
United States War Department 100,
	241
University of Oklahoma 214, 226, 233,
	258, 265-267
U.S. Army 31, 52, 54, 70, 83, 265
U.S. Military Academy 117
U.S. Weather Bureau 24
Utah Life 229

V

Vacaville, Calif. 226
Valley, Wyo. 61

W

Wadsworth, Gene 34
Walla Walla, Wash. 43
Walters, Alfred M. 75
Walter's Inn 75, 239
Washington, D.C. 231, 235, 240, 257,
	258
Washington (state of) 11, 13
Wayne, John 192
Webb, Claire 39
Webb, W.T. 39
Wegner, Bob 120-122, 159
Weinz, John 77
Western History Collections 226
Western Horseman 161, 193, 217, 226,
	231, 236, 239, 242-244, 262-
	263, 266
Western Writers of America 229
West Point, N.Y. 117
Wharton County, Texas 154
Wharton, Texas 154
Whatley, Todd 136-137, 142, 245-246,
	256
Wheatland, Wyo. 10-11, 261
Whippo, Connie 225, 234, 264
White, Lee 226
White Mountain 67
Wichita Mountains Wildlife Refuge
	106
Wild West 229
Willcox, Ariz. 4, 36, 68, 81, 123, 141,
	225, 234-235, 256, 259, 265
Willcox Community Center 41
Willcox, Gen. O.B. 36
Willcox Playa 37
Williams, "Big" John 152-153, 183

Wilson, Charles Banks 214
Wilson, Lucretia (Brown) 11-12
Winchester Mountains 36
Windsor, Mo. 11
Wood, Marty 172, 256
Wootan, J. Frank 38
World War I 85, 95
World War II 84-86, 95, 136, 158, 233, 240, 258, 265, 267
Wrangler 206
Wright, Harold Bell 25

Wyncote, Wyo. 11, 13
Wyoming (state of) 9- 12, 14, 20-22, 42-43, 45, 47, 59, 69, 77, 81-83, 87, 94, 103, 119, 124, 126, 141, 147, 183, 207, 218, 225, 231-232, 236-240, 257-267

Y

Yellowstone National Park 69, 72
Youth National Finals 207
Yunnan Province, China 100

More Ron J. Jackson, Jr. Titles From Wild Horse Media Group

Fight To The Finish
The Barge Battle of 1889: "Gentleman" Jim Corbett, Joe Choynski, and the Fight that Launched Boxing's Modern Era
By Ron J. Jackson, Jr.

This book salvages one of boxing's most legendary stories from the shadows of history — a clandestine, twenty-seven-round battle between San Francisco rivals "Gentleman" Jim Corbett and Joe Choynski on the deck of a grain barge. This gritty and colorful historical narrative chronicles the Corbett-Choynski blood feud and relives one of the most inspiring displays of determination, stamina, and courage in ring history. • 260 pages • 6 x 9 inches

Paperback ISBN 9781681791265 • Retail Price $22.99
Hardback ISBN • 9781681791449 • Retail Price $32.99
Ebook ISBN • 9781681791463 • Retail Price $9.99

Blood Prairie
Perilous Adventures On The Oklahoma Frontier
By Ron J. Jackson, Jr.

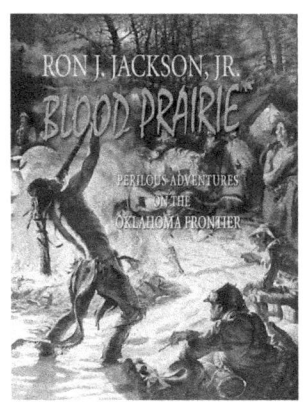

Oklahoma's history is one of triumph, but its victories were often written in blood. *Blood Prairie* brings this turbulent past vividly to life, honoring the men, women, and tribes who endured the state's enchanting yet violent frontier. Readers will journey through powerful stories of survival and defiance: the Kiowa Tribe's darkest hour, a Cheyenne woman warrior's fierce defense of her homeland, a Mexican captive's bloody struggle, and a Civil War battle seen through the eyes of an Indian Territory slave. The book also presents the most complete account yet of the legendary Buffalo Wallow Fight—a Texas last stand whose heroes, both red and white, trace their roots to Oklahoma soil. Riveting, unflinching, and unforgettable, *Blood Prairie* captures history at its rawest. • 128 pages • 5.5 x 7.5 inches

Paperback ISBN 9781681793269 • Retail Price $14.99
Ebook ISBN • 9781681793276 • Retail Price $9.99

Wild Horse Media Group
Eakin Press • NorTex Press • Wild Horse Press
P.O. Box 331779 • Fort Worth, Texas 76163 • www.WildHorseMedia.com

More Rodeo Titles From Wild Horse Media Group

Belly Full of Bed Springs: - The History of Bronc Riding
By Gail Hughbanks Woerner
Hardback - 250 page - ISBN 9781571683564 - $24.95

Best Supporting Actors: Rodeo Clowns
By Tommy Sheffield
Paperback - 160 pages - ISBN 9780977161010 - $16.95

Bob Crosby: World Champion Cowboy
By Thelma Crosby & Eve Ball
Paperback - 176 pages - ISBN 9780977161003 $14.95

The CB Cowboys: The Saga of the Legendary Christensen Family
By Billy Willcoxson
Paperback - 256 pages - ISBN 9781571688231 - $26.95

The Cowboys' Turtle Association: The Birth of Professional Rodeo
By Gail Hughbanks Woerner
Paperback - 358 pages - ISBN 9780981490366 - $24.95

Cowboy Up!: The History of Bull Riding
By Gail Hughbanks Woerner
Paperback - 322 pages - ISBN 9781571685315 - $24.95

Fearless Funnymen: The History of the Rodeo Clown
By Gail Hughbanks Woerner
Paperback - 240 pages - ISBN 9781571682826 - $19.95

The Finals: *A Complete Guide of the First 50 Years of the Wrangler National Finals Rodeo*
Oversized Book - 11 inches tall & 14 inches wide
Paperback - 240 pages - ISBN 9780615323435 - $49.95

Gold Buckle Dreams: The Life & Times of Chris LeDoux
By David Brown
Paperback - 316 pages - ISBN 9781940130132 - $24.95

The History of Barrel Racing in Professional Rodeo
By Gail Hughbanks Woerner
Paperback - 300 pages - 9781681793597 - $26.99

Pete Knight: The Cowboy King
By Darryl Knight
Paperback - 316 pages - ISBN 9780977161027 - $18.95

Ray Wharton: Champion In and Out of the Arena
By George Sharman & M.J. Schumacher
Paperback - 142 pages - $16.95

Rope to Win: The History of Steer, Calf & Team Roping
By Gail Hughbanks Woerner
Paperback - 277 pages - ISBN 9780978915025 - $26.95

They Call Me Sid Rock: Rodeo's Extreme Cowboy
By Sid Steiner & Jim Pomerantz
Hardback - 256 pages - 9781572436275 - $24.95

Wild Horse Media Group
Eakin Press • NorTex Press • Wild Horse Press
P.O. Box 331779 • Fort Worth, Texas 76163 • www.WildHorseMedia.com

www.ingramcontent.com/pod-product-compliance
Lightning Source LLC
Chambersburg PA
CBHW021145160426
43194CB00007B/690